A
GUIDE TO A
HAPPIER FAMILY

A
GUIDE TO A
HAPPIER FAMILY

Overcoming the Anger,
Frustration, and Boredom
that Destroy Family Life

ANDREW SCHWEBEL, Ph.D., BERNICE SCHWEBEL, M.A.,
CAROL SCHWEBEL, Ph.D., Milton Schwebel, Ph.D.,
AND ROBERT SCHWEBEL, Ph.D.

JEREMY P. TARCHER, INC.
LOS ANGELES

Library of Congress Cataloging in Publication Data
A guide to a happier family: overcoming the anger, frustration, and boredom
that destroy family life / Andrew Schwebel . . . [et al].
   p.   cm.
  ISBN 0-87477-531-0
  1. Family—Psychological aspects. 2. Marriage—Psychological
aspects. 3. Interpersonal conflict. 4. Happiness. 5. Self-help
techniques. I. Schwebel, Andrew I.
HQ518.R48 1989
306.8—dc19   88-39597
                                                 CIP

Jeremy P. Tarcher, Inc.
9110 Sunset Blvd.
Los Angeles, CA 90069

Distributed by St. Martin's Press, New York

Manufactured in the United States of America
10 9 8 7 6 5 4 3 2 1

First Edition

We dedicate this book to our late grandparents and our extended family, and to all people who strive for fulfillment in their family dramas.

The family is one of nature's masterpieces.
                    —George Santayana

*People travel the world over in search of what
they need and return home to find it.*
                    —Adapted from a statement
                        by George Moore

Contents

Acknowledgments

Many people helped us realize our objective of writing this book, and we want to thank them. Because we have learned so much from the innumerable families we have known professionally, we are especially indebted to them. Some appear in this book, in disguised form of course, and a few are part of composites drawn from several families.

We were fortunate that our publisher, Jeremy P. Tarcher, shared our personal interest in the subject and gave us considerable encouragement and support. Our editor Connie Zweig's challenging questions and her editorial advice were invaluable in helping us achieve the standards we set for ourselves when we began this project. We are deeply grateful to them.

We thank two young people, Davy and Sara Schwebel, for their tireless patience. During many school vacations, they accepted in good spirit the fact that their parents, grandparents, and uncle were engrossed in discussion and writing rather than play.

Foreword

When the publisher of *A Guide to a Happier Family* sent me the galleys to see if I would write a foreword to the volume, I began reading it with skepticism. I had seen so many self-help books that were full of truisms and banal, superficial recommendations for peace, fulfillment, and happiness in the family. They all left the reader unable to alter his or her situation despite the theories and directives they espoused. I started to read the Schwebels' book and was immediately engrossed. To paraphrase Henry Higgins, I had to exclaim, "By Jove, they've got it!"

Professionals in the fields of psychotherapy and marital and family therapy increasingly have been developing theories to explain family dysfunction as well as techniques to change it. Various forms of therapeutic and marital enhancement approaches have evolved. Most deal with only a part of the elephant.

Without one whit of jargon, the Schwebels integrated the best of the current theories and added their own innovative thinking and clinical experience to develop a unique concept of marital and family interaction. It is even multigenerational. They present the reader with an understandable step-by-step approach that makes it easy to comprehend how one's own marital or family system works. From there the text proceeds to teach readers how to change their interactions and gain greater relationship fulfillment.

Having written a trade book with a colleague many years ago that had the same objectives as the Schwebels' (which, I fear, were not achieved so fully), I can appreciate the extent of their accomplishment.

This book belongs in every home. It is excellent for adults and should be must reading for marital and family therapists. I hope that while the ink is drying on the first printing, the Schwebels will be busy adapting their work for use in high-school classes—we do so little to prepare our youth for love, marriage, and creating their own families.

It is clear that the Schwebel family worked together to develop their theory and techniques. They've practiced them personally and obviously enjoy their family life. They have given us a great gift—the means to fulfill our own potential for family happiness in keeping with our own dreams and needs.

Clifford J. Sager, M.D.
New York City, January 1989

Director of Family Psychiatry
Jewish Board of Family and
        Children's Services
Clinical Professor of Psychiatry
New York Hospital,
        Cornell Medical Center

Prologue

The world is filled with indescribable beauty. Yet, of all its many attractions, we, the authors of this book—a father, mother, two sons, and a daughter-in-law—treasure family life more than anything else.

We are not alone. One human attribute shared by both sexes, all ages, races, and classes, is the yearning for the intimacy of happy, harmonious family life. Many studies show that when people are asked the question "What makes your life meaningful?" they mention spouses, parents, siblings, and friends, and they say they want most of all to love and to feel loved and wanted.

The three of us who are psychologists and psychotherapists (Andrew, Milton, and Robert) have heard countless patients tell us that they are caught in a bind: they can't live with their families, and they can't live without them. Their words differ from one to another when they explain what they mean, but their difficulty remains the same.

And it's not only patients who have said this. Many of the university students we teach feel drawn to their families during school breaks, as if their homes—parents, brothers, and sisters—were magnets. Yet, at the same time, they dread the arguments that inevitably occur shortly after the warm and loving welcome.

The two of us who are teachers of young children (Bernice and Carol) have often had conferences with parents who come presumably to talk about a child but end up, often in tears, discussing family conflicts—and the anger, frustration, and boredom that threaten to destroy family life.

1

In most families, life is not totally negative. There are moments of joy too. But in between those moments comes so much pain; it seems that people endure too much suffering for the little pleasure they get in return. Some families pay a heavy price for the peace they manage to attain. "There's something missing," a husband or wife will say. "There ought to be more to love and family life than what we've got. At least we should be spending more time together and feeling closer."

Our professional and personal experiences convince us that it doesn't have to be that way. A society that can send astronauts to the moon can surely discover ways to take much of the sting out of family life without reducing its vast potential for pleasure.

We wrote this book for people who want more joy and fewer heartaches in family life. Our ideas were developed and sharpened over long years of experience and through many hours of discussion. The book is rooted in the belief that family members have far more power to control destiny than they realize. The future is not predetermined. Recently, psychologists discovered that, through heightening awareness, family members acquire greater influence over family direction, having the power to chart its course. Our purpose is to explain what stands in the way of fuller realization of that power and to reveal ways of attaining it.

In the pages that follow, we show you how your love relationships develop, what makes them strong, and what gets them into trouble. We help you understand how your *relationship script*, learned in childhood, shapes your life, marriage, and family relationships. And we tell you how to manage inevitable conflicts in more effective ways. *A Guide to a Happier Family* will help you define the stumbling blocks that deprive you of the kinds of love relationships you yearn for.

When we refer to "family problems," we mean problems like the following:

- "Something's wrong. My husband doesn't show any affection or any kind of interest in me, except when he wants sex."
- "I can't figure out what's going on. My wife is irritable all the time with me and the kids. And when I try to touch her, she pulls away."
- "I wonder why he's so aggressive when he comes home from work, bullying the children and sometimes me too."
- "I must be doing something wrong, because the kids bicker all the time, and I don't have any idea how to stop it."
- "I thought I was too suspicious. I'm not. He's fooling around with another woman, and I can't do anything about it. It makes me crazy."
- "What can I do about someone I love who won't stop drinking? She says it's just to feel good, but meanwhile the family is going down the drain."
- "Married ten years and I still carry ninety percent of the load. That's why I want out. I've had enough. The kids will just have to get used to it."
- "I can't ever please my parents—not when I was a kid and not even now that I've given them the grandchildren they wanted."
- "With the endless arguing in our home, sometimes I get so fed up I just want to run away and never come back."
- "Yes, I'm depressed. After the divorce, it wasn't easy taking care of my kids. When I married Jack, I thought it would be easier, but now, with his kids and mine, it's even harder."

If you've had thoughts like these, you're like many other people.

FAMILY IN CRISIS

No one can escape the reports in the media that tell us that the American family is in crisis. According to a recent study, the divorce rate is so high that more than 35 million adults were stepparents and one child in six was a stepchild. Professionals estimate that about one-third of married persons between the ages of twenty-five and thirty-five will end up divorced. Eventually most of those who are divorced will remarry. However, second marriages don't have a great track record: about forty percent end in divorce within five years.

Then there are the highly visible problems of alcoholism and drug abuse that tear at the heart of so many families. Even the happy fact that senior citizens live longer often creates unhappy situations when families are saddled with additional responsibility for an ailing parent or when adult siblings become entangled in bitter arguments over *who* should be contributing *what* to pay the bills and provide care. The news reports about abused children and battered wives are painful to read and hear.

Yet with all those damaging reports, marriage and family continue to be as popular as ever. Men and women still hope for more happiness. The dream for romance, affection, and intimacy goes on.

And no wonder. Nothing else can substitute for it. Our marvelous technological age can work wonders, but it can't give us the warmth and security of a loving spouse and children or the feeling of unconditional love: "Maybe I'll make mistakes, stumble on my face, but still they'll be there, loving me."

If you travel the world over, you will find the same yearning. Marriage and family practices will differ, but not the dream. People want love, and in songs and poems in hundreds of languages, they share the dream.

That dream can be realized. Through our work with families and through our own personal lives, we became

convinced that family life could be much happier than it
typically is. This led us to dedicate ourselves to solving the
problems of living together. We want to share with you what
we learned by helping others and by applying our knowledge
to improving our own family life. That is why we wrote this
book.

As professionals, our work brought us into intimate
touch with a wide range of family problems experienced by
others. But that's not the only way we learned about the joys
and heartaches of family life. All five of us gained much from
our own experiences relating to each other. Like that of any
other family, our history could be partially explained by
means of psychological theories that describe why we are the
way we are. But that was not enough. We wanted more than
an explanation of *why*. We wanted to find out *how* to cope
with our own conflicts and hurts. And we hoped that these
methods would be useful to others. So, building on theory
about individual and family behavior and our own professional experience, we developed new ideas that are beneficial
to clients and can be beneficial to you if you are trying to
improve family life.

We utilize these ideas in very practical ways when we
work with children or adults, couples or families. It's not
enough for a couple to discover that for years they have been
loving each other while trying to avoid each other. Our aim
is to help them know *why* they have been doing this, so they
won't fall into that trap again or into another like it in the
future. And with families, it's not enough to recognize patterns of behavior, such as parents tending to get into arguments at the start of every weekend, when they are looking
forward to the whole family spending many hours together.
When they come to understand the underlying reasons for
their behavior, they almost always want to change it.

In our professional practices, we aim to help individuals,
couples, and families to resolve immediate problems and also,
through deeper understanding, to avoid future ones. To accomplish our purpose, we are presenting our view of what

happens from the moment a man and woman first meet and
what continues to take place into the advanced years of marriage and family. Our point of view and the methods for
change that follow can explain how you got where you are and
how you can change.

THEATER DRAMA, FAMILY DRAMA, AND SCRIPTS

The similarities between life on stage, television, and film and
real family life are very striking. They share many common
features, the foremost of which is "drama." Everyone is familiar with drama on stage, having witnessed some plays and
perhaps having performed in them during school years or
later. The curtain rises, the players appear, and the story
unfolds; soon the interactions of the characters tell us about
their relationships, their loves, and their struggles. Sometimes we feel their joy, their suffering, and often the tension
created by their conflicts. Family drama is similar. In every
family, every single day, the curtain rises, the players appear,
and the story unfolds. And to an objective observer, the
interactions of family members reveal their relationships,
loves, and struggles.

A second feature shared by theater drama and family
drama is that both use "scripts." Everyone knows that actors
memorize their lines from the script written by a playwright
or a screenwriter. Most people don't know that family members also speak lines that have been learned in advance, some
almost from birth. While the lines spoken by family members
are not in print, they are almost as well established as those
in theatrical scripts, and family members know their lines as
thoroughly as experienced actors.

People often ask us why they keep making the same
mistakes over and over in their relationships and why they
continue to argue about the same issues. That's like asking
why Hamlet says the same lines every time Shakespeare's

play is performed. Every family drama calls for those repeti-
tious mistakes and arguments. Until the family members
rewrite their drama, they will go on and on in the same way.

You too have a family drama. Your actions and those of
the rest of your family are guided by it. You and your spouse
are the directors and main characters in this drama from the
moment you are married, and you remain so even after your
children are born, despite the prominent parts they play.
Other characters from your family and your spouse's family
may have roles in your drama: parents, grandparents, brothers, sisters, uncles, aunts, and cousins. These are mostly
minor parts, but sometimes these "players," especially parents, have a major influence on the immediate family unit,
even from a distance. Parental involvement can be helpful or
create havoc.

The family drama controls much of our lives and governs
how we relate to each other: it tells us whether we are free
to be loving and intimate while remaining independent. It
also tells us whether we face up to problems together or run
from them separately. Our methods of handling disputes—
through negotiation, compromise, and problem solving or
through power plays and revenge tactics—are spelled out in
the lines of the drama.

If the family drama you created has burdensome "baggage" that weighs you down—avoidance of problems, power
plays, too little intimacy—you're stuck with relationship
problems until you introduce the kind of changes that we call
"rewriting the family drama."

Some dramas lead people to pull away from each other
without their being aware of what they are doing. Such
dramas include the use of *family defense mechanisms,* through
which couples avoid conflict by reducing the time spent together. They may avoid conflict, but they pay a big price.
Fortunately, families can become aware of what they are
doing and can rewrite their drama to achieve more closeness.

A Guide to a Happier Family is about rewriting your
drama. It will help you to:

- Understand and identify your family drama.
- Identify burdensome baggage.
- Recognize how you avoid intimacy.
- Rewrite your family drama to allow for more joy and intimacy.

As you can see, any of these achievements requires honest and clear appraisal of your family and even of yourself. You will need to be able to put yourself in your spouse's shoes and appreciate how he or she experiences your behavior. You can do that by taking on another role associated with theater—that of the drama critic. As a critic, you take a seat in the audience and look at your family in action, including yourself in one of the key roles.

What will you see? You will be struck by the fact that any problem one person has is bound to affect the others and the family as a whole. All the members of your family are part of one system. If you change one part, it has ripple effects on everyone, like a pebble dropped into a pond. Then you may be surprised to find that some of the behavior of family members is self-defeating. They engage in activities that damage themselves and, with that ripple effect, damage the family. As you continue to function as a critic, you will probably be even more surprised to find that this hurtful behavior isn't a one-time mistake, it's repeated over and over. Fortunately, once you have discovered a source of family conflict, you have taken the first major step toward controlling it.

AN OVERVIEW

That brings us to our method of bringing about change. We'll introduce you to the concept of the *relationship script.* This is what you started to "write" as a child under the strong influence of your parents and others. You completed it in adolescence. The relationship script is extremely important because it determines the kind of partner you seek and the ways you behave in your relationship with that partner. It is unique, almost like your psychological fingerprint, fostering the kind of consistency that leads your spouse or friends to remark, "I just *knew* you were going to say that."

The seeds of your relationship script were planted years ago when, as a child, you learned what your parents valued and what displeased them, what you could do to win their favor and what brought punishment. You learned from them what to trust about yourself and others and what to like about yourself and others. You learned when it was safe to express your thoughts and feelings or when you needed to keep them hidden. You learned whether to be close to or to dominate others, to be active or passive, dependent or independent, decisive or indecisive.

What you learned became as much a part of you as your smile. You carried this into adulthood, where it shaped your relationships with your dates, your lovers, and your spouse. When you started to date your future spouse, and later when you married, two independent relationship scripts, built from two separate family dramas, bumped up against each other and began forming your new family drama. Then, if you are a parent, your children were born, and you and your spouse started teaching them *their* lines—their relationship scripts.

Your relationship script is stable. Once "written," it's there for life, unless you make a determined effort to rewrite it. One very obvious fact is that you can't rewrite a relationship script unless you know that you have one. That is, unless you are conscious of how you typically relate to other people. And most people don't know that. One of our objectives in this book is to encourage you to become aware of your relationship script—what it says about what you want in relationships and how you go about getting that.

The *family drama* begins at the moment when you meet and begin a relationship with another person. Like drama on the stage or screen, the real-life drama opens when two people come together and interact. Their dialogue comes from their own well-established relationship scripts.

To see the beginning of your family drama, picture you and your partner on stage. The dialogue between you begins. That's when your relationship script bumps up against that of the other person, and your family drama begins to unfold. To be more accurate, that's when the two of you begin to write *your* family drama by combining your own separate relationship scripts.

As you and your partner interact, you find common ground but also encounter some differences, because differences between spouses are as much the norm as similarities are. And because of those differences, conflict is inevitable.

When people decide to marry, they do so despite their differences. At that happy period they tend to ignore their arguments and concentrate instead on their strong feeling that the potential mate will be able to fulfill important needs. But, as you know, the differences can't be overlooked indefinitely. One spouse leaves the bathroom in a mess, another flirts at parties—whatever the reason, arguments break out.

Still newlyweds, at a high state of happiness, they may not yet have developed *family rules* about how they are to behave to cope with differences and minimize conflict. With each new unhappy encounter, they are motivated to develop a new rule to cope with their differences—such as "We will always cap the toothpaste" or "We take turns choosing the television program." Through these rules they manage to avoid some arguments.

The family rules also serve another important purpose. We know that love can do marvels for families, but it doesn't feed them. Love is not enough to maintain that little social community called family. There's work to be done, and if the family is to be successful and their love is not to be eroded by frustration and anger, there has to be an equitable division of labor. By one means or another, spouses work out the roles that are to be performed by them and later by the children: she balances the checkbook, he does the repairs; she cooks, he cleans.

Of all the needs a mate will help you fulfill, none is more

important than the realization of your personal dream. Your
dream is that very special aspiration that you probably fan-
cied since adolescence. It may be an image of the lifestyle you
ardently desire or a mental picture of the career achievements
you seek. You may not even have spoken about it with your
spouse, yet it is there, a powerful force in your lives, influenc-
ing your plans and decisions.

One test of compatibility is that husband and wife share a
similar personal dream. Chances are that they do, because a
common dream is one of the powerful attractions that draw two
people together. The mutually shared individual dreams will
surely become the *family dream*. Every married couple and
every family has goals, like "to own a home of our own" or "to
both have successful careers" or "to produce healthy and
happy children." At the top of them all, like a guiding star, is
the family dream, so that a couple with all three of the above
goals chooses having successful careers as their dream.

No one really has to be reminded that the family drama
is incomplete without *family intimacy*. The word *intimate*
usually brings sex to mind. However, family intimacy means
much more than that. Almost without our spelling it out, you
know what we mean, because it's what all people yearn for,
even those who are frightened by it: a closeness of spirit, a
feeling of trust that you can be who you are, say what you feel,
and still be loved and respected by those who are dear to you.
It's another kind of feeling, as well, a joy that you can give
of yourself to others when they are in need and a security that
you can lean on others when you are in need, while remaining
an independent person in your own right.

In summary, the relationship scripts interact to form the
family drama. At the core of the family drama are the following three phenomena:

- *Family rules.* The unwritten regulations—like a
  constitution and bylaws—that keep order, per-
  mitting this intimate community to attend to its
  needs.

- *Family dream.* The guiding star—hopes and aspirations—toward which the family strives.
- *Family intimacy.* The love, warmth, and trust—the heart and soul—that give meaning not only to family life but to life in general.

Perhaps this leaves you wondering about the future of your family drama. If so, you may find it helpful to imagine your family onstage five years from now. Picture the interactions among you, the expressions of love, cooperation, and joy. In trying to project into the future, you may find it helpful to answer the following questions about the present.

- Are you and your family aware of the family dream and working toward it successfully? Or are you bogged down and frustrated by conflict?
- Are you and your family guided by equitable family rules? Or are they unfair? Or not observed? Does family work get done? Are differences settled cooperatively? Or is there rampant hostility in your home?
- Are you and your spouse (and your children, in their own way) enjoying the pleasures of intimacy, free to be yourselves, to express your thoughts and feelings? Or are you bitterly disappointed by an emotional iron curtain between you and your spouse? Between you and your child?

In asking these questions, we are introducing the *happiness test.* Periodically, individuals evaluate their satisfaction with marriage and family, even if they are not fully conscious of doing so. In one way or another they ask themselves, "Considering what I am giving, am I getting a fair return?" You too make judgments about whether you are getting what you hoped for and what you feel you have a right to receive.

If you are dissatisfied, there are two paths you might take in order to gain more satisfaction. You may unconsciously adopt a *family defense mechanism*, a type of avoidance of excessive intimacy so that limited intimacy can be enjoyed. As another option, you may consciously *rewrite the family drama*. You will find this the most satisfying and enduring method of improving family life.

In the second half of the book, we take you through each step of this process. It requires effort and perseverance, but will be worth it. If you have children, it will give them a better start in creating their own relationship scripts. Rewriting your drama starts with being the critic, sitting in the audience and watching your family perform onstage. You and your spouse may do this job together.

Creating family projects. As critics, you and your spouse observe one of the following two conditions: Problems break out when family members have nothing to do but sit around, getting frustrated and irritable. Family members do most things on their own, unconnected to others in the family, and family cohesiveness and morale are low. The solution to these conditions is to rewrite your drama by collectively choosing projects in which all of you can participate.

Learning cooperative negotiation. As critics, you and your spouse have detected a source of conflict. For instance, one of you puts the other down in the presence of friends. This creates feelings of hostility that get expressed in indirect ways, like avoiding sex, which complicates your lives further. Through negotiation you establish a cooperative agreement to halt the put-downs and end the cycle of anger and frustration.

Developing intimate communication. As critics, you and your spouse observe that minor differences between you often flare up into major arguments. You notice that, when you express resentments or even offer constructive criticism, the atmosphere becomes tense. By changing your ways of talking and listening to each other, you can achieve more intimacy and harmony.

Rewriting your relationship scripts together.   As critics, you and your partner recognize that the problems between you, which are the problems in your family drama, aren't going to be overcome until the two of you rewrite the relationship scripts that you each brought to your marriage. At this moment you may be asking, "Are these authors asking us to change *ourselves*?" The answer is an unequivocal, "Yes!" Some people do change their relationship scripts, usually as a result of their strong determination to do so when they find they must either change or remain unhappy. Shy eighteen-year-olds, at college away from home for the first time, are an example. Having to choose between loneliness or disciplined effort to force themselves to take the initiative in striking up conversations, they sometimes choose the latter and are able to modify their script.

When all else fails, *part in the healthiest way.* This should be the method of last resort. When that happens, separation and divorce can be done in such a way that the costs are low and the benefits maximized. Under those circumstances, parting becomes another form of rewriting the family drama.

ABOUT US

Before we begin our journey toward healthier family relationships, we want to introduce ourselves.

Two of us, Bernice and Milton, had a unique experience that taught us the powerful influence of family life. Ten days after our wedding, we became "cottage" parents of twenty boys, ages five to fifteen, at an institution for dependent children. Some of the boys were orphans, others came from broken homes. Many were emotionally disturbed, and a few were on their way to becoming delinquents.

We lived like a traditional family of the 1940s. In the morning after breakfast, Milton went off to work, the children went to school, and Bernice maintained the cottage and attended staff meetings. After school, we played ball with the boys, and after supper, we monitored their homework and helped them write letters to parents or other relatives, some of which went unanswered. At bedtime, we told stories to the younger ones and comforted those who were homesick.

The special treat was the Saturday-night party in our tiny apartment in the cottage, where the children enjoyed games, songs, and refreshment, and most of all a lively spirit. With the passing weeks we found that a regular schedule, firm parenting, and plenty of support and love brought a large measure of harmony. The boys wanted to do their chores and help us around the cottage. Above all, we discovered how much love is treasured by those who, for one reason or another, have had too little of it.

For us, it was most painful to see seven-year-old Eddie on visiting day. Every two weeks he would go to the parking lot where the bus brought visiting relatives. He would wait until the bus emptied. His mother never came, despite repeated promises. He would run back to his cottage, fall on his cot, and weep. Eddie became for us a symbol of what everyone wants—to be loved demonstrably and dependably by those we love. As long as we were his substitute parents, we tried to give him what he needed.

Bernice's professional career has been directly related to children's needs. First as a social worker with children and their natural or foster parents, then as a teacher, she witnessed suffering caused by parents' inability to work out their own conflicts and give their children stability. Through parent conferences and especially through direct work with the children, she tried to sustain them during troubled times. One of her major challenges as a university supervisor was to prepare student teachers to cope with this most difficult task of teaching—helping the child whose family drama is failing to satisfy family members' basic needs, especially for intimacy and love.

Years after his experiences with Eddie and the other children, Milton was asked, as editorial consultant to a publisher, to read a manuscript entitled *Games People Play*, by psychiatrist Eric Berne. Milton strongly recommended the publication of what later became a best-selling book. Its appeal lay in uncovering how couples manage to go through life "playing games" in order to avoid intimacy.

Although he did not develop a theory of scripts, Berne laid the foundations for it. Milton and his coauthors have carried on his work in a new direction, using the concepts of "relationship script" and "family drama."

A few years after "cottage" parenthood Bernice and Milton had their first son, Andrew, and later, Robert. Andrew and Carol are married and have a son and daughter.

For almost twenty years as a psychotherapist, while doing research on families and training clinical psychologists, Andrew has seen families complain about problems that repeat themselves again and again. The issues change as the family matures, but not the recurring problems. It's still "Life is awful—we fight all the time" or "If it weren't for my mother-in-law, my life would be O.K." or "Why can't I ever get the children to help me around the house?" People are stuck with the same old scripts. Andrew often found that, although they complained about a lack of intimacy ("She's always busy; we never have time together"), they were using family defense mechanisms that served to keep them apart. He decided they had to discover that behavior in order to change it.

Robert studied and worked with psychologist Claude Steiner, Eric Berne's former protégé, who fully developed the concept of the individual "script" in such books as *Scripts People Live By*, *Games Alcoholics Play*, and *Healing Alcoholism*. During the last fifteen years, Robert has written about scripts, including those of clients addicted to drugs. As a therapist he has seen the script's important role in helping people to understand and alter their family dynamics. His background was preparation for the leap we have taken in recognizing that relationship scripts combine to form a family drama.

Carol has seen the varied manifestations of family dramas in her kindergarten classes. She talks about Tommy, a quiet and uninvolved student who suddenly became explosive and punched another child. In a parent conference, Carol found the same reserve in his parents, until she began to ask for information to understand Tommy's behavior. Then the parents became angry and, while more controlled than Tommy, showed the same explosiveness just below the surface. His parents had built a family drama of defensiveness, suspicion, and distrust and had passed it on to their son. The concept of the "relationship script" helped Carol to understand that Tommy was enacting the lines he had learned.

Together, our years of varied experience have led us to develop our theories about family drama, relationship scripts, family defense mechanisms, and rewriting. We have become convinced that the concepts of "scripts" and "defense mechanisms" are keys to demystifying family problems. With those tools and the others in this book you can undertake the challenge of rewriting your own family drama.

The Reviews Are In

Perhaps the greatest social service that can be rendered by anybody to the country and to mankind is to bring up a family.

—GEORGE BERNARD SHAW

1

Identifying and Observing Your Family Drama

*E*arly one evening during a Thanksgiving weekend, the five of us were strolling in a park, heading for a high-rise apartment house about fifty yards ahead. Suddenly the lights went on in one apartment on the sixth floor. The figure of a person appeared, and then another. A moment later, the two faced each other. One talked, then the other talked, and then the two at the same time. It wasn't necessary to hear them to figure out that they were having an argument.

Seconds later, the lights went on in another apartment a few floors above, and then in two more at a lower level, and people appeared in each. In one, an adult embraced a child. In another, two adults kissed.

This experience gave us an eerie feeling. With no intention of doing so, we were witnessing private human dramas. For as the lights went on, each apartment appeared at that moment to be a stage. To us it seemed as if the curtain rose, and first one character in the play appeared and then another. The dialogue began, and as the players expressed their feelings, we could see in their behavior the anger in one, the tenderness in another. Unintentionally, we were seeing one scene in the drama of everyday life.

This event prompted us to think about how family life is similar to drama on the stage, film, and television. You and all the members of your family are the characters in your

21

family drama. As an individual you perform a role, dictated by your relationship script, which interacts with those of the other family members. And you are the author of that role— the scriptwriter who, under strong influence from your parents, wrote your relationship script.

If you are single, you may be looking for a costar for your family drama. If you are married, you and your spouse are directing the play, as well as performing as the leading actors. But you are not the only ones. If you have children, they play important roles. The other players include your parents, in-laws, brothers, and sisters, and, as bit players, cousins, uncles, and aunts. You decide which of the characters play important roles because you (and your spouse if you are married) do the casting.

You are also the set designer. The settings of your drama change, as they do in a theatrical performance or movie. Sometimes the place is your bedroom, sometimes the kitchen, living room, or car. Some important scenes occur in your parents' home or in the homes of friends.

In many important ways, your drama is like those that take place behind a proscenium arch or on motion picture and television screens. Soon after marriage, you and your spouse may have enjoyed honeymoon bliss. But problems eventually arise, as inevitably as they do for the characters in television soap operas. One important difference between the conflicts you see onstage and those you experience in family life is that the playwright leads you to discover the motivations of the players. At some point you get to know why the husband is angry. Sooner or later you find out why the wife provoked his anger. The playwright provides that insight for you.

Unfortunately, in real life, you may know your anger and your reasons for it or you may not. Often you can't understand or appreciate your spouse's feelings or those of your children or parents when you have arguments. You probably are not fully aware of the influence you have in eliciting the anger—or the love—of your spouse and other family members. If you don't know what a mate, child, or parent is feeling, you will find it difficult to understand his or her behavior and therefore to cope with conflicts that arise.

Fortunately, real life has a marvelous advantage over theater. It's not static. Our dramas are not frozen. We can change them. However, most people don't know where to start. When the problems seem overwhelming, you may feel like getting down on the floor and kicking and screaming. Don't blame yourself for not knowing what to do. No one has taught you how to make a successful family. In all our years of schooling, we are rarely given instruction on family life. We are taught to name the capital of France and explain the reasons for the Civil War, but we know little or nothing about how a family functions or how a father and mother should go about settling disputes. Consequently, millions of people earn diplomas without learning the most important subject in their lives—living together with love. Through this book we intend to fill that gap.

You will learn how to be the critic of your family drama. Through the description of real-life family dramas and of families of stage and screen, you will have an opportunity to observe relationship scripts in action. Then you will prepare to practice your role as an observer of theater and movie families, and then of real-life families, including your own.

OBSERVING A FAMILY DRAMA IN ACTION

To improve family life, you need to understand the root causes of your problem. The importance of this understanding will become evident through the example of Beverly. Time after time, the same problems recurred in her life because she did not recognize their underlying causes and was therefore unable to deal with them effectively.

A Thanksgiving at Home

At twenty-seven, Beverly, who would become one of our clients many years later, was returning to her parents' home for Thanksgiving with great feelings of love and the hope that this time her family visit would be peaceful. She felt ties to the "old homestead," as she called the house in which she had spent her life before going off to college. Then, after getting her degree, she had spent most of the summer there until she found a job as a clothing designer in a city almost a hundred miles away.

Each visit with her parents after moving away had started well. That wasn't surprising, because she loved them and had no doubt that they loved her as well. But eventually the visits would turn sour. Even when the family insisted that everything was all right, Beverly sensed an underlying tension. So, as she was approaching their home that Thanksgiving, her hope for a good time was mingled with anxiety.

Beverly's parents' feelings were not different from hers. They were eager to see her, hopeful that this would be a happy visit, and a little on edge wondering if they would be able to please her. Their conversation revealed both their pride in her and the source of their concern.

Beverly's mother said to her husband, "Maybe she'll have some good news for us."

"Don't expect it, Lil, so you won't be disappointed," the father replied.

Lil was carrying a bowl of fruit to the dining-room table, and she stopped in her tracks. "I just don't understand it, Harry. She's good-looking, makes a fine salary, has a sense of humor—and no boyfriend."

"Don't push her. She's got time," Harry said.

Lil put down the bowl and came almost nose to nose with Harry, saying angrily, "What do you mean she's got time? She's not a little girl anymore, so stop protecting her."

Then in a softer tone, as she put her hand on his shoulder, she said, "Harry, you know how I love that girl even though I had plenty of trouble with her. I want her to be happy. Think how happy she is when Anna is here with her kids. Beverly is a wonderful aunt, and she'll be a wonderful mother. I just want to see her married. What's wrong with that?"

An hour later, when Beverly arrived, the first moments were full of love, everything she hoped for. She hugged and kissed her parents and told them, "It's so good to be home, to be together again."

After the well of affectionate expressions ran dry, the conversation turned to other subjects. Meanwhile they finished dinner preparations and sat down at the table. While they ate, Harry talked about his clothing business, Lil about how she handled discipline problems in her seventh-grade classes, and Beverly about new developments in clothing design.

Harry was delighted with the way they had spent the long afternoon. He felt a sense of relief but also a need to safeguard it. He proposed that they should watch the last part of a football game. Beverly felt relieved at her father's suggestion, but before she had a chance to agree, Lil rejected it.

"Our daughter comes all this way to spend the day with us, and you want to watch TV? Harry, how could you! Let's go sit on some comfortable chairs and talk." With a big smile and a hug, she said to her daughter, "I want to hear everything that's going on in your life, Bev, your friends and all that."

As they walked into the living room, Beverly had a familiar thought: "Good ol' mom, the teacher. She doesn't mean friends, she means men. She doesn't give me time to find the guy I want. One way or another, she's going to wheedle it out of me. . . . But she means well."

First, Lil asked about friends in general. Then, after Beverly talked only about her former high-school and college women friends, her mother questioned her about men. Beverly, maintaining self-control, explained that she went on dates almost every weekend but was involved in "nothing serious."

At that point, with Beverly looking at her watch, Lil asked, "Honey, what's the problem? What are you looking for in a man?"

Beverly got up and said she had to go. It was almost two hours before her originally scheduled departure, and her parents protested. But she insisted, telling them that she still had some work to do when she got home. They knew why Beverly was leaving—to avoid her mother's inquisition about the men she was seeing and why one of them wasn't good enough for her. Yet no one was prepared to bring up this fact out of fear that it would cause an emotional scene that might rupture the relationship entirely.

Each of them had a private thought about it.

Beverly's was "I'll lose my temper and hurt them."

Harry's was "If we push this, I'll hardly ever see her again."

Lil's was "I don't want to lose her."

That kind of fear is a major obstacle to finding the underlying problem. It's like a ghost locked in the closet. Never unlock the closet door, people think, or the dreadful "thing" will burst forth. Such self-defeating behavior is so common that you may well have seen it in other people, if not in yourself.

If you have confronted "ghosts in the closet," you know that the very opposite is true. You open the door, and often you find that the ghost disappears into thin air. What remains is usually human and manageable. People like Lil, Harry, and Beverly can probably cope with it in constructive ways. There may be some hurt feelings and strong emotions, but in the end that can be all for the good.

But Beverly was still a prisoner of what she had learned in the past about relating to people. In this account of her Thanksgiving visit, she has revealed the following important features about her relationship script:

Don't bring up differences.

Don't show your anger.

If people mean well, as mother does, accept their behavior even if it hurts.

You can hurt someone if you get him or her very upset.

Try to please those you love.

Escape from unpleasant situations; otherwise they will get worse.

To be safe, pay any price for peace and harmony.

With these characteristics in her relationship script, Beverly "takes it" from her family. She even excuses their behavior if she interprets it as well-intentioned. When the pressure gets so close to the boiling point that she fears she might have trouble controlling her emotions, she runs away.

Let us see how Beverly learned to behave this way when she was a child. Fearful of displeasing her mother, at a young age she became an expert at saying and doing whatever she thought her mother wanted. She knew her mother loved her and was often kind and helpful, but Beverly always felt that she had to be careful or her mother would do or say something awful.

Lil had grown up with stern parents. The oldest of four children, she had learned to protect herself against her own mother's sharp tongue and her father's harsh punishment by carefully monitoring her behavior. This practice became an integral part of her relationship script so that, first with her younger siblings and later with Beverly, she made sure they made no "mistakes." One did things "right"—and that included marrying when you were supposed to. Lil didn't *choose* to be a watchdog mother with Beverly. Her early history *made* her such a person. It led her to write that kind of relationship script, which she later brought into the family drama that she and Harry developed.

Beverly found a role model in her father. Through his behavior and even sometimes by what he said to her, she learned to avoid discussing and even thinking about unpleasant subjects. When he discovered that Beverly was upset by something that happened in school or at home, he would say, "Forget it, honey. Put it out of your mind." Beverly also observed that he did the same with her mother. Beverly could detect his anger, which he quickly suppressed. Instead of standing up to his wife and telling her off, he endured the situation.

Harry was three when his father died, and he grew up with his mother and a maiden aunt. Feeling helpless without a man to discipline her son, his mother tried different methods and found that withholding love from Harry when he misbehaved made him docile and easy to control. She had no desire to do harm to her son and no thought about the long-term effect of her behavior: he developed a relationship script that led him to avoid words and actions that he feared would displease anyone. With that strong tendency, he and Lil were compatible. His relationship script led him to want someone who would keep him on the right track; her relationship script, to monitor his behavior.

Every once in awhile, as a child, Beverly had felt like using the same angry words as her mother, but she would quickly stop herself. Even as an adult the thought would flash through her mind that maybe down deep she was like her mother. In her typical fashion, she would put it out of her mind, not even allowing herself to think about it. She had learned very well the lines of her relationship script—how she was supposed to live and what she was supposed to say.

If Beverly had known how to put herself and her parents onstage and become the critic sitting in the audience, she might have recognized the self-destructiveness in her behavior. She might have changed things and spared herself future pain. Had she done that, the last scene with her parents could have taken a very different turn, like the following: After Lil had asked, "Honey, what's the problem? What are you looking for in a man?" Beverly might have answered, "Mother, let's be out in the open about this. Tell me exactly what's on your mind."

Harry might cut in, "Let's not get all upset. Bev, it's your business. How about if we all go and watch TV?"

Lil would ignore Harry and say, "Bev, I am out in the open. I just wonder about your social life."

"I think you probably mean men, and you're telling me that maybe I'm too particular and that's why I'm not married. Is that so?"

"Well," Lil would hesitate, "to tell you the truth, I have been wondering about that."

Beverly's voice could show a little impatience, saying, "Why shouldn't I be particular? Weren't you particular when you picked Dad? Anyway, it's my business."

Lil might sit up in her chair and say, "Since when did you cut me out of your life and get so independent? You were glad to get my help plenty of times when you needed it. I'm not so sure you don't need it now. Otherwise you wouldn't be lonely."

"I'm not lonely," Beverly could insist. "I'm perfectly happy. When I find the right man, I'll get married."

"And what if you don't?"

"Then I won't marry," Beverly might answer.

"Harry, did you hear that?" Lil would say, trying to win her husband's support. But he'd just want to change the subject.

At this point, Beverly could say, "Listen, Mom and Dad, I don't want to go through subtle cross-examinations when we're together. I'm not your little girl anymore. If you ever want to ask me a direct question, do it. And if I want to ask your advice, I will. But please respect me and my way of life. Please don't try to repair me as if I were a broken doll."

With that, Lil might burst into tears, and Harry might try to comfort her. Not having seen her mother behave this way before, at least not with her, Beverly would be deeply moved. Still, she might suspect that the behavior was one more way—maybe a desperate one—of trying to control her. Beverly wouldn't fall for it. Instead she could say, "I don't want you to be unhappy. There's no reason for it. We'll all get along better this way. You'll see."

That is how Beverly might have handled her relationship with her parents if she had known how to be direct and set limits. But she didn't. If this version of her visit had really occurred, it would have been Beverly's declaration of independence. It would have meant a change in her relationship script, no longer having to follow passively the wishes of others. And it would have led, as Beverly indicated in the revised scene, to a substantial improvement in their relationship. However, it didn't happen this way. At this point in her life, she was not ready to change or even to realize that she could behave differently in relation to her parents.

Seven Years Later: Marriage

At thirty-four, with her relationship script unchanged, Beverly married John. Up to the last minute, she wasn't sure it was a wise decision. She didn't doubt her love for him, but she was unhappy about the way he sometimes made her feel cautious and on guard. She even wondered if she was going through with the marriage to please her parents.

Nevertheless, she was happy at first and began to be dissatisfied only when John would criticize her, which happened when she accommodated to her parents and friends. It didn't bother her particularly that he was hypercritical of other people. What bothered her was his criticism of her. Beverly's only defense was to ask him why he was so stern. Otherwise, she went on as she had always done, avoiding arguments and anger—and often seething within.

That kind of avoidance can't go on indefinitely, as you probably know from personal experience. After a while people find some outlet for their discontent, and Beverly's was through fantasies about the attractive guy who worked with her. Again, instead of dealing with her problem directly, she thought about escape. Beverly's solution to her marital problem—to fantasize about someone else—did nothing to help her understand or improve her relationship with her husband. It was, instead, the same mechanism she used in dealing with her parents, an outright avoidance of problems.

Fifteen Years Later:
The Drama Continues

John and Beverly have a young teenage son, Gregory, who seems to control the household. Fights flare up almost anytime, especially at meals, so that, instead of enjoying dinner, Beverly suffers indigestion. As if that were not enough, John also behaves like a teenager, sometimes shouting and making threats or retreating into a shell and doing nothing. At night, when she puts her head on the pillow, she wonders what's gone wrong with her life and how John and Gregory really feel. While there are moments when she gets satisfaction from them, mostly she turns elsewhere. And what frightens Beverly is that she is getting great relief from her fantasies of filing for divorce and from socializing with her unmarried friends.

You can understand Beverly's feelings because they are so very human. She loves her husband and son and wants desperately for her marriage to succeed. Yet, after fifteen years, she gets so little in return for what she feels she has given. And after all this time she doesn't know what to do, because she is limited in her behavior by her relationship script. She still reacts by avoiding any kind of unpleasantness and, most of all, by denying her own anger.

Her son Gregory is in desperate need of restraint. For his sake as much as for the family's, he needs to have his mother put a stop to his controlling ways. However, in her feeble way, Beverly continues to plead with him ineffectively: "It isn't good for you to talk that way." She has never been able to exercise control over him, and John has been erratic, either very strict or very permissive.

Beverly still has the opportunity to do what she should have been doing for fifteen years—be out in the open with John and talk with him about what his sternness does to her. Maybe she would begin to learn more about herself that way. At least, they could begin to address their problems head on, instead of avoiding them.

But Beverly doesn't open up, nor does John. So these three people are caught in a trap, and Beverly's only way of coping is through escape—fantasized escape, which might become real escape when she can no longer endure life in this way.

Learning from Beverly's Experience

Beverly's experience illustrates several important principles:

The relationship script is very durable. It doesn't change simply because you marry and have children. If you, like Beverly, tend to avoid facing up to differences with other people, you will go on doing it until you recognize this handicap and decide to master it.

Love by itself cannot overcome differences that lead to discontent. Love didn't do that for Harry, Lil, and Beverly, or for Beverly, John, and Gregory. The family drama that you and your mate create comes about through the union of your separate relationship scripts. If one of you consistently chooses escape instead of facing the differences, you as a couple and as a family will usually not get a chance to resolve conflicts.

For good family morale, members must feel that there are more positive feelings than negative ones in participating. If you feel you are giving more than you are getting from your family, you're bound to feel resentful like Beverly.

Escape helps some people cope with marital and family problems, but it doesn't solve them. You may have found substitute satisfaction in fantasies·or other forms of escape. In that case, you probably have gotten no more than temporary relief.

Beverly used that strategy for years, while her dissatisfactions and family problems became greater.

There is no substitute in marriage or family life for intimate communication. Intimate communication isn't just talking; it's talking about meaningful subjects, about things close to the heart. It means Beverly telling John how she feels. It means John expressing his exasperation at Beverly's avoidance of problems. It means Gregory revealing his need for strong parents to help him control impulses that might have been acceptable at three but not at thirteen. It means *you* sharing your feelings with your spouse so that conflict can be resolved.

PUTTING YOUR FAMILY DRAMA ONSTAGE

You may have wondered why Beverly did nothing substantial to improve her life. If asked, she would insist that she had tried: "I reasoned with John that he shouldn't fly off the handle, and I begged Gregory for his own sake not to shout and act like a boss. I even yelled at him a few times. Nothing worked."

Beverly didn't understand that she was very much a part of the problem. She didn't see that she helped keep the family going on in the same way. She knew very little about how John and Gregory really felt and hardly any more about her own feelings. In this respect, she was like many other people whose interactions with parents, spouses, and children are rote and mechanical, and who don't try to uncover their deeper feelings. Nor do they understand that their thoughts and feelings differ from those of the people they love.

You might ask yourself, What are your spouse's hopes in life? Besides the relationship with you, what does your

spouse desire more than anything else in life? What are your
spouse's fears? What are the hopes and fears of your children? What are yours? Are yours different from your
spouse's? From your children's?

How confident do you feel about your answers? Have
you and your spouse ever discussed your respective hopes and
fears? Have the two of you discussed the hopes and fears of
your children?

If you have ready answers to these questions, you are
quite unusual. For most people have difficulty, coming up
with something very general about "being happy" when
asked about what they want of life. That's understandable.
They have had no previous occasion to think about such
questions.

There are two ways you can discover the feelings of
others in your family, including their feelings about how you
come across to them: first, by asking them; second, by seeing
them in action. Both are useful. Here we are going to concentrate on the second method. In Chapter 9, on intimate communication, we will concentrate on the first.

Getting to know your spouse and children by observing
them in action is difficult, for the simple reason that it is not
easy to be a doer and an observer at the same time. For
example, knowing how your spouse feels during an argument
with you is complicated because *you* are very much a part of
the argument. In the language of family drama, you are an
actor performing your relationship script and a critic at the
same time. To appreciate the difficulty, imagine playing on a
basketball team while simultaneously observing your own
plays and those of your teammates, like the coach does,
watching for weaknesses and strengths.

Learning to put your family members onstage makes
being a critic easier. In your imagination, either with your
eyes shut or looking at a blank television screen, picture
yourself and them onstage. The setting could be anywhere,
such as one of your rooms, a restaurant, or your car. Observing yourselves together in real-life interactions, you can see

what makes you feel satisfied about your relationships, what makes you sad and angry, and how you can change the scene for the better.

BECOMING A DRAMA CRITIC

The job of a critic requires skill in observing interactions of family members. Like any skill, this one can be learned by practice. At first, it is easier to rehearse the skill on families other than your own, and you might find that plays, movies, and television give you plenty of families to use. Videocassette recordings of films or plays are especially helpful, because you can reevaluate your initial impressions by observing family interactions several times.

The entertainment media have another advantage over real life as a starting point in learning to put your family onstage. The playwright ignores everything that is irrelevant to the major conflict. You can't do that in real life. You and your spouse have such mundane chores as doing laundry, paying bills, and shopping, which are trivial compared to the conflict that tears at the heart. But on the stage or screen, the trivial is eliminated. Shakespeare gives us Hamlet straight, without distracting us with these everyday matters. As a result, the underlying conflict with his uncle shines through clearly.

Ideally, together we would watch a videotape, pointing out highlights about the relationships among family members in the drama we are viewing. However, because we are restricted to print, we will take the next best approach and illustrate highlights for you by referring to particular aspects of relationships as they appear in two well-known dramatic productions. We have chosen Margaret Mitchell's novel *Gone With the Wind*, which has been made into a film and is available on videotape, and the television series *All in the Family*, widely popular in the 1970s and currently telecast in syndication.

As a critic, you must guard against several traps while viewing *other* families in order to be prepared for the big job of avoiding them when you are observing *your* family. The initial one is the danger of getting caught up in the story. No matter how fascinating or entertaining the film is, you must endeavor to focus on relationship patterns rather than on the story line. The second trap is letting your emotional responses to the performances influence you. The play or movie may be sad, poignant, or enthralling, but maintain control of your emotions so that you can keep your eye on the relationships. Finally, there is the trap of taking sides with one character or another. Although one character may be saintly and another evil, let them take care of themselves, so to speak, and don't join forces with the protagonist.

We will examine briefly each of the two dramas in order to illuminate important aspects of the conflicts and of the relationship scripts of each of the main characters. As you read, in your mind's eye put the characters onstage and become an objective critic. Afterward, think about whether their family dramas tell you anything about your own and whether the ways the spouses relate to each other and to the children are similar to your ways.

Gone With the Wind

The setting is Atlanta and the Southern countryside between 1861 and 1872. The events of the Civil War and its aftermath figure heavily in the story, though for our purposes they can be ignored, along with the many characters in this long movie, except Scarlett and Rhett, with some reference to Ashley. Also, our interest in Scarlett and Rhett extends only to how they relate to each other—to their relationship scripts and their family drama.

When the movie opens, young Scarlett is the center of attention among men. She captivates them and gets them to satisfy her wishes as if they were commands. She is infuriated when a man she likes (the considerate and unaggressive Ashley), who knows her only as a young friend and neighbor, decides to marry his cousin. We see her move through three marriages, determined to have Ashley leave his wife. She marries her first husband out of spite and her second for money. Finally, she marries Rhett, whom she has spurned time and again. He loves her passionately and has wanted her almost from the beginning, although he sees through her scheming and won't be manipulated by her.

It seems now that the beautiful princess and the rich, handsome prince will live happily ever after. Not so. Scarlett's relationship script won't permit her to give up on getting Ashley. Finally, when his wife dies and he is free to marry again, Scarlett discovers that she doesn't love Ashley and really loves Rhett. But it is too late. By then, the final scene in the movie, Rhett is so fed up with her endless rejections and contempt for him that he leaves her, presumably forever. Within moments, tears streaming down her face, Scarlett is scheming again, this time about how to win him back.

At the end of the movie, you and your spouse should review the story and begin to look beneath its surface. You ask yourselves what it has to say about marriage and family and, more particularly, about Rhett and Scarlett's *relationship scripts* and *family drama.*

Rhett's relationship script shows him to be comfortable and self-possessed. He speaks his mind openly. There is no deviousness about him and no hypocrisy. Rhett makes no pretense about the fact that he is self-centered: his personal dream is to live a life of pleasure and luxury, and he uses his brain and charm to achieve that life. Finally, he reveals considerable capacity for social, emotional, and sexual intimacy.

Scarlett's relationship script shows her to be comfortable in relationships when she holds the dominant position. When she is not in control, she reverts to feeling like a child and then schemes to get into the top position again. She appears to be outspoken, but often, because of her devious purposes, she does not reveal her actual thoughts. Her personal dream is to be rich enough to live the way she wants to—and she'll use any means necessary to achieve this. Finally, she keeps intimacy at arm's length. She marries two men she has no love for, deceives herself into believing that she loves a man she can't have, and keeps her distance from Rhett, the man who loves her and whom she loves, finally driving him away. Her relationship script explains why, at the end, she remembers the words of her father, that you can depend only on the land you own. A person who must avoid intimacy is finally left only with property.

Of course, Rhett and Scarlett's story is tragic. In watching the final scene, when Scarlett asks what will happen to her after he leaves and Rhett answers, "Frankly, my dear, I don't give a damn," you probably thought of their many wasted years. As you examine the drama they created from their two relationship scripts, you can appreciate why it turned out this way.

The interaction of their relationship scripts inevitably led to serious conflict. Their personal dreams clashed—hers for independence at any price, and his for close family life— and could not be reconciled to form a family dream. They did not establish family rules that built trust between them, because she had learned to use any means to reach her goals, including deviousness, while his tendency was to be straightforward. They did not achieve family intimacy because her current incapacity for it prevented that. Taken together, you see that the foundations of a fulfilling family drama were absent, so that instead of experiencing love and contentment together, their drama was filled with misery.

In thinking about their family dream, you probably feel it was doomed from the beginning because of their antagonistic relationship scripts. However, because family dramas are not unchangeable, theirs was not permanently doomed, for Rhett and Scarlett could have rewritten it. They would have had to understand that time alone doesn't correct serious incompatibilities, nor does one partner's patience with the frustrating behavior of the other. With that understanding, they could have begun to examine what was driving them apart.

We have gone through the process of looking below the surface of the movie. We recommend that you do this as a regular practice. In our personal lives, we have found that a discussion about the family dramas in movies and the relationship scripts of the characters makes fascinating conversation and offers insight into ourselves.

All in the Family

Even situation comedies offer you a chance to be a critic and to practice observing families in action and defining relationships. Watching *All in the Family,* you see a typical sequence of events: a difference arises between Archie and his wife Edith; their daughter and son-in-law support Edith, the son-in-law with great vigor. The difference is resolved by the end of the episode, usually revealing one or another of Archie's prejudices.

These brief programs reveal the characters' relationship scripts and the Bunker family drama. Witnessing Archie's behavior and hearing his part in conversations, you can identify the features of his relationship script: he needs to feel superior to others, and he acts out this need by means of a facade of knowing everything despite his ignorance and unworldliness, and by putting down ethnic and religious groups, and individuals, including his wife and son-in-law. In his sledgehammer style, Archie is open about everything except tender emotions, which he feels but dares not voice. Underneath it all, however, Archie is an insecure man, who is very much in need of the unconditional love he gets from his wife and the not quite unconditional love and affection he gets from his daughter.

Edith's relationship script makes her warm, loving, and eager to please. She is a stronger and more sensible woman than she appears to be, even if at times she gives the impression of being a simpleton. Like some women of her generation, she learned to appear less able than she was and to compromise her own principles, if need be, in deference to her husband. She is open about love for her family and support for her neighbors, but usually not about views that differ from Archie's. Although she rejects Archie's prejudices and insulting behavior, she never fails in her love for him.

Their family drama is made up of the relationship scripts of two ordinary people who manage to make a go of their marriage because their scripts complement each other, unlike those of Rhett and Scarlett. Archie needs to feel important and on top; Edith needs to be nurturing and loving. They both know that he has to be the "lord and master" in the home. Yet, at some moments, he probably feels that she is the family's pillar of strength. She is strong enough to satisfy his need to be head of the family and happy enough in her love for him to stay in the relationship.

The Bunker family drama is a relatively happy one. Archie and Edith manage to satisfy each other's needs. They share the same family dream: a warm and loving relationship in a comfortable, livable home of their own. They follow a clear set of rules about work roles, expression of affection, and even who sits in what chair! When they come close to collision over some sensitive issue, their family rules come into play. Edith backs down, and Archie saves face. Sometimes he runs off to the neighborhood bar. One way or another they work out their differences, usually by Edith's submission or occasionally by negotiation, when each of them gives a little.

They cope with Archie's anxiety about closeness and intimacy. They have a built-in defense to protect them from a degree of intimacy that Archie would find excessive by having their daughter and her husband live with them. The effect is that Archie and Edith have much less time to spend alone together. However, even this is not enough, because, when Edith expresses affection, Archie defends himself against such intimacy by berating her for exhibiting it, although she knows (and most viewers know) he wants and needs it.

One reassuring lesson you learn by observing the Bunker family drama is that happiness in family life does not require perfection. You *can* have imperfections as individuals and still get a large measure of happiness from family life. You *can* use various ways to escape intimacy that one or more members of your family cannot tolerate or to avoid arguments you are otherwise unable to resolve. And you *can,* as Edith does (supported by her daughter and helped by the changing role of women in society), rewrite your relationship scripts and become stronger persons, better able to satisfy your personal needs.

After you practice playing the critical observer of relationship scripts and family dramas on the stage and screen, you are ready to apply the skill to real-life situations. Relatives, friends, and neighbors offer plenty of opportunity. We are not proposing that you intrude into their lives beyond your current relationship. We are merely suggesting that you put them "onstage" and observe them as you did Rhett and Scarlett, Archie and Edith, and other couples and families in film or on television. In your mind, picture how they relate to you, each other, and their children. This really means getting to understand them better.

Next, apply what you have learned to *your* family. Put yourselves onstage as the actors and sit in the audience as the critic. The objectives are the same. You're looking to define your mate's relationship script and your own and to identify the different aspects of your family drama—your family dream and the rules you live by to help you realize the dream and to meet your individual and family needs.

But we must not get ahead of ourselves, because much of this book was written to help you do just that: to sort out the scripts and rewrite them and the family drama for greater satisfaction. The next chapter will tell you how the relationship script was written and how it is used.

2

How Your Relationship Script Develops

Seven-year-old Michael threw open the screen door and searched for his mother, Margaret. He had been chased home from school by a couple of bullies. Tears ran down his frightened face as he reported the incident, hoping for sympathy.

"Wash up and go to your room," Margaret said sternly, giving the boy a distinct sense of wrongdoing. Shocked by this response, Michael meekly left the kitchen and went into the den.

That evening, Margaret spoke about the incident with Michael's father, Edward, who took his son aside for a man-to-man talk. He criticized Michael, as he often did, and told him never to run away from a fight: "Big boys don't run, and they don't cry."

Edward explained that running away is a sign of weakness. He wanted Michael to be strong and warned that any more sissiness of this sort would be severely punished.

At that moment, the young boy decided never to cry again. From then on, he would be outwardly tough and hide his fears. If he was frightened, he certainly wouldn't tell anyone. This decision, which stuck for a lifetime, made for a more workable relationship with his parents. They respected his toughness and his apparent lack of vulnerability.

Many years later, married with three children, Michael faced the threat of losing his job. Despite his fear and concern about what this would mean to his family, he could not confide in his wife Barbara. He had to face it alone—to tough it out like a man.

Although Michael never uttered a word to Barbara about the possibility of losing his job, he was angry at her because she offered no support. But because Michael's behavior with Barbara had been predetermined by his childhood, she couldn't possibly help. She didn't even know what was happening. As a child, in making his best efforts to adjust to the demands of his family, Michael had determined that he would behave with other people in the same manner.

From our early childhood experiences, we draw conclusions about ourselves and thus the workings of the world. We form certain attitudes and beliefs about what is right and wrong in relationships we make. We have dreams and fears that influence our decisions about how to behave with other people. When all these factors combine, what emerges is a comprehensive picture of ourselves in the world of people— our *relationship script.*

In this chapter you will see that, during childhood, we have all learned a relationship script that we follow as adults. It guides and governs family life and love life. You will see how relationship scripts form, and you'll discover some of the behaviors and attitudes that are part of a relationship script.

The term "script" is borrowed from the theater. The idea is that, once we write our relationship scripts, how we behave with others and whom we choose as romantic partners is more or less set—almost as if we were following a theatrical script that has a predictable outcome.

In a sense, scripts give order to life. There are countless ways that one can behave. Yet, because scripts are personal to each of us, our responses can be anticipated. Scripts dictate the choices of our behavior.

Although a script may give order to life, it can also limit our options—that is, we do what our scripts dictate even when another choice might be more appropriate. Herein lies the problem with scripts. Based on what we have learned as

children, we are attracted to certain individuals and seek out
certain qualities and characteristics in romantic partners.
Then we interact with these partners in the specific ways that
we learned. In effect, as adults, we re-create our childhood
patterns.

Some of the people we choose as partners and the ways
in which we interact with them are fulfilling. Others may be
less so, and some even downright destructive. Behaviors that
worked in our childhood may prove entirely inadequate for
coping with relationships in our adulthood. Whatever the
outcome, we are basically living by plans developed before
adolescence, when our relationship scripts were formed.

By the age of seven Michael had learned to hide his
fears. In fact, one of the dominant features of his entire script
was to hide feelings of all sorts. By the age of nine he was
capable of concealing fear, hurt, and disappointment, even
when relating to his family and closest friends. Clearly this
scripted behavior was to have a profound effect upon his
future relationships.

Michael's injunction against showing feelings led to predictable responses in a variety of situations. When hurt or
disappointed, he would withdraw from the scene or pretend
he didn't care. His thoughts were consistent: "Who cares?"
"So what?" "Big deal." As a teenager, he seemed unaffected
when he was rejected by a girlfriend. "I guess I'll have to get
another one," he said, seemingly unmoved by the experience.

Many years later though, whenever his wife Barbara was
angry or critical of him about something, such as neglecting
to do the yard work, he would ignore her complaints and
would direct his attention to other friends and activities. This
blasé but predictable attitude meant that Michael could not
directly face his relationship problems. It is evident he never
learned the skills of everyday problem solving, such as clear
thinking, examining options, discussion, and compromise.

Under the influence of his script, Michael was no more
expressive of his affectionate emotions than of any other
feelings. Only rarely would he verbalize what he called the

"mushy stuff." Michael's relationship script continued to prevent him from expressing emotions in his romantic relationships and later with his children. It deprived him of one of the most important elements of intimacy. Michael will never enjoy a truly intimate relationship unless he changes his relationship script. In that sense, he is typical of the so called "unfeeling male" who has been a popular book topic in recent years.

He is a case in point: unless you change your relationship script, you will establish relationships based on childhood decisions.

Fortunately, scripts can be changed. First we must realize that we adhere to one. Then we need to know what to look for in order to identify our own script. To help, we begin with an explanation of how a script is formed. This will prove valuable in thinking about how we became the unique people we are.

THE ROLE OF PARENTS

When Michael's parents told him never to run away from a fight, they had clear ideas about the behavior they wanted from their son.

In the Schwebel family, we sometimes laugh about how Dad (Milton) promised his sons (Andrew and Robert) that he would buy them each a couch if they became psychologists. This was back in the days when the analyst's couch was prevalent. His promise was meant to be humorous, but he must have known what he wanted. The joke became a reality—Andrew and Robert accepted the script and entered the profession; however, Milton never delivered on the couches!

If you are a parent, you probably have many ideas about the behavior you wish to encourage in your offspring. You also have ideas about how to shape and influence your children's behavior.

Although many of the ways you influence children are

planned, a large amount of your influence is unintentional. You may wish to think about these two influences as intended and unintended messages. In reading these pages you will probably remember events that helped shape your own relationship script. You also may wish to think about the messages you are currently giving your own children. The intended influences will be easy to identify, but becoming aware of the unintended ones is the challenge.

Intended Parental Influence

Intended influence is the way you consciously try to mold your children. This can be neatly summarized with three statements.

> As parents, you tell your children *dos* and *don'ts.*
>
> You tell your children *shoulds* and *should nots.*
>
> You *reward* the behavior you like and *punish* the behavior you dislike.

Even when you intend to create a certain effect, you may not actually attain the results you desire. As you look at intended influence, consider the possibility that a child has misunderstood your intentions or even rebelled against them. Intended influence sometimes produces unintended results.

The *dos,* more formally called "prescriptions," are parents' statements about expected behavior. For example, Michael's parents valued success in school and career. They said, "Do your homework every night." "Do your household chores." Other prescriptions for Michael included "Stick up for yourself if there is trouble," "Be brave," and "Do your work alone, without assistance."

The *don'ts,* more formally referred to as "injunctions," are parental statements about forbidden behavior. For example, Michael's parents were against what they considered to be displays of emotional weakness. Michael's injunctions in-

cluded "Don't cry," "Don't ask for help," "Don't run away
from fights," and "Don't let people know how you feel."

The dos and don'ts that children hear are reinforced by
the *shoulds* and *should nots*. Parents use these as tools to
communicate their values.

One of the most important values in Michael's family
was the work ethic. His parents stressed that children should
work hard in their studies, just as adults should do their very
best in their work. Michael recalls these two statements in
particular: "You should always work hard." "You should
never slack off."

Parents' expectations—expressed in dos, don'ts,
shoulds and should nots—are made even more compelling by
an array of *rewards* and *punishments*. Children who do as they
are told are usually rewarded materially, emotionally, and
verbally. Those who do not are punished.

Michael's parents were not particularly generous with
praise, although good grades were expected and well received. An excellent report card was rewarded with a gift.
Hard work and the suppression of emotions were rewarded
with compliments.

When he was eight years old, Michael's younger sister
deliberately broke his toy football game. Instead of getting
angry, Michael said, "It doesn't matter. I don't care." He was
able to hide his feelings. His parents commended him for his
restraint by frequently talking about the mature way he handled that situation. They reinforced the toughness they
wanted to see in their son. When Michael's parents disap-
proved of something, they usually talked to him about it or
became quiet and withdrew affection. They didn't use physical forms of punishment such as spanking.

Now try to be an objective critic of your relationship
script. With a journal or notebook in hand, try to remember
what your parents said to you as a child. List the dos and the
don'ts they gave you. Which of these dos and don'ts are you
still following? Which ones backfired on your parents?
Which ones do you feel you are passing on to your own

children? How were you rewarded and punished? How are you enforcing the suggestions and commands that you make to your own children? By thinking this through, and writing it down on paper, you will better understand your relationship script and be prepared for rewriting any parts of it you may wish to change.

Unintended Parental Influence

A great deal of parental influence in script formation is not planned, not consciously promoted. Parents set examples without realizing that they are teaching important lessons. Parents serve as *role models,* sometimes by conscious example, but often merely by living out their own scripts. Below we describe a few ways this happens.

Although Michael's parents described their marriage as a lofty commitment of love, they demonstrated something entirely different to their son. When Edward married Margaret, he felt no passion for her, keeping a distance throughout the years. This distance was also maintained by Margaret, who loved her husband but was often upset with him. One of her reasons for marriage was personal insecurity. She had been twenty-three at the time, two years older than Edward, and fearful that she would never find another man. Throughout most of their married life, Margaret was disappointed in Edward's social status and in the quality of their relationship. If it had not been for her insecurity, she might have considered a divorce.

With his parents as role models, Michael came to view marriage simply as an event that inevitably occurred at a certain age. To some extent, it was a means of gaining benefits through his wife performing the traditional role, but he also perceived marriage as a rather boring way of life.

Negative resolutions.   Another form of unintended influence, negative resolutions, are reactions against role models. A child observes the way parents behave and resolves never to be that way. For example, Michael realized that his father, who had worked most of his adult life as a technician for a public utility corporation, had been unhappy about his job. This awareness prompted Michael to vow never to be a slave to work. Because he had witnessed his mother nagging his father about not achieving enough, he was also determined to avoid complainers.

Rebellion.   Sometimes parental influence causes exactly the opposite of the effect intended, through rebellion, in which children deliberately defy parental prescriptions, injunctions, and values. A controlling parent who tries to deny teenagers an opportunity for autonomy is likely to create a rebellious child. Edward told Michael, "If I ever find out you smoked pot, I'll throw you out of the house." Michael's response was rebellious: "Don't worry, you'll never find out."

Rebellious responses to parental control are sometimes very creative with children who follow the letter of the law while breaking it in spirit. A teenage daughter we know who was told "never let boys touch you" subsequently got involved with older men.

Hidden scripting.   An important form of unintended influence is the script behind the script, known as the hidden script. Parental influence appears to lead to one type of behavior on the surface, while in practice the *actual* effect is quite different. For example, although Michael's parents gave him little positive support, they encouraged hard work, school achievement, and a stiff upper lip. His parents thought of themselves as selective in awarding praise, not wanting to spoil Michael. If asked why, they would probably say that they were attempting to encourage effort and hard work.

Unwittingly, Edward and Margaret created a very different outcome from what they intended. Because they gave so little positive attention, Michael eventually gave up. The attitude he developed was that he did not have much to lose by disobeying or disappointing his parents. The hidden script was "Don't even try to please Mom and Dad. You can't get much praise by pleasing them anyway."

Unfulfilled parental desires.   Another type of unintended influence in script-writing occurs when parents subtly communicate their own unconscious desires. Children read between the lines and often find themselves with scripts that incorporate unfulfilled parental desires. Sometimes, of course, parents overtly attempt to steer their children toward their own personal aspirations. The unintended influence, however, is much more subtle. Michael's mother, for example, held considerable resentment toward his father but never overtly expressed it. She found an outlet for her feelings of anger by unconsciously reinforcing Michael's rebellious behavior. When Michael fought against his father, Margaret defended Michael—even when he was being unreasonable. So in an indirect way, Michael performed the function of expressing Margaret's resentments toward Edward for her.

Looking back on your childhood, try to figure out which unintended influences may have affected your relationship script. If you are a parent, try to make yourself an objective critic of your family. What types of unintended influences might be at work with your children? Rather than trying to focus on what you want them to accomplish, take an objective look at what is happening. You might discover some unintended scripting.

Other influences.   Without a doubt, parents have the greatest influence on the life of a child, but they are not the only influence. Other individuals such as brothers, sisters, friends, teachers, and clergy each have an impact, as do institutions such as churches, scouts, schools, and the mass media. National and international events, including economic conditions, have bearing upon a relationship script. Baby boomers remember their parents talking about the Great Depression, which transmitted a sense of scarcity, the possibility that there wouldn't be enough to go around. Chance factors such as birth order, sex, race, and place of residence cannot be overlooked for their impact upon how a child views the world and learns to cope.

Conflicting messages. Children are constantly bombarded with messages about how to behave. In the construction of a script, certain messages tend to take center stage, unifying the script and dictating a life course. These important messages are generally consistent with one another. For example, it wouldn't be likely that the message "Be tough; be a man" would be accompanied by "Be a nurse when you grow up." It's more likely that the directive would be for the child to work in construction or perhaps in a high-powered profession.

Sometimes, however, script messages do conflict. In these circumstances, a dominant one prevails. A good example involved two of Michael's messages. His parents told him to "be a man." This meant he should conceal his vulnerability and handle all personal problems on his own, without the support of others. They also told him to succeed in school. The conflict between these messages arose in the tenth grade when Michael was hospitalized and homebound for several weeks after tearing ligaments and cartilage in both knees in a serious skiing accident. Even though his parents brought schoolwork to the hospital, Michael fell behind in his studies.

As his script dictated, Michael worked diligently. However, he needed more than a good effort to keep pace in three subjects—math, Spanish, and chemistry. In each of these subjects, basic skills were taught in the classroom while he was absent. Success in future lessons depended upon mastery of these fundamentals. Michael didn't realize that he had missed important material and, for the first time in his school career, began to fall behind and feel frustrated in his studies. He worked hard but lacked vital information for success. He needed help.

Michael faced the dilemma of determining which of the following directives was more important: *Succeed in school.*

(To do this, he would need to ask for help.) *Be tough. Do it
alone.* (A strong person, he was taught, doesn't need help.)

Because of his strong conditioning against seeking help,
Michael didn't even seriously consider the possibility of getting the smallest bit of assistance. Unaware of the option of
getting help (from teachers, tutors, counselors, parents, or
friends) and unwilling to be seen as a failure in school, Michael arrived at a creative solution. He began to withdraw his
energy from school, stating that it was "boring." This was his
"I don't care" attitude, a defense against the pressure to do
well in school. Michael increasingly filled his free time by
pursuing his interest in the electric guitar.

This musical pursuit, besides serving as a convenient
excuse to evade school problems, helped meet other needs.
Because Michael had learned to hide his feelings, he required
an emotional outlet. Music became that. It also helped aug-
ment his popularity with girls, an increasingly important interest. By playing in a band, he became more attractive to
members of the opposite sex.

Predictably, Michael's relationship with his parents rap-
idly deteriorated—especially with his father. More than anything, Edward wanted educational and financial success for
his son. He applied intense pressure on Michael to improve
his grades. Michael's mother tended to be more accepting,
having the notion that her son would eventually mature and
regain his interest in school. However, Michael never recov-
ered academically. To mask his failure in school and to aug-
ment his new musical lifestyle, Michael—at the age of
sixteen—started drinking alcohol, sometimes heavily.

COMPONENTS OF THE
RELATIONSHIP SCRIPT

You should have a sense of how a script is formed by now.
We will continue to follow the example of Michael's relationship script at age sixteen in presenting the specific script

components so that you may begin to get a grasp of your own script. To do this, think about what messages guide your life in each of the categories that follow. Try to put yourself in the critic's chair, endeavoring to see yourself as an unbiased observer might.

If you have children, you may want to consider the type of relationship script you want to promote and the experiences you need to provide to aid in achieving it. With older children, you may be able to discuss openly their relationship scripts.

As you read through the components, keep a pencil and paper handy so you can write down your self-evaluations.

Emotional awareness.   This is the awareness of what we are feeling. It is a prerequisite for communication. People cannot open up to others if they don't know what they feel—that is, what they want, what makes them angry, what scares them. If they can't say what they feel, it is unlikely they will have relationships that meet their needs and enable them to work out differences or problems. Michael wears a "suit of armor" against emotions. He was told to be tough and hide his feelings. Because of this, he is out of touch.

In your family life, what angers you most? What frustrates you? What bores you? Who is most responsible for stirring these feelings in you? What do you experience when you are angry? Does it leave you tongue-tied? Do you want to run away, or say what you feel and work it out with the person who provoked your anger?

Capacity for love.   This defines the extent to which we can feel intimacy and a connectedness with other human beings. It contrasts with self-centeredness. Michael's parents were poor role models, showing very little affection to each other and to their children. Consequently, Michael is underdeveloped in his capacity for love. He feels little warmth for anyone, and he is somewhat disinterested in girls except as an outlet for his sexual desires. For the most part, Michael is egocentric—totally concerned with his own needs.

In your fantasies, how close and loving are you to your spouse and children—very close, somewhat close, or rather distant? In real life, how close are you? In your entire life, with whom have you been able to show the most closeness? If closeness is a problem, have you discussed it with your spouse? If not, why? Can you say, I love you? Whom have you said it to? How do you show that you care?

Self-esteem. This is affection and positive or negative feelings that we have for ourselves. It has great bearing on our selection of a mate and on what we need in a relationship. For example, a man who dislikes his own physical appearance might seek out a good-looking woman as a trophy. Or he might feel that he is unworthy of an attractive partner. Michael's parents gave him little approval as a child, so he developed very little self-esteem. Because school success had been one of the goals forced on him—one he was failing to achieve—Michael doubted his own intelligence. Although his musical ability brought him positive recognition from others and provided an ego boost, he still lacked intellectual confidence.

Do you like yourself? If so, what makes you proud to be you? If not, who led you to feel dissatisfied with yourself? What experiences gave you the idea that you have to be different to be likable? What would have to happen for you to find yourself more acceptable? Are you taking any action to make that happen?

Cooperation. This attitude concerns our desire to work with others and share the benefits of such work. It is contrasted with a desire to be alone and work alone. It also is contrasted with a need to dominate or submit to another person. The attitude of cooperation has bearing on our ability to negotiate differences and work for compromises in any relationship. Michael is competitive. He views the world as "dog eat dog" and wants to come out on top. In terms of romantic relationships, he wants to find women who won't give him a hard time.

What feelings do you have about teamwork at home? Can you divide work fairly and do your share? Do you expect others to do their share? Is the sharing of work done successfully? What kinds of difficulties do you encounter in working with others? Do you get satisfaction from teamwork in planning and carrying out activities?

Communication skills.   This is our ability to say what we think and feel, and our capacity to listen to another person. Michael is very deficient in this skill. He lacks emotional awareness and therefore cannot communicate his feelings. Also, because he is self-absorbed, he is incapable of being a good listener.

Can you express your hurt feelings? Anger? Suspicion? How do you react when you disagree with an opinion expressed by your spouse, child, or friend? Do you express your disagreement? How free are you to say what restaurant or movie you would prefer? When you and your spouse have an argument, do you listen to his/her statements, or do you plan your own response instead?

Conflict resolution.   This is our attitude about conflict and our ability to resolve it. When a positive attitude prevails, we believe that problems can be solved. We face them squarely. Without such an attitude, we feel a sense of hopelessness. Also, in order to resolve conflict, we need to have the ability to think clearly about personal problems and to maintain our objectivity. Michael was not exposed to examples of effective conflict resolution. His parents let their problems fester for years with little effort given to resolving them. Michael is more inclined to avoid conflict than to face it.

How do you feel when you and your spouse have an

argument? Do you tend to face it squarely or try to avoid it? Do you think clearly or get flustered? If you get flustered, have you discussed this problem with your spouse so that the two of you would be better prepared to deal with your differences? Can you be self-critical? Can you offer constructive criticism to family members?

Everyday problem-solving.   This is our ability to solve the inevitable problems of daily life. For example, a woman has been asked to stay late every night at work, throwing off the evening routine of her family. Or a teenage child receives a poor report card. To deal with these situations, family members need to have everyday problem-solving skills. Your ability to think clearly about such matters will profoundly influence the quality of your relationships.

Michael is a well-developed thinker. However, he tends to avoid facing problems. Also, his rational problem-solving abilities are hindered by personal hang-ups, including his need to do it alone, his rebelliousness, his low self-esteem, and his need to dominate. For example, at times when good judgment would call for consulting with others, his need to do it alone prevents him from drawing on resources that are available.

When problems arise in your family, what are your typical reactions? Do you view problems as catastrophes, or as challenges for you to master? Do you tend to blame other family members? Or yourself? Exactly what steps did you take in coping with the most recent problem? Did you go it alone or team up with your spouse or child?

Coping style.   This refers to our characteristic ways of approaching the world, including the people we love. For example, some people avoid discussing emotional issues; some people blame others for all their problems; some bury their feelings with substance abuse; some become aggressive when they are frightened; some are "pleasers" who always put other people first.

Michael copes through tough indifference. He stands alone. He does not form strong emotional connections. He withdraws from conflict. He hides his vulnerability by professing indifference. But in many respects, Michael is also shy and inhibited. By age sixteen, he had begun to use alcohol to cope with stress.

What is your coping style? How do you adapt to the pressures of life and especially the stress in relationships? When your spouse seems unhappy or depressed, what do you do? In the case of your child, what do you do? What happens to you when a loved one gets into that state? When you yourself develop an unhappy mood, what do you do?

Values. These are your beliefs about what is good or bad, right or wrong, important or unimportant. People generally seek others who share similar values. We have an entire set of values about relationships; they concern the type of relationship we want and the type of family we envision for ourselves, including dreams we have about the ideal family life.

Michael has little interest in reflecting on personal values. He appears to be striving for success, recognition, and a sense of competency through his music. Financial success is not important to him at this time, but his financial aspirations, conditioned by his parents and incorporated into his script, will become more apparent in later years.

Michael enjoys companionship and likes engaging in social activities with others. He does not place a high value on emotional intimacy, though. He keeps his distance and does not allow himself to be vulnerable with girls. He is in no rush to marry but assumes that he will find a mate, probably in his late twenties. He says he wants a woman who won't "give me a hard time." If asked why, he would probably say that he expects to have two or three children. He values individuality above all else.

What are the three features of your family life that you value most? To what extent do your spouse and children share those values? What is one characteristic of your family that you would like to change? Have you discussed that with your spouse?

Recreation.   In part this concerns the value we place on fun. It also concerns our capacity for joyfulness—to laugh, play, and feel excitement. An important aspect of a good relationship is a couple's capacity to find enjoyment together. Some of Michael's capacity for excitement is inhibited by his injunctions against emotion. However, Michael can be playful. He seeks and enjoys recreational outlets with others. He especially enjoys his musical pursuits.

What are your values with regard to recreation?

Do you enjoy laughing? What people give you the most opportunity to laugh? Do you feel free to be yourself—carefree and open—with your spouse? Children? Friends? Parents? Do you have enough excitement in your life? If not, what would give you more? What is your idea of a good time?

Work and responsibility.   This deals with the value we place on work and responsibility. It is also our willingness and ability to work inside and outside the home. Michael is willing to work hard, though his career options will be limited by lack of education and lack of confidence about his intelligence. In a live-in situation with a woman, he would be willing to do a share of the chores, although conventional sex roles would define the division of labor.

How do you feel about shouldering responsibilities such as paying bills, seeing that the children do their homework, or doing the laundry? What is your attitude about doing family work that is traditionally assigned to the other sex? What satisfaction do you get from work at home? From a paid job? Are you usually cheerful when you get up in the morning, ready to face the day's work?

THE RELATIONSHIP SCRIPT
AND THE LIFE PLAN

All the components in a relationship script combine to form a big picture—the outlook for a life plan. Looking at Michael's relationship script, we can see the type of partners he will seek, anticipate the problems he will encounter, and predict the dramatic developments that lie ahead.

Michael is fairly outgoing and will find himself in contact with many women. He is physically attractive, and his musical talents will bring him additional female attention. Although his main interest in women partners will be in finding carefree companionship, because of his need to control, he will probably seek out a submissive and unassertive woman. When he evaluates the benefits of a relationship, his main questions will be "Do I have fun with this woman?" "Am I in control?" "Is she demanding?" and "Does she complain?"

The women who date him will find themselves involved with a man who keeps great emotional distance, is unaware of many of his feelings, is not very affectionate, and is not interested in making commitments. For the most part, Michael will want to get his own way, so many women will tend to avoid a relationship with him.

Michael dreams about success as a popular musician, although attaining success at the level he desires is unlikely. He is willing to work hard, but both his rebelliousness and inadequate education might cause him difficulty in seeking gainful employment. As a young man, finances will not be an issue, even though he grew up in a family with a level of economic comfort that he has taken for granted and will probably want to attain for himself.

His relatively low economic status may be a factor that discourages the interest of certain women partners. Another important issue is that Michael will have to struggle with a substance-abuse problem, because he uses alcohol to lessen his inhibitions. Although this may be a problem to some women, it could be an attraction to "rescuer" types who are seeking a man to save.

If he finds an assertive woman, she will make some demands. That will mean big problems because Michael lacks skills in conflict resolution. Any differences that do occur will be impossible to resolve. Further, Michael wants to avoid hassles and will reject a woman who begins to "make trouble." Michael will *not* give up control. A pushy female won't get her way. He will reject her.

Michael wants a wife and children at some point in his life. He will reach a certain age and social situation when he will finally say, "Now is the time." The scenario will probably involve a submissive, dependent woman who puts his needs first. Michael will commit himself only when *he* is ready. But the marriage will have its problems. He will be an emotionally unexpressive man who is trying to establish a family, unaware that this is a task requiring emotional communication. They will establish a dominant-submissive relationship, which is always a time bomb.

Sooner or later, one of two things will happen: He will see her lack of self-respect and lose the little respect that he has for her, and as a result want to escape; or she will get angry about his dominance and may want to escape—then one or the other may decide that the costs of the relationship outweigh the benefits. Either way, the marriage will be threatened. She may request counseling, but he won't go because it would be a sign of weakness. Predictably, Michael's script will not lead to a fulfilling family life. Unless he changes his relationship script, he will live the life plan he developed in early childhood.

Now tie together your self-evaluations of each script component and examine your relationship script as we did for Michael. Looking at each component, one at a time, write one sentence for each, no more than that. Limiting it to one compels us to reduce our self-descriptions to the most basic level, such as "I really want to cooperate with my spouse, yet

I end up always wanting to one-up him." Start each sentence on a separate line. You will end up with eleven sentences. At that point, put a plus sign next to those that please you because they are good for you and your family, and a minus next to those that limit your effectiveness and pleasure in life. Think of the effects both the plus and minus items have on your relationships with your spouse, children, and the other important people in your life. Later, we will have more to say about rewriting relationship scripts that impair the family drama.

3

Dating and Courtship: Looking for a Costar

*I*n this chapter you'll see how your relationship scripts guide your dating behavior. From this, you will get a deeper understanding of why some people make poor choices in mates. Also, we'll continue to follow the dating career of one man to see, in detail, how recurring issues in a relationship script lead to a predictable drama in family life.

In the Schwebel family, we often joke about Milton and Bernice's first date, which took place during the depression era. They went to the restaurant of the Trojan Hotel in Troy, New York, in the spring of 1936. Big spender Milton handed Bernice a menu and asked what she would like to order. More than fifty years later, we don't know what Bernice considered, perhaps a filet mignon, perhaps a simple dinner. But somehow she realized that Milton had only fifty cents in his pocket. Bernice ordered tomato juice, and Milton was impressed.

When they left the restaurant, it was raining. Bernice was wearing a new outfit. Milton, always the gentleman, offered to hail a cab. He knew the owner of the local taxi company and thought he might manage it on credit. Bernice was impressed but couldn't imagine where the cab fare would come from. She declined the offer.

We joke about the "tomato-juice date." Looking back, we know that Bernice didn't marry for money. She was undoubtedly attracted by other attributes. Today, we can conclude that Milton and Bernice had compatible relationship scripts.

RELATIONSHIP SCRIPTS AND DATING PATTERNS

Dating and courtship bring individuals together, each with a relationship script, each seeking a costar in the life drama who can satisfy personal needs. Relationship scripts explain attraction, guide dating behavior, and ultimately determine the level of intimacy that people share.

The problem is that people don't have an awareness of their relationship scripts. We may recognize that we are attracted to certain types of people but not understand what it is about ourselves that drives this attraction. We may have problems recur in relationships but not understand how we have been "programmed" for certain types of problems to occur. To understand our dating behaviors, it is important to recognize the working of our relationship scripts.

Having reviewed the components of the relationship script, consider your choice of partners. Take an objective look at yourself; be a critic and mentally put yourself onstage. You should be able to determine which factors most strongly influenced your preferences. If you are single, you can predict the type of partner that is likely to appeal to you. You can think ahead of time about the implications of the choice you eventually make.

One of the best ways to determine script influence is to look for repeated patterns. We have a friend whom we have watched choose one miserable dating partner after another. Like a magnet to iron, she has been drawn to men with serious drinking problems. She tries to save them from alcohol, and they eventually insult and hurt her. In almost every instance, they end up having an affair with another woman. Our friend's choice of partners, and the pattern of her devotion to them followed by their rejection of her, only makes sense in terms of her relationship script. It explains why such a lovely woman repeatedly would get involved with such troubled and angry men.

This is what happens: Although she is filled with self-doubt, she does feel good when she is trying to rescue someone. She finds men in need of help who like to be pampered. They want her help but resent their inferior position. Eventually, because their inhibitions are lessened by alcohol, they act out their anger by either insulting her directly or having an affair. We know that our friend grew up with an alcoholic father and learned this "pleasing" behavior as a child. She has a lot of talent and many fine qualities, but she is a prisoner of her script.

Acknowledging her script would help her to understand and perhaps alter her reality. "Yes," she might realize, "I am attracted to men with drinking problems who want to be saved. It makes me feel valuable. But the relationships fail, and I get hurt."

Only then would she have some options. She could resist the pull toward needy men. At first, it would not feel natural to her to date men with more self-confidence. She would have to find other qualities in herself to feel good about besides her ability to rescue romantic partners. It would require determination, and she would need support. But, by doing this, she would increase her self-esteem and rewrite her script for the better. She might be able to form a loving and intimate relationship that would not end with her feeling hurt and angry.

Personal Attraction

One of the critical questions people ask about a dating partner is "Does this person offer what I want?"

Initially, personal attraction starts with obvious qualities, such as physical appearance, charm, playfulness, and a sense of humor. Demographic factors, including race, religion, and social class, may enter the equation. The relationship script determines the value given to any particular trait. For example, a gold-digging woman wouldn't have seen Milton again after that first tomato-juice date. To further illustrate this point, let's compare the reaction of three different men to the prospect of dating an intelligent woman named Betty. One thinks of himself as intelligent and wants the pleasure of an intellectually stimulating relationship. A second man considers himself intellectually inferior, often calling himself "stupid" in frustration over his errors. He wants an intelligent woman to cover for his perceived shortfall. A third man also thinks poorly of himself in this regard. He avoids intelligent women because he feels his limitations are more obvious in their presence.

Now let's imagine the interactions of these three men on a first date with Betty. The first man has a delightful conversation with her. They arrange to see each other again. The second man listens in awe as Betty describes her thoughts concerning recent developments in the economy. Because of this he tries to impress her by spending a lot on dinner. Unimpressed, Betty declines an invitation for a second date.

The third man is threatened. Whenever Betty gives an intellectual opinion, he tries to pick it apart. If he can't think of an intelligent response, he makes a wisecrack, such as "Are you as good in bed as you are in the head?"

"You'll never know," says Betty, no slouch in repartee.

The third man and Betty agree to break it off after the first date.

Certain types of relationship scripts complement one another. A submissive person may seek a dominating companion. A dominating person will seek a submissive one, unless of course he or she wants a challenge.

A woman with low self-esteem who thinks she deserves very little in life might select a partner who is deficient in his capacity for affection. Because she feels she has little value, she might be willing to do much more than her share of the work around the house.

An extremely passive man rejects an unassertive woman. "It just didn't feel right," he says. He doesn't know it, but nothing will feel right until he finds a woman who will "mother" him.

Two individuals who share the value of deep religious commitment discover closeness by sharing spiritual beliefs. They enjoy discussing religious issues and participate in numerous church activities.

As people start to get acquainted, relationship messages influence timing, expectations, and commitment. Some scripts are oriented toward finding a costar fast. An individual with this message would probably latch onto the first person who came along. Other scripts are more inclined toward the playful side of dating. Many scripts have different requirements at different times. The early years may be designated for fun, and the later ones for the serious pursuit of a mate.

Problems are inevitable when the needs of a dating couple are divergent—for example, when one wants a casual good time and the other wants commitment.

If a dating person intends to get serious, attraction to a partner may be increasingly influenced by life goals. An aspiring female socialite seeks a successful professional or businessman. The successful male provider, for his part, wants an attractive woman by his side. He thinks she will handle the emotional needs of the two of them. She will arrange the dinner parties and social calendar while he provides the earning power. Sometimes the first date tells it all. When a suitor asks an aspiring socialite for dinner and takes her to a McDonald's, their future together has been determined—he's history. They have shared their last McNuggets.

Poor Choices

Some of the factors that pull people together contribute to positive relationships, and others do not. Some produce long-range compatibility and a satisfying and fulfilling family drama, whereas others produce irreconcilable differences. In some cases, a person will look for one factor in a costar while overlooking other ones that will become important in a relationship as time progresses. People can find one attribute in a partner that is very important to them, get married, and still be extremely dissatisfied because they overlooked other important requirements of their relationship script.

One of us counseled a creative, hard-working man who suffered from low self-esteem that stemmed from childhood neglect but focused largely on his physical appearance. He had been married only two years when he came for help, perplexed by his relationship problem.

"She was everything I wanted," he said. "As soon as I met her, I knew I wanted a relationship. I can't figure out why I'm so dissatisfied now."

"What was the attraction?" the therapist asked.

"She is absolutely gorgeous. She is so beautiful."

"What else did you like?"

"I don't know. I guess she was nice."

This man got involved in a relationship with a very narrow focus of attraction. He could not see beyond one thing—her looks. Physical appearances can't hold a relationship together forever. This man's relationship script was so dependent on one factor in his search for a costar that he didn't think very carefully about his true needs.

In some relationship scripts, the traits that attract people to each other can be a cause of problems. As clinical psychologists, Milton, Andrew, and Robert have worked with couples composed of dependent women married to take-charge men. The man makes all the decisions; the woman defers willingly. She gives up her power; he runs the show. They appear to be a perfect match except for two things: she eventually resents his dominance, and he eventually has disdain for her low self-esteem. With this matchup, we see a script in which people are attracted and repulsed for the very same reasons. Certain psychological needs that pull people together are quite simply the wrong ones on which to base an intimate relationship.

Sometimes dating partners pay attention to certain qualities that they find attractive but overlook the importance of shared values. For example, a religious churchgoer could marry an atheist, while a man who wants a big family might marry a woman who doesn't want children at all.

WHEN RELATIONSHIP SCRIPTS MEET

Put two people together, each with his and her own relationship script, and you have an interpersonal reaction much like a chemical reaction. The couples who hit it off stay together. The greater the compatibility of the relationship scripts, the longer they stay together. As their relationship scripts mesh, they begin to define a new entity—the family drama. The seeds of this drama were in the relationship scripts, but a family drama has certain dimensions of its own that are unique.

Regardless of the quality of the match in terms of attraction, when people form relationships, they will have conflict. People have their differences about what they want out of life and how they plan to work together to attain it. Conflict is inevitable.

The way in which a couple copes with conflict is built into their relationship scripts. The couple may ignore their differences, fight incessantly over them, or possibly resolve them as they arise. Another way couples cope with differences is by finding excuses to keep away from each other. They may, for example, bury themselves in career activities, even wedding preparations, in order to have some distance.

We have worked with many couples in which the household division of labor had become a big issue. David and Marsha, who got married in their early twenties after a short courtship, each had certain assumptions about responsibility, especially household duties. He thought she should do everything. She expected a fifty-fifty arrangement. They didn't talk about their assumptions ahead of time and fought over who made the bed and cooked the meals. But they had good problem-solving skills and a cooperative attitude. Eventually, they learned to negotiate and found satisfactory resolutions.

The outcome of conflict in a family depends largely upon certain critical aspects of the relationship scripts of the people involved—specifically, their skill in conflict resolution; their skill in communication; their ability to love; and their desire to cooperate. Disagreements will not be successfully resolved and intimacy will be limited if the relationship script is weak in these areas.

In thinking about your own relationship script, crucial questions that determine how you get along with others include: Can you commit yourself to another person? Can your partner commit? Do you want to cooperate? Does your partner? Are you willing to be vulnerable? Will your partner be vulnerable? Do you know what you feel, think, and value? Does your partner know what he or she feels, thinks, and values? Can you talk and solve problems effectively together? Can you make good agreements? Can you negotiate differences?

CASE HISTORY: MICHAEL'S DATING PATTERN

To clarify further the role of scripts in dating, we'll continue to examine the dating history of Michael, the young man whose relationship script was presented earlier.

For Michael, dating in his teens and early to mid-twenties was geared toward having fun. He enjoyed the company of women, but he was neither interested in nor capable of emotional intimacy. He assumed that he would get married and have children—sometime in the distant future. He had an "I don't care" attitude about dating. He never pursued anyone; it would be too much of a commitment. Women came to him.

Though his social skills were not well developed, he worked as a singer and guitar player in a rock band that played at bars where he could meet women. Alcohol lubricated his social interactions. There was little personal communication. Relationships were casual and brief. He remained interested as long as women friends didn't, as he put it, "hassle" him.

One of Michael's partners as a teenager was Maria, who first had been attracted to him when she saw him performing onstage. Maria and Michael had only a few dates. Michael never realized it, but Maria broke it off because he didn't conform to her idea of a gentleman. Her script called for someone who would dress stylishly and open doors for her. Michael didn't fit the billing for a costarring role in her production.

Shortly after his twenty-first birthday, Michael met Carolyn at a friend's wedding. She was a cosmetics sales clerk in a big department store. Three months later, they began living together, without a formal discussion or, for that matter, a verbal commitment. She gradually moved her possessions into his apartment. He never would have committed himself to such closeness, so the living-together arrangement had to sneak up on him.

Michael and Carolyn shared common interests in attending sports events and listening to music. Carolyn admired Michael's dream of musical success, was impressed by his dedication to his work, and liked going to hear his band play. He enjoyed Carolyn's attention but kept great emotional distance. There were no "I love you"s, never a serious discussion, no commitments.

Carolyn grew very attached to Michael and wanted more. She thought the problem was his drinking. Michael drank whenever the band played and often had a couple of beers at home during the day. She saw herself as someone who could save him from his bad habit with alcohol and eventually win him over by solving his drinking problem.

In Carolyn's effort to reform Michael, she started to

follow him at parties and count his drinks. She chastised him for drinking too much and urged him to cut back. She complained that too much of his time focused on partying and too little on her.

Michael didn't want to discuss his feelings or problems. His script didn't allow for it. He didn't take well to being told how to behave. In fact, he had a very strong rebellious streak. The more she complained about his drinking, the more he drank. He began to see Carolyn as a nuisance and withdrew further from her. She kept chasing. At this point, she would do anything for him. He wanted to end the relationship, but because of his script injunctions, he could not tell her how he felt except when he was drunk and angry. Finally, Michael started bringing other women to the apartment. It worked—Carolyn moved out.

Irene was attracted by Michael's toughness. She liked partying with him and moved into his apartment shortly after they met. All the attraction was there for her, but there was one serious problem: he never said what he felt, never expressed warmth, never showed emotions. Irene didn't know where she stood and felt unloved.

She wanted to talk about the problem, but he balked. The more she pressed for affection, the further he withdrew. She became enraged, and he started to refer to her as a "hysterical broad." Finally, after all the hurt, she moved out. Michael barely noticed it. He said to a friend, "Too bad. She was crazy, but she was a good kid anyway."

Michael was twenty-six years old when he met Barbara, the woman who was eventually to become his wife. She lived down the block and worked as a high-school teacher in the public school system. After they met through a mutual friend, Barbara would come by to visit. One night they started kissing and ended up in bed.

As they saw each other more frequently, Barbara tried to reach Michael through his stomach. In the evenings, Michael's apartment often smelled of baked goods. Occasionally the two of them would go to a movie together. Her father

owned a small music store in town, so she grew up in a
musical environment and liked to go to clubs to hear Michael's band.

Barbara was a middle child with an older brother and
younger sister. As a child, she had been able to win favor by
being a good little girl and doing nice things for others. She
had helped Mom clean around the house. She had been a
major caretaker for her younger sister. Though she had done
well in school, her personal achievements had not been recognized at home. Her older brother, in contrast, had always
been encouraged to achieve.

This had influenced Barbara's script. She saw men as the
achievers. Women were the helpful ones behind the scene.
She saw, for example, that her mother provided the emotional
support that her father needed to keep operating their small
but successful music store. Barbara's script was to be a good
little girl and give to others. Selfishness was defined as the
ultimate misbehavior. When Barbara assertively asked for
what she wanted, she was told to stop being selfish. Her father
warned her that "selfish girls never find husbands." Her
mother told her that she had to win a man's love. Once the
love was won, the man would give back and the generosity
would be returned.

In keeping with her script directive to give, Barbara was
extremely generous to Michael. She liked the role of supporting him in his career quest. Good givers develop their intui-
tion so, Barbara could see that Michael didn't want to be
pressured into anything. She enjoyed the fun they had together but never asked for a commitment.

About a year after Michael and Barbara had begun their
relationship, Michael's band was booked for a three-month
engagement in a much larger city. This meant good exposure
for the group. On the road, none of the anticipated musical
success occurred. To Michael's surprise, he realized that he
had grown attached to Barbara and missed her, although his
relationship script would not allow him to admit such vulnerability. She called almost every day and arranged a visit that

he looked forward to. When she came, they had a great time together. Near the end of the musical engagement, the keyboard player and the drummer announced their intentions to leave the band.

Michael returned home with his dreams diminished. Worse still, his good friends in the band stayed behind. He was lonely.

With the band dissolved and his best friends absent, Michael filled the void with Barbara. They spent more time together. She moved into his apartment and started doing all the housework. Other than an occasional argument about him leaving his dirty laundry on the floor, they got along well.

Michael still did not verbalize his affection, but his willingness to live together encouraged Barbara. She began to think she could win him over to a marriage commitment, though she never uttered a word, knowing that he would react against such a suggestion.

Barbara was extremely supportive of Michael as he began anew, taking a sales job and working evenings as part of a musical duo with a friend.

He was twenty-eight years old. Several of his friends were married within the period of a few months. Michael was living with Barbara, and his relationship script called for a marriage in his late twenties. He decided it was time. They set a wedding date.

The first part of their family drama had been written: Barbara pleasing Michael and not asking for much in return. Michael was allowed the emotional distance he needed. But the marriage had special meaning in Barbara's script: it meant commitment. Barbara remembered her parents' words that unselfish people were eventually rewarded for their giving. Barbara felt she had a great deal to look forward to.

But Michael didn't change. He remained emotionally remote and never provided the warmth she expected. She blamed herself at first and kept giving. Although they had three children, he still withheld his affection.

Tension mounted between them. Barbara wanted to go

to a marriage counselor. Michael refused—it would be a sign of weakness to ask for help. Finally, Barbara became very angry. Her script said that she should give, and that the man would eventually reciprocate. The reciprocation never occurred.

Michael had serious career difficulties. He held in all his feelings and frustrations. And as a result, he drank to excess. The pressures at home and work were overwhelming. He said, "I don't care," and withdrew. Barbara filed for divorce.

4

Learning Your Part in the Family Drama

Men and women bring their own relationship scripts into their romantic relationships, as we have seen. When two individuals interact, they establish something new—their characteristic way of being together as a couple. This pattern of interaction is what we call their "family drama." Once the family drama is established, the die is cast. Family members will interact in predictable ways. Even their future areas of conflict can be anticipated. By understanding our family drama and knowing how it works, we can learn how to deal more effectively with inevitable conflicts.

The family drama develops as you and your spouse create three vital components of family life: the *family dream,* which gives direction to many of your decisions and activities; *family intimacy,* the actual or potential love and emotional ties that give meaning to your life; and *family work,* which gets the necessary, day-to-day jobs done and enables you and your family to work toward the dream while enjoying the benefits of intimate relationships.

We will discuss each of these separately, paying special attention to potential sources of conflict. Then we will show how to regulate these three components of family life through the use of *family rules.*

Reading this chapter will equip you to better understand and evaluate your own family drama. You will be able to identify your family dream and decide whether you, your spouse, and your children share the same dream or if you are working at cross purposes. You will learn to assess and determine whether you are satisfied with the level of intimacy in your home, the extent to which you and your spouse can express feelings, affection, and love to each other and to the children. Finally, you will be able to examine the way work is assigned and carried out by family members and whether you both consider the work loads equitable or one of you is resentful about unfairness in work assignments.

You will learn that making changes involves altering family rules. Most people, when asked about their family rules, are puzzled. Perhaps you too don't realize that you have rules at home. Although you may never have set aside time for the expressed purpose of establishing rules, you have built a set of them to regulate your lives, usually without being conscious about it. An improved family life begins with the job of identifying existing rules and intentionally considering the costs and benefits associated with each.

The family drama is crucial in your life because it is so enduring. Once you write it, you go on acting it out. University of California psychologist Harold H. Kelley and his eight distinguished coauthors of *Close Relationships* write that the give-and-take between husband and wife or parent and child follows recurrent patterns. For instance, a husband's criticism of his wife's physical appearance may be expected to lead her to weep, which in turn arouses his anger. Families have many such patterns that give the family drama its consistency. That consistency works well if the drama makes family members happy and fulfilled. But it is tragic if the drama entraps the family in an emotionally deadening state that leads, at best, to unfulfilled lives and, at worst, to drug addiction, depression, or suicide. Like drama on stage, the family drama varies widely from delightful comedy to fateful tragedy.

THE FAMILY DREAM

Families are complex communities made up of the unique qualities of each individual and the unique features of the family as an entity. Despite differences, family members tend to be more satisfied if they have reached agreement about their goals, especially the one that stands above others—the family dream. There may be several prominent family goals, but this one represents the family's highest aspiration.

The family dream is derived from the parents' two relationship scripts and from their experiences and education during their formative years. While growing up, each spouse acquired values, interests, and ambitions. The predominant one came to be the individual's personal dream. For one person, the dream is to be first in the graduating class and to rise to the top in the chosen profession. For another, the goal is to marry, have a family, and acquire a house and garden. For a third, it is to devote as much time as possible to recreational pleasure, such as golf, dancing, and winter cruises in the Caribbean.

The two personal dreams come together to form the family dream. During the early years of the relationship, from dating well into marriage, the partners talk about their goals in life, especially the most precious ones, their personal dreams.

Many marriage partners are drawn together because of the compatibility of personal dreams. In those families, these are so similar that the spouses reach agreement on a family dream without much effort. In other families, where personal dreams are incompatible, any one of several different paths to the family dream may be followed: One partner's dream is so compelling that the other happily adopts it, or one partner persuades the other, or one partner simply imposes his or her dream on the other.

The family dream profoundly influences family life. For example, a family with the dream of gaining great wealth might forsake pleasurable opportunities for vacation and recreation in order to spend time with influential people who could help with a business deal. They might put opportunities for financial success before those for family closeness, personal fame, social status, and a wide variety of other activities.

The family dream gives meaning and purpose to family life. The absence of a family dream, which usually occurs when partners cannot contend with incompatible personal dreams, spells trouble. Under these circumstances the family functions like a ship adrift at sea.

With passing years, families may change the dream. The first one—for example, two successful careers—may have been realized, and the partners are ready for another. Or they may find they have changed their values. Instead of striving for wealth, they now may have a strong social commitment, choosing to devote themselves to speaking out against nuclear war.

We will discuss ten of the most typical types of family dreams in order to help you identify your own. Please keep two ideas in mind as you read on: first, your family's choice of a dream is a driving force toward its destination in that it becomes your prime objective and flavors much of your life, including your interests, activities, and even your selection of friends; second, the choice of a dream does not determine how well your family functions. A family with any dream can get along well or not.

Pleasure.   With this dream, work is mainly a means to enable the family to engage in activities that give pleasure. Conversations at mealtime are mostly about past, present, and future pleasurable events. The topics, drawn from experience, may be sports, music, art, or travel. Except for job and school, and those hours needed for housework and homework, the rest of the time is devoted to favored activities.

Achievement.   Personal achievement by the father or both parents is the dominant theme in this family. In the case of one parent's achievement (such as becoming a successful politician or businessperson), the spouse and children are expected to share the glow of the spotlight when the parent attains recognition. Generally, all family members are instilled with the value of being first in any competition.

Wealth. The accumulation of wealth and prized possessions provides the highest satisfaction in this family dream. Being rich is associated with the parents' favored values, which in turn are passed on to the children. While success in becoming rich is clearly an achievement, this family gets its satisfaction from the sheer accumulation of money, rather than from recognition of success.

Social status. Recognition for the family name and its reputation in the community is what these family members strive for. The family reputation may have been derived from community service, achievement, or philanthropy. No matter how it may appear to the outside world, as far as the family is concerned, social status is what family members value most of all.

Upward mobility through children. Families committed to this dream gain satisfaction and pride through every action that is believed to help their children rise to a higher educational and social rung than the parents. The relationship script of these children is dominated by the goal that they should rise above their parents, use more educated language, and marry a person from a "good" family.

Religion. The dream of this family type is to live the proper religious life, which means observing the rituals faithfully and instilling these values in their children. Life for them is centered around religious activities. Because of this, the social and spiritual significance of the place of worship dominates their daily lives. Family members derive great satisfaction and security from being part of the religious community with the network of support it provides.

Cohesiveness. These family members desire close family ties. Their first priority is to share happy hours together in daily life, work, and play and to maintain these feelings even when circumstances lead to physical separation.

Individuality. This type of dream is to provide circumstances that permit each person to live his or her life in separate but favored ways. The highest value is development of individuality and independence. Spouses may spend much of their free time with their respective friends, rather than with each other. Though they share some daily experiences, their work, recreation, and vacations are understood to be their own.

Social commitment. Service to others is expressed through involvement in activities concerning health, social welfare, education, labor, ecology, or peace organizations. Strong commitment may carry over from parents to children because the family is socially linked to a network of like-minded people.

Survival. Unlike the previous types, families with survival as their dream have no choice. They cannot choose other family dreams until they can provide the bare necessities of life—that is, all their energy is devoted to meeting survival needs. Millions of families who live below the poverty level must settle for this goal. The fact that the attention of family members must be given to sheer survival does not mean that they are lacking in self-esteem, only that their energy is too drained to devote themselves to other aspirations.

Clarifying Your Family Dream

In reading about these dreams, you may have found that more than one seems to describe your family experience. Even though you have only one primary family dream, other goals influence family life. To determine which is the primary one, first narrow down the possibilities. Then ask yourself, Which activity would we let dominate? If, for example, the choice is between family cohesiveness and social status, consider the following. Would you rather accept a prized invitation to a Saturday-night annual charity ball or go on a long-planned weekend vacation? Answers to questions such as these will help you identify the family dream.

One test of family happiness is to find out whether members feel they have agreed on a dream and are on their way to achieving it. Those who believe they have made significant progress are likely to be content and to have met the following conditions.

The family dream is the dream of both spouses.

One did not impose it on the other, and therefore there is no covert sabotaging of it.

Children old enough to understand share the family dream or at least are not so unduly affected by it that they actively or covertly oppose it.

The family dream is realizable or very nearly so. The aim is not to replace the royal family in Britain, but rather to own a home near the woods.

You may not meet these conditions if you and your spouse don't share a common family dream. However, you may be able to rewrite your family drama and develop a mutually agreeable dream. Cooperative negotiation and intimate communication are methods for working out conflicts between your two personal notions of the family dream. These differences may be reconcilable, perhaps by deciding that one will be the first dream you will aspire to, and after that is achieved, the other will replace it. Or your two dreams may be integrated so that one spouse's dream of social status is combined with the other's dream of achievement. But if the two of you are working at cross purposes—for instance, one favoring a high degree of individuality and the other a high degree of cohesiveness—you will need to negotiate a different solution.

If you discover that one of you has imposed your family dream on the other, prepare for open or subtle conflict—one of you will carry a burden of resentment that will be unloaded in the future. Through cooperative negotiation and intimate communication, you can deal with this problem too.

You may find that older children (teenagers especially) do not share the family dream. This can occur as part of the normal growth process, as they strive to achieve their individuality by differentiating themselves from you and your spouse and making choices reflecting their preferences. Or their opposition to the dream may have little or nothing to do with the dream itself but reflect adolescent rebellion against all adult values. Either way, these differences will be a source of friction in the family.

We recommend that you encourage your children to express their thoughts and feelings about the family dream. Of course, if you find evidence that particular aspects of working toward the dream affect them adversely (for example, both you and your spouse work all weekend), you will want to make whatever changes that are necessary to correct the situation. If they continue to oppose your family dream, you can explain to them that they have a right as individuals to choose their own values and goals. Also, when they have their own families, they will be free to choose their own family dreams, just as you as parents chose yours. Invite them to help you achieve your family dream—pointing out, for example, that you helped your parents to achieve theirs. If, however, your family dream is antagonistic to their values, ask them to respect the differences.

Assessing Your Family Dream

Once you understand the concept of a family dream and identify yours, you are in a position to make one more important assessment. You can ask yourself if the benefits you derive from striving for your family dream are greater than the costs or if the satisfaction is greater than the pain.

If the answer is no, you can look further and explore

three possible reasons: First, the problem may be that the family dream is unattainable. If this is the case, then you have probably put your finger on a major source of frustration and conflict in your family. A dream may become unrealizable because you have aimed your goals higher than circumstances permit. Second, the dream may no longer represent your family values. In that case, the family has been working without enthusiasm for a goal that has no appeal. The passing years may have changed your values, but the change may not have translated into a new family dream (for example, from social status to social commitment). The third possible problem is that the dream is still your family's choice, but you have not selected suitable methods to achieve it (for example, speculative financial investments based on inadequate information). As a result, the cost of striving has been greater than the payoff. To solve this problem, you will need to change the dream or find new ways for achieving the dream.

DEVELOPING INTIMATE BEHAVIOR

While the family dream is important as the family's guiding light, something else provides the glue that binds the family together. That is love—and love is expressed through intimate behavior. When two people meet, the emotional aspects of their relationship scripts interact. The resulting drama is a happy one if they share mutual desires to give and receive affection, tenderness, and sexual pleasure. It is not so happy if one wishes only to be on the receiving end or one cannot ask for or accept affection. Differences about what spouses want for themselves and expect from each other are a potential source of conflict. That is why it is necessary to look at the quality of intimate behavior when a family is in trouble.

Love is an activity as well as a feeling. It is incomplete without loving action, and people show their love through intimate behavior. The word "intimacy" is commonly thought

of in a very narrow sense—that is, to mean sexual relations.
We, as therapists, use it more broadly to refer to the capacity
to open up, allowing yourself to know your true feelings and
to be able to share them.

You are trusting of those you love when you can bare
your soul without fear of embarrassment or humiliation. You
are capable of intimacy when, knowing you love someone, you
are able to express it; when troubled by something your mate
has said or done, you can talk openly about it; or when as an
adult you are still treated as a child by your parents, you are
able to set them straight with loving firmness rather than
brute hostility.

As people establish relationships, they reveal their capacity for intimate behavior. They set their boundaries; they
let each other know, by words and by silence, how much they
are able to share of themselves (their desires, aspirations,
anxieties, guilts and fears). As they interact, they find how
much love, affection, and support they can give or receive.

Among the various forms of intimacy, tender feelings do
not get much press. In contrast, what makes the daily news
is stories about sexual intimacy or brutality. Recall your own
school experience and how seldom tender feelings were discussed. Although you may have had some instruction about
sex, you probably had little education about other forms of
intimacy such as the expression of loving feelings out of bed
or between parents and their children. Because of this lack,
people learn intimate behavior mostly at home, and this factor
is crucial in the formation of relationship scripts.

Problems develop when husband and wife have different
expectations. When she is upset, she might want to talk about
it, sitting close to him and feeling his support. However, he
might say it is best to put it out of mind. He may think that
morning is no time to kiss each other and the children,
whereas she, accustomed to that practice while growing up,
feels neglected without it. He believes that talking about an
argument after it's over is a waste of time, whereas she wants
to clear the air and feel better. She thinks they should sit and

talk about their day's activities after returning from work, instead of silently watching television. He says that he needs to be alone to calm down, while she feels rejected when he does this.

Four Areas of Intimate Behavior

The rules that families establish about intimate behavior affect the quality of their lives. With some, the rules call for closeness and support, with others, for distance and competition. As you begin to evaluate your own capacity for intimacy, keep in mind that there is not just one kind of intimate behavior. Instead, you can think in terms of four major areas of family activity in which intimate behavior develops. We want you to see that there is no such experience as general intimacy. Some people can express one form of intimacy (sexual) but not another (supportive loving). Knowing the four different expressions of intimacy is helpful when you put your family onstage and become a critic. You will be better prepared to see your part in encouraging or discouraging intimacy in your family drama. You will then be in a position to decide which changes you need to make.

Supportive loving intimacy.   This kind of intimacy refers to caring, tenderness, and understanding. Supportive love makes people feel valued and important. You can observe a parent whose actions are accompanied by loving feelings and one whose actions are not. You can notice the atmosphere in a home where the mother noisily drops the platters of food on the dining-room table in resentment over her cooking assignment. In another, the mother may take pleasure and pride in what she prepares for her family. Compare the father who resentfully repairs his wife's car with the one who does it lovingly. Supportive, loving intimacy is quiet and undramatic. Yet no type of intimacy is more important to family happiness.

Families can endure a great deal of hardship and pain

when their family drama is marked by supportive loving
intimacy. At times of stress an individual is able to stand more
firmly and confidently knowing that others care for and will
assist him.

A thirty-two-year-old family friend described his experience of supportive, loving intimacy:

> I always loved Jan, and I thought we had a pretty good
> marriage, which had all the love possible in it. But I
> learned there was even more to a marriage when my father
> got sick. Dad was in his late fifties when he got terminal
> cancer. My impression was that I was a strong person.
> Other people thought so too. But this made me snap, and
> I couldn't bear what was happening to him. And he and
> I were just beginning to get close.
>
> I never was a very emotional person, didn't show
> affection and all that sort of thing. But one day near the
> end I couldn't get Dad out of my mind. I left work early
> and went home and into my bedroom so the children
> wouldn't see me when they got home from school. I just
> sat. A long time later I heard the bedroom door open. My
> back was to it, but I could sense that Jan was looking at
> me. She came over to the chair, put her hand on my
> shoulder, and said nothing. After a while she said,
> "Honey, stop holding back. Cry! Let it out."
>
> I couldn't then. I could only go on brooding and
> feeling sorry for myself. But Jan kept after me until I let
> myself go. I hadn't cried since I was a kid, and it wasn't
> easy.
>
> Day and night she stayed close to me. It really helped.
> It gave me more than relief. It enabled me to get in touch
> with Dad and to develop a closeness that I'd never had.
> That helped me handle his death. The support and love Jan
> gave me has even improved our marriage.

The kind of supportive loving that Jan gave her husband
is a key to successful marriage and family life. Sociologist
F. Ivan Nye has found that the "therapeutic role"—one family member helping another in need—is closely linked to

satisfaction in marriage and family life. There is no substitute for this kind of intimacy in building the family morale. To know that your spouse and children are there when you are in need, to back you up, help, and support you, makes life easier and creates feelings of family loyalty.

You may recall the last time your spouse was in need. Now, in your mind's eye, place the two of you onstage. What did your relationship script permit you to do? Were you emotionally giving and supportive? Did your spouse get relief from the interaction? If not, why? Did your spouse's needs make you uncomfortable, and did you pull away? If so, what made you uncomfortable? Try to pinpoint feelings, such as "I can't stand it when an adult cries" or "I don't know what to do when someone is depressed."

Supportive, loving intimacy can help adults cope with severe problems at work and children with academic or social problems at school. Each of these calls for sympathetic listening, reassurance, and helpful advice.

This kind of intimacy manifests itself on happy occasions too, especially when cooperation among family members is stronger than competition. Then, when one has a success, the others rejoice and give loving support. Family members don't have to be worried that their victories will be seen as a threat to others. They can feel free to be themselves and use their resources to the fullest.

Finally, we want to emphasize that supportive loving intimacy is not only for occasions when one member is hurting emotionally or is happy over an award. It is for all the time in between. It means creating an atmosphere that pervades a home and shows itself in a smile, a touch, or a joke. You will feel it if it is there. And if it is not there, you'll want to know why. The best way to find out is by putting your family onstage and taking the role of critic.

Sexual intimacy. This refers to sexual relationships between husbands, wives, and lovers. The physical aspects of sex cause far fewer problems than the emotional ones that stem from the relationship script. Two people bring to their encounter many ideas they acquired growing up, which could enable them to attain exquisite pleasure in bed or cause abysmal frustration. For example, no one but the bride may know that she was sexually abused, and even she may not know the effect this may have had on her relationship script and her ability to give sexual pleasure in the marriage.

People are sometimes hesitant to talk freely about sexual intimacy, especially concerning their needs and feelings about various sexual practices. When the dialogue about preferred sexual activities is limited, one or both partners may be frustrated for years without saying a word.

For most people, enjoyment of sex is affected by what happens between spouses the rest of the time. You will find that, when you and your spouse show a great deal of supportive loving intimacy (understanding at times of need, praise at times of accomplishment), the sexual relationship is considerably improved. Unexpressed anger, on the other hand, typically blocks the free expression of sexual intimacy.

Making sure both you and your spouse find sex enjoyable is important. The drama of the healthy family contains the rule that sex be pleasurable to both partners. You will find these guidelines helpful.

- Give sex high priority. Plan it for a time when you won't be hurried or tired, whether that's in the early evening, at 3 A.M., or in the morning. And also allow room for spur-of-the-moment sex.
- Give your attention entirely to this physical and emotional encounter and to nothing else—especially not work.
- Find out, if you don't already know, what your partner enjoys.
- Tell your partner, if he or she doesn't know, what you enjoy.
- Be imaginative, especially if you and your partner like diversity. But if you both like a particu-

lar way all the time, don't feel pressed to do something else.

- Feel free to take the initiative in sex.
- Remember that quality counts. That may mean orgasms for both partners after long and fulfilling lovemaking, touching, fondling, or holding each other, or any other activity that pleases both partners.
- Don't use sex for ulterior motives, especially for control or to prove one's manliness or womanliness.
- Don't expect every love encounter to be perfect. One of Ernest Hemingway's characters said about a great love experience that "the earth moved." But it won't every time.
- Be aware that, with age, everything changes. Yet couples can go on having sexual satisfaction into old age as long as they maintain relatively good health and follow the adage about sex. "Use it or lose it."

These guidelines are helpful in promoting good sex with your spouse, as well as in bringing the two of you emotionally and spiritually closer. If you have trouble applying them, perhaps you are caught in the rut of a family drama that denies you sexual pleasure. But you can overcome the problem by rewriting your family drama.

Intimate playfulness. In most families, members take off in different directions, to work or school, five days a week. Evenings, weekends, and vacations give families opportunities to enjoy leisure time together. During these interactions, family members get more than fun and games. They get a deeper understanding of each other. Free of the pressures of school and work, families can be more relaxed, open, and intimate. They can allow themselves to be vulnerable.

A wife, laughing heartily, will say to her husband, who

for the first time has revealed some of his school-day pranks, "John, I never knew this about you." Children will say to their parents, upon hearing about their first date, "You mean you two hitched a ride to a dance!" It is not so much what is said, but rather that family members open up to each other and find it pleasurable.

Letting yourself go in a playful way is more than just fun, it's good for the healthy development of the family. Intimate playfulness in the family drama has its best chance of expressing itself when the parents believe that recreation and freedom of thought are important.

Psychology dictates that, to a considerable degree, people have the power to make themselves feel good or bad depending upon what they choose to think about. This is easily demonstrated. You need only think of a warm and loving relationship to feel good, the loss of a dearly beloved person to feel sad, or a deeply embarrassing or humiliating experience to feel tense.

We are not Pollyannas. We know that anger, pain, and grief are unavoidable in family life because conflict, sickness, and death are inescapable. Given all the negatives in life, we strongly urge you to take active measures to put the positive into your family life: love that is actively expressed and demonstrated; approval and praise for little things, as well as big achievements; stimulation and fun in many settings, such as at play, during dinner conversation, with outdoor activities, at concerts, and during sex.

One aid to intimate playfulness is humor. Although it has received popular attention since Norman Cousins reported at length on the role of humor in overcoming a disease that physicians had considered incurable, its power is vastly underestimated. Humor makes us feel good, and we like to be with people who make us feel good. It brings people closer together and helps to reduce tension.

Lew, a friend of ours and a widower with two children, married Joyce, a divorcee with two children. Faced with the typical problems of the blended family, Lew called on his sense of humor to keep the tension within manageable levels. On a gray Monday morning during their first month of marriage when the family was eating breakfast silently, Lew told them a story that lifted everyone's spirits and got them laughing.

"I want to tell you a Monday morning story. It's about a criminal. He was being led to the gallows to be hanged this Monday morning. The criminal said: 'Well, this is a good beginning to the week.' "

Lew said that his story sent the children off to school laughing with comments like, "Oh, Dad, what a story!" and "Where did you dig that up?" Pretty soon the children were bringing comic stories to the table and eventually were looking for the funny side of life without having to rely on ready-made jokes and stories.

Humor can be used for other serious matters in family life, such as when a husband/father fails to carry out his work roles. Not long after she married Lew, Joyce was pained that for three successive nights Lew watched the TV news instead of doing his job of clearing the dinner table. By the time the news was over, she had cleared the dishes and Lew seemed oblivious to it. Her initial impulse was to burst into the living room and confront him. She controlled herself and chose a different way. She posted the following notice on their bedroom door:

SUMMONS

Husband Is Required to Appear in Domestic Court
Hear Ye, Hear Ye,
Court Orders Trial of Delinquent Husband
for Violation of Contractual Agreement
Regarding Dinner Clean-Up

When Lew read it, he burst out laughing. That was a lesson he said he would never forget.

Joyce, like other stepparents, knew she had to be sensi-

tive to the feelings of her new children, and at the same time
be responsible for their welfare and safety. When her four-
teen-year-old stepdaughter arrived home from a friend's
house an hour late, Joyce was irritated but turned her annoy-
ance into humor. She made a show of looking at her wrist-
watch, almost under the girl's nose, saying, "Hmm. I guess
my watch is an hour fast and needs to be fixed again." This
way she made her point without creating a head-on collision.

Spouses who show tendencies to see themselves as superior to the rest of the family can be helped through humor to
see their true selves. For example, one wife used the following
anecdote: Charles de Gaulle and his wife are sitting in their
living room. He's reading, and she is knitting. "Oh, God,"
says his wife, "It's so cold." Then he turns to her and says,
"When we're alone, you can call me Charles."

Humor is no substitute for confronting the hard issues
in family life, but it can lighten the tone. As we have seen
from Lew and Joyce's blended family, it provides a way to
deal with problems before they become conflicts. Humor also
helps us maintain a balance and protects us from a consuming
preoccupation with serious matters.

Intimacy with the extended family.   For some families,
life is enriched by intimacy with the parents and siblings of
spouses, as well as grandparents, aunts, uncles, and cousins.
These relatives represent a support system. At times of grief
and uncertainty and at happy times as well, we turn to the
extended family.

The extended family is so important that those who live
far from home crowd the airports on Thanksgiving and
Christmas in order to spend even a short time with distant
loved ones. If family members aren't available, people distant
from home form a network of friends who satisfy some of the
social and emotional needs usually provided by the family.

To enjoy the benefits of their kin, newly married adults
need relationship scripts that are relatively free of jealousy

about each other's extended families. They also must be free of dependency on parents, so that they can make independent judgments as a couple.

It is important once again to highlight the central position of supportive loving intimacy. If your family drama contains such intimacy, it probably carries over to the other areas of intimacy, such as sexual, playful, and the extended family. If it doesn't, you can rewrite your family drama so that it does.

SHARING THE FAMILY WORK

The old saying "You can't live on love alone" needs to be modified for our purposes as follows: "You can't live on love and the family dream alone. A family must eat!"

You can't strive for a family dream (other than survival) if you don't have enough food, shelter, and personal safety. Consequently, there is work to be done by parents and children. The successful division of family work enables family members to keep the family ship afloat and permits it to reach for greater harbors. The way in which the family assigns roles and in what spirit they are carried out are both part of the family drama. Mopping a kitchen floor or changing a baby's diaper may seem out of place in discussing drama, but in real life the mother with the mop and the father with the diaper may be filled with resentment about the task.

To help you put your family onstage, we have organized the tasks that families must perform into five major work roles. We assess each role in terms of its potential for creating conflict. As you read the roles, ask yourself, How are work roles divided in my family? How do I feel about the division? Do I think others in my family feel good about it? What resentments do I or others feel about the current work assignments? What conflicts arise as a result of dissatisfaction over these assignments? And what benefits do I get from the way the roles are divided?

Provider role. When families had to build their own homes, grow their own food, and make their own clothing, their time was devoted to the provider role. Today, the provider role is the income-producing activity of one or more members of the family. In more than half of American families, both parents work at income-producing occupations. Some older children and teenagers also contribute to the total family income through part-time work. Wages are used to pay for goods and services to meet family needs. The provider role satisfies family needs and gives wage-earners a position of control, although this control is a potential source of conflict.

Money-management role. Families make many financial decisions about the allocation of their assets. They may have to choose, for example, whether to live in a more elegant home or have funds for travel, whether to buy a new wardrobe or redecorate a room, whether to eat out regularly or buy a new car, whether to send the children to summer camp or enroll them in private school. In a less affluent family, they may have to choose whether to economize even more so that one or both parents should not have to work such long hours. Money management is an important role. Whoever controls the purse strings in the family possesses power, so that competition for this role often leads to conflict.

Housekeeper role. This role includes decision-making about housing, food, and clothing. Some tasks are unpopular, such as cleaning bathrooms or washing dishes. Competition for decision-making power and avoidance of undesirable tasks are another common source of conflict.

Child-care role. Through this role parents attend to the health and security needs of children. It refers to such responsibilities as protecting children from physical danger and illness, as well as feeding, cleaning, and clothing them. Until recently this role typically has been the mother's, but with an increase in two-career families and busier schedules, the sharing of child-care assignments has become more common and a greater source of conflict.

Child-socialization role. This means raising your children to be the kind of people you want them to be. In fulfilling this role, you are shaping your children's relationship script. How you do this stems from your own relationship scripts, and therefore disagreement between spouses about what to expect and demand of children is common.

If you are content with the current assignment of these roles in your family and how they are being carried out, and if you believe your spouse and children feel the same, you are fortunate. If you feel the division of work is unfair and you hold resentments about it, or if conflicts arise about family jobs, then a new plan of action is in order. Continuing in the present way will only breed further resentment and conflict.

A plan of action calls for a discussion with your spouse, using the drama rewrite methods of cooperative negotiation and intimate communication. You want your spouse to know you are distressed about work assignments, and you want your reactions to be a frank exchange of views. Then you need to negotiate differences.

Below, we give you the beginning of such a discussion, which is usually one of the most difficult parts of making changes. The two participants are "You" and "Spouse."

You: Can we talk? Something's bothering me.

Spouse (defensively): Something bothering you? . . . Well, let's talk now.

You: For a long time I've been feeling I'm carrying too much of a load. And it's upset me. I see now that I should've opened up to you earlier and. . . .

Spouse (with an edge of anger): Are you telling me I'm not doing enough around here?

You (controlling yourself, because your aim is to have a productive discussion, not an angry argument):   No, not at all. I'm just honestly sharing my feelings with you and hoping the two of us could talk about them—and your feelings too.

Spouse: What good will that do? What good will it do if I tell you that I get so fed up at times that I wonder if it's all worth it?

You: At least it will clear the air. We'll know where we stand, how we feel, and then maybe we can do something about it. We won't be worse off than we are now. To tell you the truth, I feel a little better already—just the fact that we opened up about it.

Spouse: Well, I don't feel any better. But I'm willing to try.

When you and your spouse reach this point you will have come a long way.

KNOWING THE RULES YOU LIVE BY

No matter how compatible they may be, when two people come together in marriage they bring their own relationship scripts and are bound to have differences. Add a child or two and the differences are compounded—and further compounded for a stepparent. So it is not surprising that partners run into conflict in day-to-day family life. The conflict is settled by establishing family rules—the laws of the land.

Whether in their first or third marriage, partners develop rules intended to enable them to agree upon the family dream and seek to achieve it, assign and carry out family work roles, and enjoy the pleasures of intimate behavior with each other, their children, and members of the extended family.

Some rules help families become effective, close, and loving, while other rules make them ineffective, distant, and competitive. You probably know families in which the general tendency is for members to be supportive and helpful to each other and other families in which it seems everyone is clawing at everyone else from morning to night.

Collectively, the family rules—and there may be hundreds of them—can be looked upon as the family's "constitution." It resembles the United States Constitution with its stated purpose "to establish a more perfect union, to insure domestic tranquillity, to provide for the common defense, to promote the general welfare. . . ." The family constitution is written to provide order to family relationships.

Just as the Constitution is subject to amendment, so are family rules. They are created by the family and can be modified or replaced. The process of initially establishing rules begins before marriage. During the dating period, sooner or later, the man and woman come upon a sharp difference between them. He wants one thing; she wants another. Their relationship scripts come banging up against each other. How they work out this conflict and the next one, and the one after that will set a pattern—a rule—for the future, becoming part of their family drama.

Rules are developed to govern all family activity. Below are examples of two different rules for family activities.

Work Roles

Each person carries out his or her work assignment faithfully.

Each family member, except mother, resists and avoids work assignments until mother explodes in anger.

Intimate Behavior

Family members exchange hugs and kisses before retiring for the night.

A formal kiss on the cheek is given only when a
family member is departing on an extended trip.

Family Dream

The family dream is known and supported, and
plans for implementing it are often discussed.

The family bounces from one dream to another and
makes little progress toward achieving any one.

The way rules operate in real life is apparent almost at
the outset of a relationship, as we'll demonstrate in the case
of Susan and Dan, who had been dating for a month. They
considered themselves lucky to be going together because up
to this point everything about the relationship had been love
and kisses. One evening, though, they seemed to be coming
to an impasse: Dan wanted very much to go to a basketball
game, but Susan was tired and wanted to spend the evening
together in her apartment.

Their emotions began to grow stronger and their voices
louder as conversation turned into argument. Dan shouted,
"If that's the way you feel, I'll just go myself." Susan burst
into tears and said, between sobs, "You don't really care
about my feelings." Dan felt guilty. Relenting, he embraced
her, and they spent the evening in her apartment, where
Susan went all out to reward him for following her wish.

Two weeks later, when a difference arose again about
how to spend a weekend, they settled it in the same way. The
pattern repeated a few times. Dan stood up for his position;
Susan put on an emotional performance. Dan backed down,
and Susan won and rewarded Dan. Pretty soon, Dan didn't
even put up a fight for what he wanted.

If this pattern had been kept up, Dan eventually would
resent losing. And under these circumstances, another rule
would develop about how Dan demonstrated his resentment.

Possibly the rule would be that he would save resentments until he could justify a secret affair or perhaps end the relationship. Maybe the rule would be that he would give in, resent it, then cut down Susan in front of her friends. With Dan persisting in angry resignation, Susan eventually would reappraise the situation. After a time of enjoying the satisfaction of dominating him, she might grow impatient. Her thought could be, "What a wimp. No matter what I want he gives in. I've had enough of him." Or she might stay involved because of her affection for him and the pleasure of being in control while, at the same time, having a secret affair with a "real man." She could also reach the point of sensing a conflict: she wants him as he is, and she wants him stronger. This might lead her to discuss the issue with Dan in a healthy and constructive way.

As it turned out, Susan's insistence on getting her way was more of a passing fear about Dan leaving or dominating her than a deep-seated need for control. Also, Dan realized that he would come to resent always giving in. He was the one who finally raised the issue. Although it began as an argument, it became a constructive discussion.

We will put them onstage. The setting is a little restaurant a few blocks from their apartment; the time is six months after their marriage. During most of the meal they have talked about their workday, then about their plans for the upcoming weekend. Now they are discussing where they are to go for Thanksgiving. Susan announces that she has already promised to spend the day with her parents.

Dan: Wait, Sue. That's not fair. You know my parents asked us a long time ago.

Susan: We can go there next year.

Dan: We spent Christmas with your folks. The only fair thing is to give my folks a turn.

Susan: Aw, come on, Dan, Christmas was so long ago.

Dan: It's not just Christmas. We spend a lot of time with your parents. You know I like them, but I want to be fair.

Susan (tears beginning to appear): You used to see my point of view before we were married. *(She begins to sob.)* Now you don't care.

Dan: Let's not have a scene in public. Let's get out of here and talk about it at home.

They walk home silently, except for Susan's occasional sob. When they get home, Susan stretches out on the couch in their living room, sobbing more loudly.

Dan (with controlled impatience): All right. I don't want to go through this again. If it means that much to you, we'll do what you want.

Susan: I can tell from your voice you don't really want to. You used to want to do what I wanted. *(She sobs even more.)*

Dan: No, I don't want to go there. It's not fair. And I know there were a lot of times I didn't want to do what you wanted, but I couldn't stand to see you crying—and I can tell you I was plenty angry about it. *(Susan lowers her head and begins to wail. Dan lifts her face toward his and speaks firmly.)* What in the world are you bawling about? *(Susan goes on wailing. Dan raises his voice.)* Stop crying! Stop crying now!

Susan is stunned. She has never heard him shout like that. She wipes her tears and sits up, trembling. Dan takes her hands and asks her what she's afraid of that makes her tremble.

Susan: You.

Dan (puzzled): Me?

Susan: I don't know why I said that, but I do feel it.

Dan: We can't pass it off like that. What are you afraid of? What could I do to you?

Susan: You could leave me. I don't know why I said that either, but it's what I'm thinking. You could leave me. Or. . . .

Dan: What else?

Susan (sitting up stiffly and speaking aggressively):   Or you could boss me around and try to control me.

Dan: Have I ever done that? You know I haven't. Do you know who's been doing the controlling?

Susan (realizing what Dan means and looking sheepish):   You mean, me?

This was the beginning of intimate communication between them. As a child Susan had seen her young aunt abandoned by her husband, and the adult talk in Susan's home was that the aunt had allowed him to control her. Then Susan's oldest sister (eight years older) experienced something similar when her fiancé broke their engagement after two years. What she picked up in her young mind stuck with her and became part of her relationship script. It showed up years later as she and Dan began developing their family drama.

But they were still in the process of writing their drama. They worked out a system of compromises to resolve differences about recreational and social activities. They pretty much decided to take turns choosing. Later they discovered that, although sometimes their first choices differed, they could find second and third choices that they shared. They developed a rule for the resolution of differences: openly discuss preferences, listen to each other, and negotiate for fairness.

Even though Susan had a tendency to use tears to get

her way and Dan tended to give in and quietly resent things, both of them had relationship scripts with highly developed problem-solving skills and with a high premium placed on cooperation. Because of this, they recognized the need to negotiate.

Like Dan and Susan, every newly formed family makes rules. This principle applies even if this is the second or third marriage. The coming together of two or more people demands a new set of rules—a family constitution. Because each partner's relationship script reflects the rules in the parental home, the two must reconcile differences between their relationship scripts, especially in cases of young married couples. In cases of the previously married, the situation is complicated in that the spouses bring an influence from the earlier marriages in addition to their respective relationship scripts. But in the end all that counts is that they be able to work out differences in mutually satisfying ways.

The rules in your family drama may be quite obscure. We find that, when we ask people about their family rules, we get a blank stare. This is because there is little reason for anyone to think about them if family life is proceeding smoothly. And when problems come up, people don't think in terms of rules. But because they are very much part of everyday life—your everyday life—we want to show you how they relate to the family dream, intimate behavior, and family work and to help you identify and work toward rewriting some of the rules.

Rules and Your Family Dream

The family dream is usually derived from the personal dreams of both partners, although sometimes one partner imposes a dream on the other. Rules are used to decide which personal dream or combination of the two becomes the family dream. Rules are also used to make plans and assign responsibility for doing whatever is necessary to achieve the dream.

What are the rules that apply to your family dream? If

you already know your family dream, list the rules you used in developing and working toward it. You can identify them by answering the following questions.

- What is your personal dream in life?
- What is your spouse's?
- If they are different, how did you go about choosing your family dream? (Your answer to this is a description of the family rule you used in choosing your family dream.)
- Assuming there is a plan of action to enable the family to achieve its dream, how did you and your spouse decide on the action to be taken? (Your answer to this is a description of the family rule on decision-making about action to realize the dream.)
- What steps have been taken to carry out the action? (Your answer to this is a description of the rule about what action your family takes to realize the dream.)

Now is the time to evaluate the effectiveness of the rules connected with your family dream. Do the rules produce a family dream and action plans that represent each of you? Or do they permit one of you to impose one dream on the other? If so, and if you want family harmony, you will want to consider developing new rules to select the dream. Have the action plans been carried out? If not, then the rule about implementing plans is probably faulty and needs to be replaced.

Our clients Bud and Jody Coleman wrote the following about their rules during a course on marriage enrichment.

Our rule was to decide together. We began talking about our dream when we first got serious. We didn't call it that. We wanted to live well, that's all. For us, that meant having a house and garden and a little place in the mountains for skiing. We had no trouble agreeing on what we wanted.

Also, we had no trouble in making plans about how we'd get these two homes. We decided to save a certain amount from our salaries.

We had problems when it came to action. Up to that point we had no big differences between us. But when we had to decide where we wanted our house and our ski hut, we had differences, and I mean great big ones. Our problem was that we didn't have a rule to settle differences. It finally hit us when a close friend said to us one day, "Why don't you go for mediation? An expert will show you how to work out your differences." Well, we liked that idea but decided that first we would try to do it for ourselves. If it didn't work out we could go outside for help. That's how we set up this rule that, when we don't agree about a decision, we just sit down and work out something that satisfies both of us. And we did that about the house and the ski hut.

Rules and Intimate Behavior

Intimate behavior is love made explicit. Love becomes explicit when two people begin to shape their intimate behavior during dating days. Actually, they are establishing rules about intimacy. They come prepared with their respective relationship scripts, which contain models of how close they could and should become, not only in sexual terms but all others. The rules they develop may allow them to be loving and demonstrative. Or they may permit physical and emotional closeness only during sex, and even then to a limited degree.

Men and women, young and old, yearn for intimacy. A problem in some families is that their rules limit the experience and expression of intimacy, leaving husbands and wives, parents and siblings feeling deprived. The family drama in such homes is marked by stiffness and awkward silence.

When Fran, a friend of ours, was honest with herself,

she would admit that her marriage to Peter was not a complete success. She felt he was never himself. When she told him that, he was genuinely puzzled, even when Fran explained that he never let himself go. He just said that he guessed he didn't have a lot to say. Fran felt she never really knew his feelings—about her, about himself, or about anything important.

Fran's older brother and his wife came from out of town for a short visit, giving Peter further opportunity to get acquainted with them. One evening after dinner, Fran and her brother began talking about their early family life, their jealousies and loves, the idiosyncrasies of their parents, and other issues that Peter found to be painfully personal, but he said nothing. He excused himself and went off to his bedroom.

Fran was furious because he left and didn't return—and even more so when Peter later accused her and her brother of talking about issues that should be kept private. He was very upset, and she didn't know why. She asked herself how she had gotten into a marriage with someone so different from her, someone who couldn't tolerate the very closeness and openness she needed.

The only rule Peter could tolerate was avoidance of all but sexual intimacy. Fran couldn't live that way. She couldn't tolerate a family drama filled with frustration and conflict. She knew she needed more intimacy or she would remain dissatisfied. She knew that she and Peter had to talk and resolve their differences or come to another solution.

Knowing your family's rules for intimate behavior can make you more aware of what you and members of your family expect of each other.

In order to identify your personal rules about intimacy, answer the following questions.

- How does your family react when you are obviously distressed?
- How do you react when your family is obviously distressed?

- What is the mood or atmosphere in your home on weekday mornings? Evenings? Weekends?
- When one of you has a success, such as a promotion, honor, or award, how do the others react?
- To what extent do you enjoy sexual relations with your partner?
- Are you free to discuss sexual intimacy with your spouse and to explain what you would like?
- Do you and your family share in making recreational plans?
- Is there a spirit of playfulness in your home? Or is it one of grimness?
- Do you and your family enjoy relationships with your extended family or, if you have none, with friends?

The answers to these questions should reveal the rules about intimate behavior, showing whether your family atmosphere is warm, playful, and cooperative or leans toward coldness and hostile competitiveness. They will indicate whether there is support and understanding when a family member is in need.

Rules and Your Family Work Roles

Work roles enter the conversation of lovers during dating days, even if they are not living together. Whether two people discuss the following issues or not, they surely make decisions about them: who picks up the check at the restaurant and leaves a tip, who chooses recreational activities, and who buys the theater tickets. Even before sharing an apartment, they may choose to travel together, which could compel them to make decisions about budgets, payments, first use of the bathroom, and coping with differences about such items as dirty laundry and bathroom orderliness. A couple doesn't have to be married to begin arguing about underwear dropped on the floor or hair left in the sink—and about who is going to do what about the problems.

Once two people are living under the same roof, the allocation of work roles becomes more complex, and differences, sometimes leading to conflict, are certain to appear. Arguments are especially likely over the issue of decision-making. Some adults prefer to have authority to make policy and then assign work to a partner or an older child. For example, the mother sets the rule that the children will do their chores promptly, and it is the father who will see to it that they do so. Or the father tells his wife that credit-card bills must be paid upon receipt and that she should do it.

Jeff and Sandra, both thirty-five, were newlyweds, and their household included two of Sandy's children, ages nine and eleven. For the most part, when differences about work roles cropped up, they outwardly made light of them because they were determined to make a success of the marriage. Each had thoughts such as, "He(She) should really be doing more. But why make a fuss? We're so happy." It wasn't long, though, before they came up against an issue that provoked their first major argument.

Their relationship scripts differed sharply on who would manage the family's money. Jeff grew up in a home in which his father was the sole proprietor of the checking and savings accounts. Father discussed money matters with his wife, but both had no doubt that his word would be final. Jeff expected to play that role. Sandra, on the other hand, had grown up in a home where the mother distrusted the father, so that while he was presumably the money manager, she surreptitiously accumulated funds in a private account. When Sandra married her first husband, her mother advised her to keep a private account. Sandra followed this advice and later told her mother it was good that she did so because her husband wanted to control everything.

Jeff was an easygoing person who had given Sandra no worries about being overpowering. However, on this matter, he argued that there must have been something wrong with her because she had to "wear the pants." For her part, Sandra began to think that Jeff was like her first husband, except that he had kept his need to control her hidden until now.

The arguments began to get out of control as some of the buried resentments about the other's work roles began to spill over into this argument. At one point, in a rage, she shoved him against a wall. His immediate impulse was to retaliate, but he stopped himself, grabbed his coat, and went out of the house.

Sandra heard some sounds. She looked up the stairs and saw her two children weeping. They had been awakened by the argument. Suddenly, she felt engulfed by a wave of fear. What if he should not return? What if she and the children should have to go through the mess of divorce again? What will her friends think if she can't make this marriage work? She comforted the children and sent them back to bed. Then she made a decision. It's not worth fighting over this. I don't like giving in. I resent it. But I can't afford to do anything about it.

When Jeff returned, she mollified him, saying she was sorry for making an unnecessary fuss and assuring him they would follow his way. A rule was established: on money matters, Jeff was the final arbiter. Jeff also got his way about other gender-linked roles—housekeeping and child care were Sandra's ultimate responsibility, although Jeff would help. Life seemed to go smoothly, but Sandra never forgot and never really forgave Jeff. There were times he approached her amorously, and she would turn him away, with one excuse or another, as a form of punishment. She got satisfaction from that even when she knew she was depriving herself of intimacy.

This is a case in which a rule is made that deals with the immediate conflict and provides a guideline for the future. The way it was made—with one winner and one loser— means that this family is left with unfinished business and ultimately two losers. Sometime in the future, maybe when the children are self-supporting, the conflict will surface again in another form, and Sandra will let Jeff know that he is a power-hungry macho man. In the meantime, she will covertly take out her resentment toward him.

What are the work rules in your family drama?

Answer the following questions in order to identify the rules used to assign and perform work roles.

- What are the different categories of work performed in your household?
- Who makes the work assignments? How are they made?
- What are your feelings about the work assignments?
- What do you believe are the feelings of your family about the work assignments?
- How do you know this?
- What do you and they do about those feelings?
- How well are the work assignments carried out?
- What changes are needed in the assignment and performance of work roles?
- Have you discussed those needed changes with your spouse?
- If so, what were the results? If not, why not?
- What conflicts stem from dissatisfactions about work assignments or how they are carried out?
- What steps do you and your spouse take to cope with the controversies?

Your answers reveal important characteristics of your family drama because rules do more than guide your family's daily life. They set the pattern of how you relate to each other and thus contribute to the psychological atmosphere in your home. If your family rules are imposed by one person, chances are that the others are carrying silent resentments.

If the rules call for inconsistencies, in all probability you and others are experiencing frustration. And if they disallow affection, you and others may be hungering for it.

If you are dissatisfied with your rules, remember that nothing about your family drama is set in stone. You and your spouse wrote your rules and your family drama—and you can rewrite them.

5

The Happiness Test: Your Critical Review of the Family Drama

Most people unknowingly apply what we call a "Happiness Test" to family life. They test family life to determine if they are getting a fair share of benefits from the family drama to justify the costs associated with it. Spouses generally conduct these tests at a low level of awareness, and this works to their disadvantage.

We hope here to be able to help you utilize your best thinking for conducting high-quality happiness tests that will aid you and your family in realizing your goals and making progress toward your family dream.

CASE HISTORY: AMY

Amy, a dental hygienist and mother of three, is having a typical Wednesday afternoon with the children. During the past hour, these questions have flashed through her mind:

Should I nag the children to pick up their toys?

Should I be affectionate with Bill tonight?

Should I explain to Mom why I want to go back to school?

Should I ask my sister to kick in half of the money I spent on Mom and Dad's gift?

Should I drive crosstown to shop at the mall's white sale?

Should we have another baby?

Should I confront Bill about making Saturday-night plans without consulting me?

Should I ask for a divorce?

Choices, choices, choices. And, except in the last case, Amy was uncertain enough to shrug her shoulders and pause a moment before deciding.

When we asked Amy how she goes about making these decisions, she replied, "I have no idea. I don't really have a way. I just do what seems best." If you analyzed Amy's decision-making you'd discover that, in fact, she does have a system. She unknowingly uses the Happiness Test to make decisions. It is composed of evaluating the pros and cons of each option or, to put it more mathematically, subtracting the costs associated with each choice from its expected benefits. We call it the Happiness Test because, through its use, people make the decisions that they think will make them happiest.

For example, the first question Amy raised—should I nag the children to pick up their toys? brought the following thoughts rushing through her mind.

Pros

If they get away with it today, they'll be messier tomorrow.

I'll teach the children an important lesson.

I'll feel better if the toys are put away, and I'll be nicer to the kids.

I can fix dinner while they clean the room.

Bill will complain if things are scattered around.

If they clean up, I'll be protected in case Mom drops in. There will be no mess.

Cons

The little one will cry if I yell.

The kids will fight over who played with which toys.

I hate myself when I nag and then I become grumpy.

If I push the kids, they'll be agitated when Bill gets home.

Amy weighed these arguments, subtracting the costs from the benefits, and decided not to nag. The Happiness Test showed Amy that complaining to the children wasn't worth it—the apparent costs exceeded the possible benefits. The test persuaded her to reshelve the toys, appreciate a few moments of peace and quiet, and enjoy the preciousness of her children who had collapsed on the playroom floor watching *Sesame Street.*

THE HAPPINESS TEST IN EVERYDAY LIFE

You, like Amy, face a barrage of decisions daily. You weigh the costs and benefits of your alternatives using the Happiness Test as a guide. Most decisions are minor and are easily tackled with the Happiness Test. These small but pesky issues are reflected in questions like "Should I get out of bed now or catch five more minutes of shut-eye?" "Should I drop the children at Mom's before I go shopping or afterward?" and "Should I switch lanes or follow this slowpoke a bit further?" We make these either/or decisions without much thought, automatically weighing comparative costs at a low level of awareness or even unknowingly.

Other minor decisions involve sorting through many options. For example, "What time should I go shopping?" is a trivial issue that offers almost infinite choices. Nonetheless, you still apply the Happiness Test, modifying it to meet the demands of the question. In this case you evaluate each reasonable choice by subtracting its costs from expected benefits. If more than one option has benefits exceeding costs, you choose the one with the greatest surplus of benefits.

To illustrate, the Happiness Test might first narrow down your decision to two choices of shopping time, either 7:30 P.M. or 10:00 A.M. If you shop in the evening, a friend will accompany you, but you will be away from your family and the crowds will be larger. If you shop at 10:00 A.M., you will avoid the morning rush hour and the stores will be nearly empty, but you will have to go alone because none of your friends share your vacation day. Although both options are attractive, providing benefits in excess of their costs, the Happiness Test might lead you to choose the first because having a shopping partner makes that option far more appealing.

You also use the Happiness Test to guide major decisions: "Should I take this job?" "Should I move to a new city?" "How should I react to my mother-in-law's request to move into our home?" In making important decisions, people typically conduct the Happiness Test more consciously than with minor ones.

The Happiness Test is very personal. Given exactly the same options in exactly the same situation, two people applying it may make opposite choices. For example, one person might choose to move to a new job or city, the other to stay put. One might welcome the mother-in-law, while another may decide to place her in a retirement home. This makes sense because people have their own personal ideas about what would maximize their happiness, and they weigh the costs and benefits of the options in their own unique way.

The Happiness Test at Home

The same Happiness Test is applied in making crucial decisions in family life by people who are dissatisfied with their relationships: "Should I remain a member of this household or pack my bags and move out?" For these people, the Happiness Test poses the question, "Do the benefits of being a household member exceed the costs?" The pros and cons of remaining in the home might include answers to questions like "Am I getting as much from this relationship as I'm putting in?" "Is the family effective in helping me satisfy my own needs?" and "Am I getting as much happiness living in the home as I would living outside the home?"

Of course, people usually ask these questions subconsciously, seeking to determine whether marriage and family life are sufficiently worthwhile. One day when Amy was ill and the children's toys were scattered over the floor, her husband came home and scolded her explosively. She was taken aback. Although she said nothing, she was so deeply resentful that the next day the thought of divorce entered her mind.

In applying the Happiness Test, however, she realized that his outburst was unusual. She saw that, although her husband and children frustrate her more often than she would like, she was content. Later that day when she walked past the family photos on her dresser, the broad smile that crossed her face indicated the test's favorable outcome.

Happiness Tests: Selfishness or a Healthy Reality

Happiness tests may sound selfish, but they do not necessarily lead people to take actions at the expense of others. In fact, happiness tests can do just the opposite. After people act to help themselves, they are often better able to provide benefits to other family members. Because this concept is counterintuitive, we will illustrate it with a concrete example.

Before every commercial airline takeoff, a flight attendant reviews safety procedures for the passengers, such as the possibility that during the flight the air pressure could be lost in the cabin. Passengers are instructed, "In that unlikely event, oxygen masks will automatically drop in front of you.

If you are traveling with small children, put on your own mask first, then attend to the children."

On your first flight, these eyebrow-raising instructions might have sounded alarmingly selfish. After some thought, however, you might have decided that the Federal Aviation Administration has recognized a reality: once the adult's need for oxygen is met, he or she is better able to help the children.

Likewise, if you, the adult, find your needs fulfilled in your family, you are better able to give of yourself to help your children and spouse realize their own fulfillment. If the Happiness Test guides your decisions so that you are satisfied, you will be more energized and willing to provide love, attention, and support to others.

Happiness tests become tools of selfishness only when one family member uses them to continually exploit others. In such situations, there is no equity in the home. If this is the case in your household, you can take steps to improve matters. First, raise the issue with your spouse. Second, discuss whether you have an equitable system for sharing benefits and dividing costs. Try to produce a more bountiful supply of available benefits, such as love, opportunities for fulfillment, and so forth.

Conducting Your Happiness Tests More Effectively

As we stressed earlier, you already perform happiness tests to assess your marriage and family life, but seldom with full awareness and in well-planned ways. Your relationship script may allow you only to be partly aware when you conduct tests and may direct you to feel as if you were doing something wrong. You may tell yourself, "It just doesn't seem nice to think so pragmatically about marriage. It seems too materialistic, maybe even selfish."

We disagree. You owe it to yourself not only to conduct happiness tests, but to perform them with maximum effectiveness. Love and family life are too important not to do so.

Although so much depends on the outcome of happiness tests, too many family members conduct them incorrectly, producing seriously flawed results.

Most people conduct happiness tests at a low level of consciousness and therefore are unaware of when and why they make certain decisions that may have major impact on the quality of family life. You should avoid performing tests in the back of your head. Instead, tap your full potential for disciplined thought. Many people also conduct happiness tests in unplanned and illogical ways, shooting from the hip. Don't conduct assessments only when the urge strikes; intentionally conduct some tests when the family drama is running smoothly.

When people are aware that they conducted an assessment, problems often arise because they resist sharing the results with family members. Discuss the results with your spouse and, when appropriate, with the children. Provide them with an opportunity to react, correct wrong assumptions, and help bring about needed changes in family life.

The results of happiness tests are often dominated by the most immediate experience and the feelings and thoughts elicited by that experience. For example, Nate just finished a battle with the children and is full of anger and frustration. In conducting the Happiness Test at this moment, Nate should also pay heed to his feelings of pride when a few weeks ago his daughter won an academic honor and his son achieved Eagle Scout status.

LEARNING FROM THE BUSINESS WORLD

The family is like a small business organization, and therefore you can learn much about successful family life by studying successful business practices. One most important observation, for instance, is that successful businesses have managers

who work hard at guiding their organizations toward their
goals.

Managers try to avoid financial calamities by monitoring
sales and determining whether productivity is at its peak. But
a successful enterprise does not stop with this assessment. At
the end of each quarter, accountants balance the books and
calculate whether company earnings for that period exceed
costs of operations. Based on these calculations and assessments, executives gauge progress, spot problems, and make
adjustments to improve operations.

At the end of a fiscal year, the chief executive reports to
stockholders, explaining the bottom line and the firm's plans
for the short- and long-term future. Such business plans are
crucial. They shape the company's future. In other words,
well-managed business enterprises build mechanisms into
their operations that enhance the likelihood of success. Here
is a lesson for families: sound evaluations promote success
and the achievement of the family dream. You and your
spouse can put this idea to work in your family by regularly
assessing whether or not your family drama is developing in
the direction you desire.

When he was well into his nineties, Grandpa Schwebel
(Milton's father) explained how decades earlier he had
managed money problems at home and in the family business. In contrast to the business, he explained, heading the
family was much more complicated: "I knew how well I did
in the store. Every day I counted the receipts. But at home,
how could I arrange things so everybody could get what they
wanted? That was a problem, especially during the depression when we had very little. There were so many people to
try to please in the family. During those gloomy days I had
to forget what people wanted and just be satisfied to provide
for what everybody needed."

Grandpa identified a key challenge in conducting logical, well-considered happiness tests in the family: identify the
full range of costs and benefits for family membership.

Identifying the Benefits of Family Membership

An important problem in conducting businesslike happiness tests is identifying the full range of benefits associated with family membership. Few people are even aware of how many needs they have and, of these, how many could be satisfied in the family.

To help you identify the personal needs that are being met by your family, consider Abraham Maslow's classic "Hierarchy of Needs." Beginning at the bottom of the list with physiological needs, move upward through safety, belongingness, and so forth. For each level, write down on a sheet of paper some benefits you gain from family membership. Then make another list of needs that are not now being met but could be. Save this list of potential benefits—we'll be able to use it later.

Production

Maslow's Hierarchy of Needs

Self-actualization needs: fulfilling your unique potential, becoming all you can be, having rich emotional experiences and a desire to help others

Esteem needs: gaining self-esteem that stems from competence and achievement, while gaining the approval and recognition of others

Belongingness and love needs: having love, affection, and acceptance from others

Safety needs: having protection from hazards, freedom from financial worry and crime, and an orderly predictable environment

Physiological needs: having sufficient food and water and opportunities for sex and rest

Identifying the Costs of
Family Membership

Over the years Grandmother Davison (Bernice's mother) enjoyed sharing wisdom with her children and grandchildren,
often conveying insights that she had undoubtedly learned
from her parents and grandparents. Among her favorite
pieces of advice was "You get what you pay for." The implica-
tion is, if you want quality, you have to pay for it.

Family life has plentiful benefits, but the bounty does
not come free. Each member has costs to pay, including doing
a share of the work necessary to run a family, making the
compromises needed when people live together, and helping
to cope with the conflicts involving marriage and family life.

Costs, like benefits, are individually determined and
measured. Therefore, whatever a person experiences as a cost
is a cost—it takes a toll from him or her. However, few people
have systematically listed their costs, a necessity in making
business-quality assessments for happiness tests.

In developing a complete list, you'll need to identify the
range of costs, from the stress that accompanies mealtime to
the worry about the budget, from your spouse's lack of concern about your needed dental surgery to the way the yard
work is divided, and from the tension caused by in-laws to the
lack of time for personal hobbies.

One way to develop your complete list of costs is to carry
a notecard for several days or more. As costs arise, record
them. People who have tried this procedure have been
pleased with the results.

USING WRITTEN HAPPINESS TESTS

All of us attended Tara and Ron's wedding some nine years
ago. That same year they moved away and began teaching
careers. During a recent New Year's Day visit, Ron shared the

following story, explaining that a year earlier he had reached a low point, primarily because he felt joyless and frustrated at home. At the time, he did not understand this feeling because he had nearly everything he thought he wanted.

Ron began by talking about a day following a miserable night spent fighting with Tara. After a long battle, Ron had no success in sleeping. Ill-prepared for the morning's arrival, Ron overslept, argued with the children, and then screamed at his car after it overheated en route to delivering the boys to the day-care center. That day even the tow-truck driver treated Ron badly.

When a taxi finally brought him to Kentwood School and the peaceful refuge of his classroom, which would be blessedly empty until the children arrived twenty-five minutes later, Ron figured he had a choice. He could rent a car and run away or treat himself to a cup of coffee. He chose the coffee. Sitting with a steaming cup in hand, Ron sighed, furrowed his brows, and pondered, "Is my marriage and family life worth the hassles?"

A few years earlier he had learned from us about happiness tests. He wondered. "Do the benefits of my family life justify the price?" Various forms of the question had flashed through his mind ever since he first married Tara, but never in a disciplined way. Now he needed to address it consciously and concretely if he was going to shake the blues.

Ron considered the benefits he had received from the relationship with Tara. He chuckled, recalling their dating days and the excitement of having a girlfriend, the fun they had driving his old convertible, the joy of giving her a friendship ring one Valentine's Day, the pleasure of bringing her home at Christmas, the thrill of being in love and planning the wedding, the specialness of the honeymoon and introducing Tara as Mrs. Ron Gunther, the adventure of buying a first house and acquiring a huge mortgage, and the indescribable wonder of having children. These were highlight moments— bits of time during which he and Tara stood on the peaks they had struggled to reach.

Next, Ron wondered about the benefits he had never expected to be important: the security Tara provided, the physical comforts she offered, and the fact that she had been a friend he could count on. On a sheet of paper Ron began preparing a list of costs and benefits. He continued working on it that night, later sharing his efforts with Tara.

Ron explained that he was generally happy with their marriage but thought they could improve it. Tara was impressed with Ron's work and candor. She too wanted to enrich their family life. For several days Tara and Ron carried notepads and built their lists.

The next weekend they exchanged their lists, and following a procedure for rewriting their family drama, they developed a mutually suitable plan to improve their family life. According to Ron's last report, they made substantial progress. He was happy again, and so was she.

Although Ron and Tara's story vouches for the value of businesslike happiness tests, people balk at the notion of using paper-and-pencil techniques to improve marriage or family life. The idea is new and alien to them. Hollywood has done a disservice by portraying a mystic view of romantic and family love, leading people to believe that love spontaneously springs only from the heart. But time and again, hefty applications of thoughtfulness and planning have strengthened family relationships, maximizing everybody's benefits and identifying small problems before they grow out of hand.

NEW UNDERSTANDINGS OF
YOUR FAMILY

If you, like Tara and Ron, wish to gain more insight into your family drama, a sensible starting point is involving your family in a meeting to conduct happiness tests. This undertaking pays immediate dividends. First, it enables every participant to generate a personal list of costs and benefits. From this, he or she can develop plans to bring more fulfillment into family life. Second, as everyone learns about one another's lists, they gain a deeper appreciation of one another's lives, which fosters harmony among them.

Sharing happiness-test information also can help you rewrite your family drama. Once family members have a sense of their own needs and those of others, good things happen almost spontaneously. A husband may see his wife's day-to-day tasks in a new way and offer to help her achieve her goals. Once a husband has expressed previously unspoken needs, he may feel comfortable in asking his wife for support. Parents and children may decide to work together on several Saturday mornings toward the goal of landscaping the yard, or they may jointly plan to make more progress on their family dream.

Once happiness-test results are shared, plans for improving the family drama almost inevitably develop. And if they don't, we encourage people to push gently for commitments from each other before ending their meeting. Whether plans develop spontaneously or are coaxed, we recommend scheduling a three-month follow-up session to evaluate the plans and to retake the written happiness tests.

Follow-up sessions offer tremendous advantages. They provide accountability for the promises people made to improve matters during the first happiness-test session. And during the second happiness-test session, families evaluate whether the plans were realistic and adequate. If not, further adjustments can be made and assessed later during a third session.

Although happiness tests are subjective by nature, they provide concrete information to your family if they are conducted in an open, thoughtful, and objective manner. To promote careful work and to facilitate the discussion of everyone's results, we have developed two types of written happiness tests. Type 1 involves spouses who discuss what they feel about their own costs and benefits. Type 2 involves parents and children in age-appropriate discussions about every family member's costs and benefits. Choose which Happiness Test you wish to pursue according to the problems at hand and whether you want to involve your children.

Directions for the Type 1 Happiness Test: In preparation, you may want to carry notepads for several days in advance, recording costs and benefits as they come to mind. Plan the session when there is ample time and good feelings prevail.

Each spouse divides a piece of paper in half. On the left side you enter the benefits received from family membership, writing the major ones on top and the minor ones at the bottom. Follow the same procedure on the right side, listing costs. Take time and think deliberately. When you decide your lists are complete, make a third list, recording your ideas about how family life could be improved for you.

When you've both finished, take turns explaining your entries. When all your information is shared, and only at this point, discuss what you learned and evaluate each option in terms of how it would affect each family member's costs and benefits. You may develop new ideas during this discussion, which also should be evaluated. Before ending the session, set goals and reach agreement on plans you will carry out to improve family life.

Norm, a member of our psychotherapy group, tried a Type 1 test with his wife Marilyn. Although they found no surprises when they looked at their costs and benefits, the session prompted an examination of their lives.

Norm's written document confirmed his beliefs about being overworked. He could only issue a deep sigh after tallying the time he spent at the office, handling household repairs and family finances, and commuting so the children could attend suburban schools. His entries told him why he felt like he was living on a treadmill. With his figures in hand he said to Marilyn, "Can we talk?"

"Sure," Marilyn replied, ready to share her test results,

which indicated that she was equally overloaded with responsibilities.

Comparing their notes, Norm and Marilyn found they
had named the following benefits: joy from knowing that they
were loved; feeling a warmth from family membership; support from being part of a family and having a partner in a
shared mission; a goodness from fulfilling their religious commitments; satisfactions from raising children; comfort from
having a familiar, predictable environment; sexual fulfillment; and satisfaction from knowing they had a romance,
even though they spent little time nourishing it.

Norm and Marilyn listed as costs having to: spend too
many hours working; devote energy to suppressing stored
anger lingering from past disputes; overcome lost pride from
last year's financial setback and this year's empty bank account; cope with nagging children and intrusive parents; endure for several years a downward spiral in their closeness
and intimacy; and live in a home in which the children were
constantly fighting.

Both spouses wrote corrective strategies for mending two
major problems—their finances and their difficulties with the
children. They decided to center their efforts in these areas,
giving top priority to their financial worries. After some discussion, they rejected the idea of Norm taking a second job.
They decided that this would tire him further and harm their
marriage.

Another suggestion, however, hit the target. They would
give up volunteer work for the time being and ask the children to assist in extra chores around the house. This would
provide them with more free time to spend as a family unit
and allow them to save energy for Saturdays, which they
would set aside to work together on the mail-order business
they had long been dabbling in. The children would help with
that too, becoming the official envelope stuffers. Norm
thought that, by giving the youngsters more responsibilities
and by better structuring their time, they might fight less. If

these plans failed, Marilyn suggested, they could seek help from the guidance counselor at the school.

They took this Happiness Test on April 25. On December 9, Norm and Marilyn each took their second tests and established that the changes had benefited them greatly. As Norm later told the therapy group, "The family atmosphere has improved considerably, which is not surprising. After all, neither one of us feels as overwhelmed as we did, and so we certainly bark at each other and the kids a lot less."

Directions for the Type 2 Happiness Test: The first major task here is simply getting everybody started, particularly teenagers. While Type 2 tests may not deal with issues in great depth, involving children has the obvious benefit of gaining their cooperation in the process of rewriting the family drama and the less obvious payoff of teaching them important social problem-solving skills. Here are specific instructions.

First, parents and children individually prepare cost/benefit forms as described for Type 1, adjusted for the children's ages. Parents explain the task to the children and define the terms. Parents and children then list their benefits and costs of family membership. Next, everyone writes down their ideas about how family life might be improved.

The family shares their lists as follows: Each person reads through his benefits, without interruption. Then, alternating the order of presentation, family members share their costs, without interruption. (Blackboards or easels can be useful tools at this point.) A discussion of one another's lists of costs and benefits follows. People may suggest (but not mandate) additions to one another's lists. Finally, parents and children read and discuss their ideas for improving family life. Before beginning, remind your children that:

- Some benefits, like love, are available in unlimited supply; others, like time and money, are not. Therefore, Johnny and

Mary can get all the love they want; however, when Mom and Dad buy presents,
they must work within a budget.

- Sometimes trade-offs can be made. This
  month, extra cash pays Mary's Saturday art-
  school tuition. Next month it will be used
  for Johnny's school trip.
- Sometimes one person's need and another's cost can be matched to benefit
  both. Grandma has too much free time
  now that she's retired from her job. She
  helps Dad, who is overworked, by keeping
  his books, and as a result everybody in the
  family benefits.
- Family members have different needs and
  opinions. People feel differently and want
  different goals.

Before ending the session, plan the next one. Choose one
of the children to save the written material until the next
meeting.

These steps are deceptively simple and straightforward.
While some families breeze through them, others discover
that it takes practice before parents and children get the
maximum yield from Type 2 happiness tests.

Type 2 tests can be effective, even with resistant children. When Nina Johnson suggested the Type 2 Happiness
Test to her husband Mel and her teenagers Pete and Tracy,
their reaction was less than enthusiastic. Pete's comments
captured the feeling: "Mom, you've got to be kidding!"

Nina expected the resistance, but won compliance by
explaining, "Our home is constantly filled with tension; this
is worth a try."

In fact, after the family members completed the written
happiness tests, everybody felt a sense of relief. Long-
harbored feelings had been released. Besides airing frustrations and anger, each family member shared hopes and

dreams and received recognition, if not support, from the others. They ended the session by making plans to improve their family life.

At least for the moment, they were pleased that they had taken time to sit down together, express feelings, and work out a plan. Although they stuck to it for only a few days, all was not lost. A couple of months later, they tried it again with greater—but not complete—success. As they recognized, partial success is better than none, and it leaves the possibility open for another try.

Creating Realistic Expectations

With happiness-test results in hand, families gain a better sense of their needs and a deeper understanding of the forces that stand between them and their family dream. But there is a myth that can get in the way of applying the Happiness Test appropriately—the myth of "perfect families."

While conducting happiness tests, you may picture perfect families dwelling somewhere in your neighborhood or community. You may visualize husbands, wives, and children living trouble-free lives, filled with love and intimacy without a fight or significant difference of opinion. Such families, however, do not exist, except in the imagination.

You need to know that real families have real conflicts, so that you are not forced to wrestle with unrealistic expectations. Differences inevitably occur among family members dwelling under one roof and extend to grown siblings, parents, and adult children housed perhaps thousands of miles apart. Fights can be sparked by events of the day or by decade-old jealousies. Conflicts can end at sunset or at death, or sadly, they can endure beyond a lifetime if passed on to children. Family members can find unlimited sources of conflict. Loved ones can debate the distribution of family resources, power, and control. Imagined injustices can polarize or sour family members as quickly as real ones.

As you and your spouse move forward after conducting

your happiness tests, it is important that each of you recognize that, though you may strive for perfection, you seek really to be satisfied with substantial progress. If you insist on perfection, you only set yourself up for disappointment and defeat, because perfection is unattainable.

If either you or your spouse has even a sliver of belief in the existence of a perfect family, we suggest a technique that students in our classes find helpful. They conduct an abbreviated interview with one person in a family they believe runs smoothly. They do these interviews in private to promote candor.

Ask the interviewee if his current family has had serious problems. If married, inquire as to whether he or his spouse has feared or thought privately about divorce. Inquire about children. How do the youngsters behave, relate to the parents, interact with siblings, and so forth? Gently probe into school behavior and performance. Has either been a source of irritation or embarrassment?

Next, ask him to recall the family in which he was raised. Are there serious problems among family members today? Have past arguments curtailed contact between adult siblings or between adult children and parents? Is there unhealthy competition among siblings, arguments about who receives what benefits from the parents, or disagreements about contributing money or assistance to aging parents? Are there scars remaining as a result of substantial difficulties stemming as far back as childhood?

Whether the interviewee describes open, biting warfare or a subtle dueling cloaked in silence, in all probability he will confirm some instances of significant conflict that disrupted family functioning. Our students always reach the same conclusion—families inevitably encounter significant conflict that can't be easily handled by everyday problem-solving techniques. We predict this result with confidence, and cannot underestimate the importance of your recognizing this reality.

Once you believe that conflict is inevitable in families,

you can see that, although you cannot prevent all conflict in your home, you can assume the role of observer and figure out how to cope with and manage it effectively.

THREE WAYS FAMILIES HANDLE CONFLICT

Everyday problem-solving skills, like straightforward communication, discussion, compromise, and generating options, serve an important function in every home. They smooth out minor differences and lead to acceptable solutions. They uncover answers for spouses who differ over issues ranging from how to squeeze the toothpaste tube to which home to buy. They also aid children in ironing out differences over toys, going first or last, sharing candy, and who has to do a particular chore. Finally, everyday problem-solving techniques enable parents and teens to reason with each other and provide a vehicle through which Mom or Dad can teach reluctant preschoolers.

Eventually some issues develop that cannot be handled with everyday problem-solving skills. These problems have the potential to cause persistent difficulty in the family and can bring with them great hardship, adding much to the cost of family membership and nothing to the benefits. Because problems such as these have negative effects on happiness tests, they are a threat to the family.

These problems involve matters crucial to each party's relationship script. For example, consider Lacey and Steve. She wants a large circle of friends and weekly opportunities to socialize. He wants quiet weekends by the fireplace or on the patio, depending on the season. Every week they argue about this matter. Friends are crucial to Lacey's self-image; she was taught as a girl to be social, and it is an essential part of her relationship script. Steve, in contrast, was taught that the most important quality of a wife is to provide the husband with comfort and rest so he can "recharge his batteries" and ready himself for the harshness of the work world. Every week their level of anger and frustration seems to creep upward. The costs of this issue to each of them will continue to grow until they must act because their happiness-test results have become unfavorable.

Similarly, Lee and Chris have a problem based on their relationship script differences, which centers on how strictly to discipline Chris's child. The bickering that mars their home life grows worse by the week, and so does the child's behavior. The source of the conflict does not matter; the nature and persistence of it does. If such inevitable differences are not managed, homes become battle zones.

When a person's costs outweigh the benefits—and he or she cannot fix matters using everyday problem-solving methods—happiness-test outcomes become unfavorable. Because individuals find this situation intolerable, they will take other corrective action to reduce costs and/or increase benefits. In Part II, "Rewriting the Drama," we'll provide five approaches you can use to improve your happiness-test results when everyday problem-solving tools don't work.

Rewriting the Drama

A successful marriage is an edifice that must be rebuilt every day.

—ANDRÉ MAUROIS

6

Family Defense Mechanisms to Improve Your Happiness Test

*I*n this chapter you will learn about Family Defense Mechanisms (FDMs), which are prescribed patterns of behavior that people unintentionally follow. FDMs work by regulating the amount of shared family time and by directing shared time into activities that cause minimal friction between people. They bring immediate improvement in unfavorable happiness-test results and are often the first way family members try, unknowingly, to rewrite their dramas. This chapter contains methods that will help you identify and evaluate the role FDMs play in your home. Knowledge about FDMs is powerful. Once you identify those that you use, you will be in a position to make positive changes that will benefit the lives of everyone. Here are some examples of FDMs.

- Jim works late nearly every evening. On weekends when he is home for extended periods, his wife spends much of her time shopping at the mall or visiting friends.
- Sherman and Vanessa, married twelve years, have started taking separate vacations. Last August he went fishing in Alaska while she took her mother on a South American cruise.
- Seven-year-old Diana rarely plays at home. She can always be located at one of her friends' houses.

- Evelyn, twenty-three, lives with her parents and was very pleased when her younger sister decided to go to an out-of-town college, because the two of them have been extremely competitive for years. When Evelyn's sister comes home for weekend visits, Evelyn sleeps at her boyfriend's apartment, claiming that she wants to be generous to her younger sister and give her the run of the house.

You may know people like these who, with their families, use FDMs to reduce family conflict. People do not seek out FDMs. Rather they happen upon them. And, although most people are not aware that they are using them, once they discover the behavior patterns, they continue to follow them because they bring needed relief from conflict and tension. With hostilities reduced, people are able to more fully enjoy the leisure time they do share as a family.

FDMs are not the healthiest solution to a family's problem, because they do not deal with its basic cause. Rather, FDMs bandage the symptom, allowing people to avoid rather than confront their differences. But they are a natural part of the human experience, and they do improve happiness-test outcomes, providing time both for individual independence and family intimacy.

A few years back, Rick and Patti Stone were fighting constantly, and both had developed short tempers with the children. As the costs of family membership began exceeding benefits, they unwittingly stumbled upon a solution—a FDM that called for physical escape, allowing them to enjoy as much time together as they could comfortably tolerate. Their story is described below.

Around 10 P.M. on weeknights, Rick pulls his Mustang convertible into the driveway. Patti is fast asleep, giving in to the fatigue induced by her strenuous day at the office and then at home, cleaning, cooking, and chauffeuring the children. The net result of the Stones' weekday schedule: for five consecutive days Rick has practically no interaction with his wife and children. Both Patti and Rick complain to friends about their tough schedules, but they never discuss changing them.

Weekends involve more contact. Rick, Patti, and the children eat breakfast and watch Saturday-morning cartoons together. Later, Rick spends the afternoon golfing. When he returns home, he stokes the grill and cooks dinner for the family. Everybody enjoys the barbecue—especially roasting marshmallows. When the children tire and go to bed, that's Rick's cue. He pours chilled wine into frosted glasses, and he and Patti, who have not seen much of each other during the week, ready themselves for an intimate evening of flirting, tenderness, and love. They usually become living proof that absence makes the heart grow fonder.

Sunday's schedule is as invariable as Saturday's: church, breakfast at the pancake house, and a trip to Poppa and Nanna's, where Patti and the children spend the day. After a brief hello, Rick journeys to the golf course for a businessman's match and then to his office for a headstart on the week.

Before Patti and Rick happened upon the FDM of physical escape, they argued incessantly but settled nothing. On a daily basis, they managed to make each other miserable. Their FDM reduced shared time and consequently the amount of conflict and distress. During the week, Patti and Rick had no opportunity to fight over dinner or the children's bedtime routine, and with Patti asleep before Rick came home, the number of bedroom battles was reduced dramatically. Because the FDM made both parents happier, it also allowed them to give more fully to the children. Because Patti and Rick are happier, so are the children.

As the Stones' case illustrates, FDMs do not provide the kinds of solutions typically seen in old-time Hollywood movies or in today's romance stories. A pessimist might evaluate them as mere safety-valve changes: they artificially make the home environment tolerable by releasing just enough steam to enable families to survive.

Recognizing the limitations of FDMs, we liken their function to grease in a pump for reducing friction—once friction is reduced, people are spared unnecessary discomfort, have a more satisfying family life, and enjoy more intimacy, even if only from time to time. In short, FDMs provide struggling family members with more favorable outcomes on their happiness tests.

HOW TO DETECT FDMS

To ascertain whether a pattern of behavior is an FDM, you need to know its main purpose. For instance, you observe the neighbor across the street leaving for the office every evening after dinner. His night hours could stem from a need to earn extra dollars, from career aspirations, or from an FDM. Similarly, you know a couple with jobs on opposite coasts. They may have chosen these positions as a sacrifice necessary to their family dream, or they may have chosen them to preserve their marriage, following the dictates of an FDM.

Visiting the home of an acquaintance, you may have difficulty determining the purpose of a behavioral pattern. From your outsider's perspective, it is often difficult to establish whether a pattern represents an FDM. To determine this, look for the following characteristics that are associated with FDMs.

The main purpose of an FDM is to decrease the incidence of family conflict. It limits the time family members share or directs them away from activities that are conflict-prone, such as unstructured leisure or nonroutine decision-making. An FDM nearly always gives the impression of serving other purposes and it may actually bring useful secondary benefits. Rick and Patti's long work hours brought them financial security. Furthermore, their dedication won social approval from their parents.

The behavior of an FDM is in excess of that which is necessary, and family members do not act to stop the behavior, even if one or more complain about it. Instead they implicitly support it. In one family we know, the husband, wife, and only child watch the same TV program on three different television sets in three different rooms. The father gripes about the electric bill, the mother about the three messy rooms, but neither acts to change the viewing habits.

Although family members behave as prescribed by an FDM, most are unaware that their behavior is protecting the family. For example, Patti believes Rick's long workday and her own early bedtime are necessary. She told us, "We love each other, but we don't have time to be romantic or go places together or share what's happening in our daily lives. I don't like the setup. But who can choose? Our friends face the same thing. Raising kids these days is hard work and expensive. You don't have time to pamper a marriage."

Patti's children believe, "Daddy can't come home for dinner. Poor Daddy, he has to work so hard." Nobody recognizes the hidden motives in Rick's behavior. The atmosphere in their home, however, improved dramatically once they established their FDM. For example, by Saturday morning, Rick misses Patti and the children, and they miss him. Five tranquil days set the stage for a great weekend at their household.

Once in place, FDMs protect the level of intimacy in a home. They serve this function by allowing the attractiveness of each person to shine brighter during periods of closeness. Therefore, the home becomes more joyful, enabling parents and children alike to have more fun. They enjoy each other's company, and they can again look forward to the future and achieving the family dream.

In homes in which the level of conflict has been severe or threatens to become so, FDMs preserve the physical integrity of the household. Because of this, when spouses review their family life, it looks healthier and happier to them than it did before. Although they remain unaware that FDMs are functioning, they are aware of reduced fighting and more displays of affection. That recognition, by itself, will lead people to conclude that their marriage and family life are going better. And this thought, in turn, will brighten people's feelings and help them to act more optimistically and lovingly.

Before the Stones discovered physical escape, Patti rated the chances of her relationship improving as minimal. After they discovered the FDM, however, she and Rick had fewer fights, which improved her happiness-test results. As she told us, "No fighting with Rick, a good home, and the children. I had hoped for more, but I would have settled for that." Also, once Patti and Rick started using physical escape, Rick's behavior began changing. There was no chip on his shoulder when he walked into the house. Instead of being demanding, he took care of himself when Patti was asleep. And a month after the change, Rick said "I love you" to Patti several times during one weekend. This moved Patti, and she started wondering, "Maybe he does really love me like he used to; maybe when we were fighting all the time, Rick just hid those feelings or kept them bottled up inside."

IDENTIFYING FDMS

Be prepared. Nearly everybody who reads the descriptions of the following FDMs will recognize one that sheds light on familiar family-behavior patterns. After studying a list of FDMs, one graduate student exclaimed, "Did you interview my husband before you wrote this?"

There are four general categories of FDMs, some of which break down into various FDM types that we'll explore in detail. The four categories are:

Escape FDMs, in which one family member or more withdraws.

Driven-person FDMs, in which one family member or more focuses such great attention on an activity that it hampers the full development of intimacy in family relationships.

Mood-swing FDMs, in which loving and unloving feelings alternate.

Multi-household FDMs, which link two or more parts of the extended family.

FDMs most often prescribe behavior for one or both spouses. This happens because the spouses are the hub of the family circle, and their relationship is the one most often troubled and in need of support. However, FDMs also serve to reduce conflict in relationships between lovers, parents and children, adult siblings, and adult children and their parents.

Escape FDMs

The Escape FDMs lead one family member to physically, emotionally, or psychologically withdraw from the others. This improves the happiness-test outcomes of family members who collude in—or do not object to—the escape. Although the escapee may be working toward a valued personal goal, the principal purpose of the escape is to limit shared time and conflict, thereby reducing the costs of family membership. With family-interaction time a scarce commodity, family members better enjoy the time they share. There are three types of Escape FDMs—physical escape, psychological escape, and escape through drugs and alcohol.

Physical escape. With this FDM, a person withdraws, spending substantial blocks of time away from other family members. Regardless of how the family understands and explains it, the main purpose is improving happiness-test outcomes. So the specific activity a person escapes *to* is less important than the fact that he escapes *from* others.

The story of Phillip and Jane and their children Ashley,

Todd, and Jodi illustrates physical escape. Jane told us, "I serve dinner at six sharp, and as soon as we finish, Phillip grabs two cigars from his humidor and marches down to the den. That's where he spends the evening, smoking, shuffling business papers, and listening to a ball game. If anybody wants to talk to him, they know where to go—into his 'hideout,' as the kids call it."

Although the children joked about Dad and his hideout, they were well aware of how important it was to his routine. This awareness was illustrated in an essay that daughter Jodi, age nine, wrote for her English lesson.

My Father

My father's name is Phillip Williams. He was born January 14, 1946. My father works at the telephone company. My father went to Indiana University. My father's favorite sport is baseball, and his favorite color is green. He's older than forty, and I call that "over the hill." He likes to spend a lot of time in the den doing his work. I hate that. The end.

Psychological escape. With this FDM, a family member, in physical proximity to others, withdraws psychologically, thereby reducing interaction and friction. When this FDM is in use, family members feel out of touch with the escaper. It may take repeated requests to pull him or her into conversation—for example, "Mort, for the third time, please put away your MBA course material. You've been studying all weekend. Our guests are due in one hour, and I need your help." After an escape, feelings of anger and frustration toward the others dissipate to some degree, and family members are more ready for periods of meaningful contact and some level of intimacy.

The following practices are examples of psychological escape.

- *The aching body:* When Phyllis' lower back both-
  ers her, she spends ninety-minute stretches in
  silent meditation.
- *The couch potato:* After dinner Henry dozes on
  the couch until bedtime, when the rest of the
  family goes to sleep. At that point, Henry suffers
  from insomnia, so he stays up to watch the late
  movie.
- *The Walkman addict:* Teenager Libby wears the
  stereo earphones to her portable unit the way
  women might wear earrings, during all waking
  hours and sometimes during sleep.

Escape through drugs and alcohol.   Some people who con-
sume drugs and alcohol are not using them as part of an FDM.
When drugs and alcohol are part of an FDM, one person
distances himself by being under the influence of substances
during family time. The escape can appear to lower costs and
increase benefits over the short run in three ways: by distanc-
ing family members physically or psychologically, thereby
limiting conflict; by the effects of the substance, which temporarily close down negative feelings, reduce tensions, and permit him to be a "happy drunk"; and by warmth and intense
hope generated after a binge, when the escaper makes up or
promises to improve family life.

Although escape through substances often involves aspects of other FDMs, we singled it out and categorized it
separately because of the unique consequences it has over the
long term. Compared to other FDMs, which can help families
maintain satisfactory happiness-test outcomes for many years,
alcohol and drugs inevitably cause health and other problems
for the user and his family.

The following are examples of this FDM.

- *The husband tamer:* During Bill's busy work season, Donna sips wine coolers all afternoon, enabling her to tolerate his awful after-work moods.

- *The high teenager:* A sloppily dressed, seventeen-year-old client in psychotherapy discusses drugs and her parents:

  "I really love my parents, but they'll never know because they never listen to what I say."

  "My parents suffocate me. Want examples? When I go to my room and close my door to study, within five minutes Mom comes barging in. What is she so nosy about? I'm sick of it. One day Scott asked me to get high. He was so cute. He said, 'You know why they call it high school? 'Cause you are supposed to be high.' So I got high, and it was nice. No worries. Now, when I'm home and Mom or Dad hound me—no problem. If they don't back off, I pop a pill. They're cheap enough, easy to get, and I can afford them, even on my puny allowance."

Driven-Person FDMs

With driven-person FDMs, one family member or more invests substantial amounts of time and energy in an all-consuming effort directed toward a particular family concern or goal. This all-out effort improves happiness-test results by limiting the time available for unplanned shared activity, during which conflict could develop. This effort also eliminates potential family controversy over the use of resources such as time and money. The driven-person FDMs also improve happiness tests by providing the satisfaction associated with a shared mission. There are three types in the driven-person category.

The solitary driven person. With this FDM, one family member, supported by others, labors alone on a family goal in an obsessed manner. Like physical escape, this FDM reduces family conflict by keeping people separate. But a key

difference between the two is that this FDM requires commitment to a common family goal, which, if achieved, will provide others with shared satisfaction. The activities involved
are often geared toward social or economic advancement and
therefore are often found when the spouses' relationship
scripts direct them to seek money, power, or status.

The solitary driven person is illustrated in the following
examples.

- *The stamp collector:* Bernard, with Emily's full
  support, occupies hour after hour organizing his
  stamps and attending postage-stamp auctions
  and club meetings. He and Emily hope the collection will supply funds for their retirement home.
- *The husband's practice:* Rosemary participates in
  a dozen charity organizations. She and Don justify the time as necessary to promote his veteri-
  nary practice.
- *Beat the others:* Ned agrees with Louise, who
  wants him to stay on the road past midnight if
  that means one last sale and outdoing the other
  salesmen.
- *My child focus:* Sheila, a single mother, took on
  a part-time position besides her full-time job so
  that her children could take dancing and tennis
  lessons.
- *Keep up with the Joneses:* Both Connie and Dan
  work double shifts so that every year they can
  afford designer wardrobes, glitzy vacations, and
  two new cars.

The driven team.   With this FDM, two or more people work
toward a family goal in an obsessed manner. They invest
enormous amounts of time and effort in the goal, substantially
limiting the amount of unstructured time available during
which difficulties might develop. Furthermore, given the

shared purpose of the FDM, family members are less susceptible to differences over the use of resources such as time and
money.

This FDM differs from projects that families might
choose to share because the activity is not practiced out of
deliberate choice, but rather out of unrecognized necessity.
Instead of fostering intimacy, family members use this FDM
to maintain a tolerable distance, focusing on the goal instead of an appreciation of their teamwork. Family members
using this FDM are a bit like two young boys, each playing
his own game with his own toy truck, while sharing the
same floor.

The driven team is illustrated in the following example.

Wilma and Junior Webster were broke but happy early
in their marriage. Though their income was limited, they
contentedly added children and then Wilma's mother to their
household. When Wilma's mother died, Wilma couldn't re-
bound from her depression. Nothing perked her up. Junior
grew discouraged, and the marriage grew stormy. They could
not spend more than an evening together without yelling at
each other about the children, Wilma's health, or whether
they would ever have enough money.

Fate smiled on the family, however, when Junior's boss,
a successful real-estate entrepreneur, decided to retire. Because he deeply trusted his longtime handyman, Junior, he
offered him the first option on a long-term package deal for
buying the properties. The opportunity snapped Wilma out of
her depression. During their first years in business, the couple labored side by side in sixteen- to eighteen-hour workdays
to make their monthly payments. But, much to their surprise,
although overworked, their marriage improved.

In time, the Websters established themselves financially
and could afford to hire help. Wilma begged Junior to relax
at home and travel. Several times they tried to take time off
together, but they would end up on each other's nerves again.
That led them back to their old plan of work, continuing to
spend long hours working together in the rental units.

The problem-driven family. With this FDM, family members divert time, energy, and other resources in an obsessed manner to handling a special family problem. The investment in a clear-cut goal benefits family members and limits the amount of free time during which conflict might develop. This FDM depends on two factors: one family member displays a problem or has a goal that requires attention, and the spouses' relationship scripts are such that they focus their energies on attending to the special need. Nobody is aware that the family system might have created the problem or overstressed its importance. Ironically, spouses may complain about the burden they have to bear.

The problem-driven family is similar to the driven team, except that the targeted goal is internal to the family, an important distinction. In the problem-driven family, one family member takes on the responsibility for receiving the time and attention of others, diverting it from issues that might otherwise lead to family conflict. If that person changes and no longer needs attention or becomes unavailable through leaving the home, the FDM cannot work. In that case, the family will encounter new conflicts or will have to find another FDM, as in the following example.

Mr. and Mrs. Lopat had four daughters and one son, Gary, who had persistent academic and social difficulties. For years Gary's troubles cemented the marital relationship, giving it a common focus that displaced arguments about work roles and intimacy. It also gave his sisters a focus—to be always ready to defend their brother in school, on the playground, and in the neighborhood.

At age fourteen, Gary was sent to a special boarding school where he quickly made an adjustment. However, within a matter of weeks, his parents were having great difficulty in their marriage. Soon, Marti, Gary's youngest sister who had never had difficulties before, began developing problems with her girlfriends, in school, and on the playground. Unconsciously, she began assuming Gary's former role as the focus for her family's attention.

Sometimes the use of one FDM leads to the discovery of another. The examples below illustrate what happened in two families, as parents reacted to the escape FDMs their children were using.

- *Save the kid:* Dee and Bradley fought incessantly, until their son Bert developed a drug problem. Besides working together to solve Bert's problem, they now co-lead a parents' support group.
- *The cult focus:* After teenager Suzanne joined a religious cult and focused her life on praying, volunteering, and donating to the guru's fund, her parents pulled together and have spent the last two years trying to convince Suzanne to return home.

Mood-Swing FDMs

The mood-swing FDMs operate in a cyclical way, allowing family members to have alternate feelings of closeness and distance. There are three types, and all improve happiness-test outcomes by allowing people to have the periods of closeness that they want between periods of psychological distance that they need.

Aggression/closeness. We call this the "aggression" FDM. With it, a person displays intense anger or verbal aggression toward one or more of the family members. The barrage continues, perhaps with retaliation, until the attacker is sure that the recipient is sufficiently hurt, angry, intimidated, or disgusted to stay away for a period of time. After the separation, angry feelings dissipate and family members crave and seek out a period of closeness.

This behavior pattern is often found in families that contain one spouse who has an aggressive, macho relationship script or a passive-aggressive relationship script. Temporarily, this FDM improves the happiness-test results by allowing family members to release pent-up emotions, by separating people and limiting shared family time, and by providing opportunities for tenderness and love as people make up and deal with hurt, pain, and guilt.

Over the long run, aggression introduces unforeseen costs into the lives of every family member. Victims of aggression can suffer from lowered self-esteem, psychological difficulties, and ineffectiveness in day-to-day life. Perpetrators must cope with the feelings generated after hurting loved ones, and they may never learn to deal adequately with personal problems. Witnesses to family aggression are also harmed, often developing relationship scripts with warped outlooks and with ineffective tools for coping with frustrations.

The aggression FDM is displayed in many forms, as the following practices illustrate.

- *Physical aggression:* Jerome loses his temper periodically and shoves his wife. She will not remain in the same room with him for a period of days afterward.
- *Guerrilla warfare aggression:* When Juan angers Marisol, she immediately goes on a shopping binge, charging hundreds of dollars of clothes on their credit cards. The two remain at arm's length for a day or two.
- *Provoked aggression:* Nine-year-old Lew presses Mom's button by walking into the house through the front rather than the side door, leaving dirty laundry on the hamper rather than in it, and playing in the snow without wearing his coat and gloves. Mom lets Lew have it, but before he goes to sleep, she comes into his room and they make up and have a lengthy chat.
- *Aggression combined with escape:* During a recent psychotherapy session, Annette reflected on her childhood years. "Remember the Saturday-night

fights on television during the 1950s? They had
nothing on our family. We had a ten-round match
at about 11 P.M. every Saturday night. Dad
worked six days a week, although he could have
worked five. On Saturday he'd come home at 7
P.M., and we kids hid in the closet. He'd pretend
he couldn't find us, although we were always in
the same place. We'd play with him until dinner.
After we ate, we'd go to bed and wait, knowing
what would follow. Soon, Mom and Dad would
discuss, then yell, and finally scream their heads
off. The fight always started the same way:
'Should we go to the early church service or the
late one?' This would go on until one would
insult the other, and that parent would cry,
'That's it,' slamming the bedroom door. We'd
rarely go to either service; usually Mom and Dad
didn't talk most of Sunday. Sunday evening, just
before dinner, they would make up with a big
kiss, and all was well. It happened every week
without fail."

Resignation/anger/closeness.   We call this the "resignation" FDM. With it, one person gives up doing a task that he
is capable of accomplishing, inducing others to rescue him.
For example, a spouse may give up an important goal, such
as earning enough money to support the family, or an essential chore, such as competently keeping tax material organized, forcing others to take care of him in new ways. The
resigner typically has a dependent relationship script, which
leads him to act this way. Another family member with a
compatible relationship script rescues others by doing their
work or attending to their personal needs.

Over time, this FDM causes the feelings of family members to fluctuate from the closeness and caring that is associated with the help-giving process to the anger and
frustration that is generated when one gives more than his

share or is treated in a condescending way. After these negative feelings dissipate, family members make up, completing the cycle and producing loving, warm feelings. Temporarily, this FDM improves happiness-test outcomes. The resigner will not compete for what he wants, reducing conflict. This relieves household tensions because people no longer have to struggle with him over power. He has abdicated direct control.

Happiness-test outcomes are further enhanced because resignation produces a clear-cut family goal: invest time, energy, and money into helping the resigner regain his full abilities. Striving toward this goal eliminates conflict and makes everybody feel good. The resigner sees that his family cares. The competent family members enjoy "saving the day" and, feeling sorry for the resigner, let the anger toward him melt away.

From time to time, however, the resigner and the rescuer(s) become angry at each other. This anger creates the distance family members need after their period of closeness, but it eventually fades, producing new opportunities for family intimacy and expressions of love. Although resigners and rescuers may be very vocal in their complaints about each other, they nonetheless collude in practicing this FDM. An example of the resignation FDM is presented in what we would call "the royal resignation."

Thirty-five-year-old Roger waits for Wednesday, which he calls "hump day," and Friday, which he calls "made-it-through-another-week day." Because a buddy at work was promoted ahead of him, Roger has felt shafted by the world. His initial reaction was to go home, drop on the sofa, and become a fixture. After Roger surrendered his career dreams, it was easy for him to decide his life was about as good as it would ever get. Upon sharing his resignation with Mona, things at home changed immediately. Mona waited on him hand and foot and let him abdicate most household responsibilities. Roger even gained new attention from the children, who were ordered by Mom to respect Dad.

"Hey," Roger later explained, "the kids let me pick which cartoons we'll watch on Saturday mornings."

Within a few weeks, however, Mona developed a short fuse and nagged Roger about resuming household chores. He became enraged and said thaᴛ she hadn't been treating him like a man. She was taking everything over, acting like she wore the pants in the house. Following a few days of distance between them, they made up and were close for a while. Eventually, however, arguments developed about household chores, and Roger again responded with feelings of resignation. This time, however, he mentioned suicide. That scared both Mona and Roger, leading them to seek psychotherapy.

Psychological distance/buy-off/closeness.   We call this the "buy-off" FDM. After a period of psychological distance using this FDM, one person gives a family member something he desires, fostering closeness in the relationship. One spouse may present the other with dinner out and an evening movie or perhaps with a gift. Children make offerings too. They may deliver a prized crayon drawing or promise their parents a straight-A report card.

Family members collaborate in using this FDM, allowing the buy-off to draw them together for a period of time. The closeness can last for hours, days, or weeks. In time, the buy-off wears thin or family members grow angry about having to offer the deal or accept it. At this point, the relationship reverts to its psychologically more distant state. Although the giver and recipient of buy-offs may complain about the deals, this mood-swing FDM improves family members' happiness-test outcomes by cyclically providing closeness in amounts they can tolerate.

Examples of the buy-off FDM include the following.

- *The distance arrester:* Although they are married, Reed and Kay live like college roommates for weeks at a time, eating meals separately and following their own sleep schedules. Although most of the time they are content to coexist in the house, periodically Kay misses the closeness they once had. She purchases a catchy greeting card and hand-delivers it to Reed. He usually responds favorably to her gesture, and they spend a string of good days doing things together.

- *The TV payback:* Gail feels badly about not sharing much time with the children during the week, so on some weekends she lets them stay up late and enjoy TV with her.
- *Bedroom bribe:* Kirk brings home a box of chocolate-covered cherries, hoping the coldness that has prevailed over the past few weeks will melt in the bedroom.

Families using the buy-off FDM may find that the deal needs to be varied and its worth matched to the circumstances, making the exchange equitable for the giver and receiver. Karl and Bonnie's marriage had grown stale some time ago, and they were taking each other for granted. Maybe that's why Karl was delighted when the young group at the office invited him to join them for a Friday happy hour. Karl accepted, believing the socializing would serve him well with the staff, but he felt guilty about his decision and failed to call Bonnie until after he had missed dinner.

Karl returned home late with a faint smell of alcohol on his breath. Still, Bonnie accepted his brief explanation, partly because she had enjoyed a peaceful evening with the children. Bonnie's calm reaction impressed Karl and sparked generous feelings in him. He surprised Bonnie, "Honey, get a baby-sitter for tomorrow night. I'm taking you out to dinner!"

Bonnie accepted immediately, although she was surprised by the offer because the two of them had not been out alone for months. Karl selected Bonnie's favorite restaurant, and the couple had a tasty meal and enjoyed each other's company. The buy-off magic broke the next night, giving way to a heated argument because Bonnie asked if Karl's secretary had gone drinking with the gang on Friday.

Two weeks later, Karl found reason to work late at the office, but this time he remembered to call Bonnie, assuring her of his early return. However, he missed the 8:12 P.M. commuter train, and by the time he managed to get home, Bonnie was livid because she had postponed eating her own dinner to wait for him. Karl promptly offered a weak apology and dinner out together. "After all this," Bonnie stated flatly, barely hiding the smile coming to her face, "I deserve more than that. Look at all my waiting and worrying."

Karl increased the booty, pledging a dinner and movie to rectify the situation. Bonnie accepted the buy-off, enabling the couple to dodge a battle about Karl's tardiness, while also providing them with an evening out and the promise of a period of closeness. The pattern of their FDM was now established: distance leads to a buy-off, and that in turn brings them closeness.

Multi-Household FDMs

Multi-household FDMs exist with two or more physically separate living units, often tying together extended family, different generations, the homes of adult siblings separated by many miles, and the new families of divorced ex-spouses. The multi-household FDM operates when members of the participating households adopt FDMs that interlock, connecting through individuals in the unit, such as when an adult child links with a parent, or it can connect unit to unit, such as when two households square off to battle each other.

To better understand this FDM, consider Hanna Townley and George Bayard, who had two children before their marriage ended five years ago in divorce. Since then, both have remarried and have had children with their new spouses.

Now, Hanna and George's new families are involved in a multi-household FDM, which operates because the Townley and Bayard households each use driven-person FDMs, focusing their attention on court battles involving child support, visitation, and custody issues. The ongoing legal entanglement provides each family unit with a common enemy and a substantial problem requiring time and energy.

As this example illustrates, multi-household FDMs can take place regardless of family members' feelings toward each other. Siblings, ex-spouses, and other kin, whether they love, hate, envy, compete, or feel indifferent toward each other, can create linked households and find their behavior prescribed by an FDM. Although the people involved might vigorously deny any link or complain about the activity required, members of the different households are actually colluding in the use of the multi-family FDM. The reasons why they take no definitive steps to stop its operation are the same as the reasons for continuing any of the FDMs: they improve the short-term happiness-test outcomes by providing people with a way to cope with inevitable conflict.

As the following example illustrates, multi-household FDMs operate by using many different combinations of FDMs within the connected homes.

Winnie, a registered nurse, resigned her position in the hospital emergency room the day after her engagement to Jeff appeared in the hometown newspaper. Jeff, however, did not earn enough money to satisfy the new family's needs, and because he was a high-school dropout and a civil servant, there was little prospect of a financially comfortable future.

Winnie's father, a successful salesman, volunteered to contribute money to the couple's budget, provided that his new son-in-law allow his daughter to stay home and raise his grandchildren. Jeff consented, realizing that if Winnie stayed home she would be best equipped to attend to him.

Meanwhile, Winnie's parents agreed that Dad would stay on the road one extra day a week to earn additional dollars. The parents' driven-person FDM interlocked effectively with their offspring's mood-swing or resignation FDM, immediately providing benefits to both home units.

YOUR FAMILY FDM REVIEW

FDMs help people maintain balance in their marriages and families. Although FDMs treat symptoms, rather than solving basic underlying problems, they allow difficulties to be avoided or dealt with indirectly. Because solutions are often not easily found in certain kinds of relationship problems, FDMs can be a blessing.

Of course people pay a steep price for skirting conflict: they sacrifice the opportunity for maximum intimacy in marriage and family. However, even with several FDMs operating, people can experience a good measure of family joy and pleasure, making the trade-off a reasonable one.

Now you can put your family onstage and play the role of the critic, identifying FDMs operating in your family and the costs associated with using them. The following is a set of questions about FDMs that may be operating in your home. For illustrative purposes, we have included the answers given by Lisa Alpert, a thirty-nine-year-old mother of three. Keep a pad of paper handy so you can write down your answers.

From the FDMs described earlier in this chapter, identify any that you have seen operating in your family, in the past or present.

Lisa: When I was growing up, my parents often used physical and psychological escape. Dad always seemed to be playing golf during the weekends. Sometimes he would leave the house before we were awake, so he could get a good tee time. The image I have of my mother back then is of her sitting in her chair reading paperback novels. Although she'd do anything we wanted, no matter the time of day, her one request was, "Please don't disturb me when I'm in my chair." Regarding my present family, I think my husband Scott and I use physical escape.

To help you identify any FDMs you may have missed take time to ask yourself these questions:

- Did your family suddenly begin doing something different at home and find that life was improved?
- Do you have any regular patterns of behavior that may function to prevent conflict?
- Are you linked in any remarkable ways to parts of your extended family?

If you answer yes to any of these items, think about whether an FDM is involved.

Lisa: As I think about those three questions, I see the answer is yes, yes, and yes. Some time ago, Mom and I started shopping together. It began suddenly. Now we go every weekend, and it helps me avoid fights with Scott and the children. It sounds like physical escape and multi-family FDMs are involved.

Families adopt FDMs by trial and error. Can you remember when and how your family came to use the FDMs you've now identified?

Lisa: I cannot recall how my family FDMs developed in my childhood, but I certainly do remember when Scott and I started using physical escape. One weekend Scott was steaming mad at me over nothing. The fifteenth time he yelled at me, I grabbed the children, whom I had been nagging because Scott had upset me, and stormed out of the house with no destination in mind. Well, I always liked shopping. After a

few minutes of driving, I cooled down and headed for the
mall. When I came home, Scott and I made up and all was
well. The next weekend I invited mother to join me at the
mall. We soon became shopping partners, giving birth in both
of our homes to the Multi-Household FDM.

FDMs bring many benefits. List those gained by your
family from the FDMs you identified before.

Lisa: The major benefit is that we have more relaxed weekends. Scott and I don't fight like we used to, so we get angry
less often at the kids. Besides having more family fun, Scott
and I started enjoying each other's company again and have
become much more romantic. An unexpected benefit of all
this has been that, for the first time in my life, I can build
a more rewarding adult-to-adult relationship with my mother.
She still gives me advice, but we have become friends, so her
ideas don't seem critical like they used to.

FDMs bring costs as well as benefits. List the costs that
your family incurs from FDMs.

Lisa: My costs include being away from home a good part of
Saturday, piles of undone housework, and the distance I
sometimes feel from Scott. If you asked my husband, he
would measure his major cost in dollars and cents. It's tough
for me to resist sales, so he would be right in saying I spend
some money needlessly. The children have some extra work
because I'm not around as much to serve them. But they've
managed, and they've learned by doing more for themselves.
Anyway, for the kids and for all of us, the benefits have far
outweighed the costs.

Look ahead a few years to when your children will be
out of the house. Consider the long-term impact of these
FDMs on your family.

Lisa: This will take some thinking. Without much difficulty, I can imagine fleeing to the mall five years from now; although the children will be older, my family will be basically the same. But, it's mind-boggling to think that Scott and I might be using this FDM in the distant future, when we have an empty nest or after we've retired. By then I hope we'll have less pressure in our lives and more time to build marital intimacy. I certainly hope we won't need FDMs.

Invite your spouse to complete this questionnaire and to discuss the results with you.

Lisa: That's a helpful suggestion. I'll give Scott a description of these ideas and have him take this quiz.

The knowledge you develop by completing the FDM Review puts you in a position to make informed decisions about your family's functioning. Once you have identified FDMs operating in your home and considered how they affect your family life, you can take the critic's role and choose whether to continue using them. Recognizing that not all difficulties need to be overcome or can be surmounted with a head-on approach, you may decide FDMs provide sufficient benefits to justify their use. Or you may choose to work with family members in the process of rewriting the family drama, making FDMs obsolete.

The next chapters discuss various ways in which you can intentionally rewrite your family drama, directing it to more effectively meet your family's needs and to more quickly move you toward the family dream. The first rewriting technique we consider is family projects.

7

Creating Family Projects

*B*rides and grooms approach the altar with high hopes for what lies ahead. Riding the wave of honeymoon bliss, they look forward to writing exciting chapters in their new family dramas. In a matter of time, however, a good many find themselves blocked, unable to sustain the momentum. When the initial excitement is over, marriage and family life become dull and routine.

However, as we will show, families can use projects to rekindle the spark and to raise family members' spirits. A "project" is any undertaking that family members choose to provide themselves with a shared challenge and greater closeness. Although family subgroups (like husband and wife or father and daughter) may participate in projects, often the entire family is involved. As people work side by side, they experience enhanced feelings of intimacy, as well as the joy associated with accepting a shared challenge and making progress on it.

Projects can be short-term undertakings, lasting a matter of hours, or they can be enduring, lifelong pursuits. The types of projects people select vary with family members' ages and tastes. Projects can take forms ranging from building a doll-house to engaging in sports activities, from operating a family business to sharing hobbies. The possibilities are endless. Volunteer groups, club memberships, service organizations, church involvement, entertaining, baking a birthday cake for grandma, home improvement, preparing and serving breakfast in bed, gardening, crossword puzzles, the stock market, business opportunities, a picnic, coordinating events like a family reunion, planning and taking a vacation, arts and crafts—these and hundreds of other activities could become your projects.

Projects bring pleasure, and most families use them for this purpose. However, projects can also be employed to fulfill individuals, heal a tired marriage, and reduce interpersonal conflict. Each of these uses is explored in this chapter, as well as how you can convert an FDM into a project. But first, let us explain how you can distinguish the two.

HOW TO TELL A PROJECT FROM AN FDM

At first, you may have difficulty distinguishing an FDM from a project. This is not surprising, because the activity involved in an FDM may be the same as that in a family project. Furthermore, an FDM may appear to be designed to foster intimacy or create excitement. Although the behavior involved in FDMs and projects and their purposes may appear to be the same to an outside observer, the meaning of the activity to the family involved is quite different. When you are engaged in an FDM activity, you feel very different from when you are engaged in a project activity, even if the activity involved in both cases is the same.

There are several reasons why FDMs and projects feel different. Of primary importance is that people intentionally choose projects, but people *happen* upon FDMs. The purpose of the projects is to provide a shared activity that provides family members with the opportunity to spend time together, while the purpose of FDMs is to reduce family conflict by regulating contact and the use of shared time. Projects foster greater intimacy between family members by providing shared challenges, excitement, and accomplishment; FDMs merely permit people to share the limited intimacy they can tolerate. People commit themselves to projects because they provide joy and enable them to become more fulfilled as

individuals and as a family unit. Although people may complain about how tiring FDM-prescribed activity is, they are
driven to it to make family relationships manageable.

We want to help you feel comfortable in the critic's
chair, so that you can determine whether adding a family
project would overload you or kindle new excitement and
perhaps greater passion in your marriage.

To make this decision you will want to consider the
balance between routine and predictability in your life and
change and challenge. Psychotherapists know the balance is
delicate; inappropriate amounts of change at a given moment
cause distress. People who encounter excessive change see
the world as chaotic and uncertain, whereas those who experience insufficient amounts feel stagnation and boredom. What
you probably want is a good degree of certainty and routine
along with enough newness and challenge to keep the spark
of excitement bright.

Take a moment to consider whether in recent weeks you
have had too much newness and uncertainty, too little, or
appropriate amounts. If you've had too much change, you
probably crave a period of routine and quiet. For instance,
during the few days following the Christmas and New Year's
holidays, many people want nothing more than to "vegetate"
at work and home.

After more extreme periods of change, the readjustment
time is longer and more pronounced. For example, after a
miscarriage, Jackie put it this way: "Since Billy and I lost the
pregnancy, I've felt a little crazy. Around the house and office
I want everything done exactly the right way, the way I do
it, the way it always has been done. And that's all there is to
it. Period." We explained to Jackie that her newfound need
for stability and predictability was a normal reaction to the
unexpected discontinuity she was coping with.

If you've had too much routine and too little newness,
you would probably appreciate an activity that introduces
variety into your weekly schedule. Consider school-age children. In the months of May and June, all they talk of is

summer recess. They seek change in the form of escape from classroom routine. By mid-August, however, they grow bored with vacation activities, and although they may deny it to the end, most look forward to the challenges school presents them.

Families can use projects to add excitement when their home life becomes humdrum. One way they can accomplish this is by converting an FDM into a project.

USING PROJECTS TO REPLACE FDMS

FDMs serve a valuable role, minimizing disharmony in your family. However, behind each FDM there is an underlying problem. If you successfully transform an FDM into a project, you will have opportunities to address and resolve the cause of the disharmony while fostering closer feelings among family members.

The Hardens converted an FDM into a project and were very pleased with the results of their efforts. When we first met Becky, aged fourteen, she could not remember the last time her family ate dinner together. Her dad, Sheldon, had always come home from work, changed into casual clothes, and left for the club where he spent several hours. She didn't know exactly what he did there, except she knew he used exercise machines, the swimming pool, and the jogging track.

When Sheldon returned from the club, fresh and showered, Becky was usually studying or watching television with her mom, Trish, in the den. Sheldon would heat his dinner and eat in front of the kitchen television.

Becky's junior-high graduation shocked Trish and Sheldon. Recognizing that Becky might be living with them for only four more years, they decided to work on improving their family life. They saw that they used physical escape as an FDM and decided to convert it into a project. Although well motivated, it took Trish and Sheldon a period of weeks to explore the frustrations they were harboring and to delineate

what they needed from their relationship. And they spent
several additional days developing a plan for a project.

However, the time they invested paid handsome dividends. They agreed that Sheldon would continue spending
evening hours at the club because it was healthy. But his
workouts would be part of a shared effort for family fitness.
Trish would get herself into shape, and so could Becky, if she
wished to join them.

Trish and Becky bought club memberships and went
with Sheldon every day. At first, Sheldon concentrated on his
own workouts, joining the others in the swimming pool. Once
they demonstrated commitment, however, Sheldon spent
more time with them, teaching, observing, and cheering them
onward. When the family finished exercising, they ate dinner
together, often chatting about how good their aching bodies
were looking and what they would be accomplishing in future
athletic competitions.

Soon after the project began, all three Hardens began to
feel better psychologically. And, in time, Trish and Becky
worked themselves into tip-top physical shape. With the FDM
gone and family members sharing several hours each evening, Sheldon and Trish might have found themselves arguing like they had several years before. But they didn't. As is
often the case, Trish and Sheldon had become more tolerant
of each other, partly because they felt good about their joint
activity and accomplishments.

As Trish and Sheldon's experience suggests, the steps
for transforming FDMs into projects are simple:

1. Jointly identify FDMs operating in your home.
   This alone can help you better understand
   each other's feelings and improve Happiness-
   Test outcomes.
2. Jointly consider each FDM and decide
   whether the activity prescribed by it should be
   continued, abandoned, or modified. After dis-

cussing your options you should feel more in control of your family life.

3. If you agree that the prescribed activity should be discontinued (for example, excessive television viewing), use your problem-solving skills to accomplish this. If you agree that the activity should be continued (for example, as in the Hardens's case), you have achieved an important step in converting the FDM into a project. Use your problem-solving skills to plan how to accomplish this.

4. Next, consider your children. How will the intended changes affect them? Given their level of maturity, ask yourself, "What are the benefits and costs of informing or involving them in the discussion?"

5. Identify what kind of conflict might emerge when you replace the FDM with a project. Plan how to attack, if not overcome, any problems you expect might develop.

You might accomplish these steps in one evening. However, the work involved is usually more time-consuming, particularly if one spouse has a controlling personality or if an uncooperative child is involved. Once you have taken these steps, you are ready to make the change.

Patience is a blessing for those wishing to convert an FDM into a project. Darlene had to repeat herself several times over a period of weeks before Dick even vaguely understood that she was serious when she said, "Dick, our marriage is in trouble, and we'd better fix things soon."

In talking to us about her marriage Darlene said, "I've wanted children for years. Dick still isn't ready. He's ignored me every time I talk about a baby. I introduced the topic again on Valentine's Day. Cupid's night would have been a dazzling time to conceive, and it was the right time of the month. But

Dick wouldn't budge. That night when he leaned over for a
kiss, I quoted Gloria, from an episode of *All in the Family*.
I screamed, 'Don't touch me unless you mean business.'

"That comment seemed to penetrate Dick's thick skull,
but it didn't bring the results I wanted. From then on Dick
spent an increasing number of evening hours working at his
convenience store. We weren't fighting as much, and I
thought things might get better. But they didn't. And he
hasn't cared enough about my needs to bring up the topic of
the baby.

"About ten days ago I gave up and mentioned it again.
Dick pushed me aside again and griped about his needs: 'You
have to help in my store. I'm building our future. I need you
at the cash register, not playing nursemaid. In a few years
we'll have kids.'

"That's why we came for counseling."

During the next few sessions the couple identified and
discussed an FDM they wanted to convert into a project:
Dick's evening hours at the store. Darlene surprised Dick,
warning, "I like the idea of working by your side. It's a
perfect way to build intimacy. But, if it's going to be a family
project, it's going to be *our* store not *your* store. And we better
plan on painting the storeroom and converting part of it into
a nursery."

After some clear thinking and good discussion, they
agreed that Darlene would work full time in the store—which
would be jointly owned—both legally and psychologically.
They would also begin their family as soon as possible, hope-
fully in the current tax year, Dick joked.

One year after they began their project, the couple, now
proud parents, described the changes in their marriage as
miraculous. Although Darlene and Dick had difficulty beginning rewriting their family drama, once they began, they
produced healthy changes that recognized and respectfully
treated the goals of both.

Although most families can use projects successfully,

not every family can, particularly those in which one person is domineering, extremely manipulative, or suffers from a significant psychological disorder.

USING PROJECTS TO OVERCOME INTERPERSONAL CONFLICT

As discussed earlier, conflict is inevitable in family life. Interpersonal difficulties, whatever their cause, will eventually upset your Happiness-Test outcomes and force you to react. When everyday problem-solving techniques fail to remedy a particular conflict, you might try to find a project to manage the problem or eliminate the source of it.

Identifying a project to cope with or eliminate an interpersonal conflict is like trying to solve a crossword puzzle. First, you search your mind for ideas, applying full measures of creativity and determination. Next, depending on the circumstances, you ask other family members for suggestions. Finally, after giving it your best effort, you sometimes have to depend on trial and error or a stroke of luck.

The following examples illustrate how you can try to tailor projects to particular types of interpersonal difficulties. Notice how some people choose projects that succeed by capitalizing on the needs and wants of family members, while other people start small by selecting short projects with a high probability of success. These give family members a taste of what is possible, which whets the appetite for more.

Anna, age eight, and Robin, age nine, essentially ignored Paul, their stepdad, although they had been living with him for over a year. Paul worked an afternoon shift and was the girls' morning caregiver during the summer months. Last summer he let them go to the basement to watch cartoons until he went to work at noon, but this summer, with full support from his wife, he began a project with them. He set up a computer in the family room, knowing the girls wanted to learn to use one, and offered to teach them. The girls resisted at first, hoping their mother would allow them to take lessons at school. When she refused, they reluctantly accepted Paul's invitation. Within a couple of weeks, Anna and Robin had learned a great deal, including the fact that it could be fun to be with Paul.

Wayne, Sharon's husband, invested her retirement funds in a fast-food outlet, although she had preferred to buy safe government bonds. A year later, when the Hamburger Palace failed, Sharon lost hope for a secure future and, in her fury, began to berate Wayne endlessly for his poor judgment. Following months of hostility and struggle, they recognized their relationship was in jeopardy. Rallying together, Sharon and Wayne planned a money-making project, building and selling souvenirs of their hometown. The first summer was so successful that they began another project—studying the art of investment and formulating long-term financial goals.

Karen and Rick, raised in different religious faiths, married against the advice of both sets of parents. However, differences in their religious upbringings had little effect on them until they were ready to place their oldest child in Sunday school. At this point, each spouse pleaded, argued, and tried to convince the other of the wisdom of having the child attend classes in either his or her church. Almost overnight, their marriage became so fragile that they scared themselves into an agreement. They decided to pursue a spiritual-enrichment project—fully involving themselves in the activities of both churches.

Anita, age fourteen, and her brother, Troy, age sixteen, quarreled constantly. With the teenagers' battles becoming increasingly nerve-racking, their parents decided to act definitively, identifying a project they thought might reduce the squabbling. One day their mother came home and told them to dress in tennis clothes as quickly as possible. She had entered them as a mixed-doubles team in a tennis tournament, and their first match was scheduled in an hour. The children fared well, placing third and making the project into a success by practicing and playing together all summer-long. Equally important, they fought less and found new closeness as siblings.

Cynthia and Dennis joke about having found their project accidentally. The last time they vacationed, Cynthia forgot to cancel newspaper delivery. It happened that thieves broke into their home while they were away, and Dennis blamed the burglary on Cynthia's carelessness. He was so angry that he could hardly speak to her. By the weekend, however, Dennis, Cynthia, and the children began a home-security project. They borrowed books from the library, bought new tools, and installed alarms, locks, and other equipment.

As these examples show, well-chosen projects enable family members to turn conflicts into opportunities for shared challenges, intimacy, and excitement. By adding these ingredients to family life, projects often serve a secondary purpose of reducing future conflict. Shared challenge means family members have joint goals and joint successes, and this reduces their competitiveness, a major cause of interpersonal problems in the home. Greater intimacy makes family members more tolerant of each other and less likely to fight about trivial matters. New excitement in family life means that children and spouses will no longer need to fight boredom by arguing.

FINDING PERSONAL FULFILLMENT THROUGH PROJECTS

Besides supplying families with shared challenges, projects can be used to provide individuals with opportunities for personal fulfillment, as shown in the examples that follow.

Kimberly and Mitch, by their interminable squabbling and other attention-getting techniques, say, "I want recognition. I want you, Mother and Father, to accept me for who I am, to love me." They would benefit from a project that called for children and parents to work together.

By her stomach ache on Monday morning Tina tells her parents she's not much of a student and has no wish to go to school. By his avoidance of after-school play with the boys in the neighborhood, Roy tells his parents that he's afraid to compete in sports. Tina and Roy would gain most from a project that built their skills and confidence in schoolwork and sports.

Unspoken feelings such as those acted out by Kimberly, Mitch, Tina, and Roy are not dramatic, and usually go unnoticed in countless discussions on the causes of family discontent. But they are important. If nothing is done about these quiet irritants, they eat away at family morale and lead to resignation. Talking, thinking, planning, and trial and error would probably enable the families of these children to design suitable projects. It's as simple as that. It becomes complex and difficult only when family members lack problem-solving skills or when they don't want each other to become fulfilled. Consider the story of Linda and Joe, who suffered from both of these problems.

Linda, thirty-five, needed a project to beat feelings that had been haunting her. "I want to make something of my own life. I love being a wife and mother, but that's not enough. I long to be someone in my own right," she said. But she and her husband had difficulty talking about this wish, partly because he resisted the idea of Linda being out of the house all day. But Linda persisted and eventually initiated what became a family project.

In one sense, the story began when Linda quit her job as a clerk in a jewelry shop. At that time, she was pregnant and within two weeks of her due date, pleased to be a homemaker who would fully devote herself to Joe and their baby. Eventually the couple had two more children, and for several years Linda was satisfied and busy. Once her youngest entered first grade, however, Linda began feeling restless, confused, and guilty.

She felt restless because, with the children in school, she had spare time and energy and no place she wanted to apply them. She felt confused because she wanted to work outside the home, but not at her old job. Linda wanted a career but had no marketable skills and did not know what options were available to her. Because she wanted to begin her career now, she felt guilty: long ago Joe had clearly stated his opinion that young children need a full-time mother at home with them. At the time, Linda had agreed with him.

For a long while Linda suffered silently. Because she never voiced her concerns, they did not emerge until Joe noticed changes in Linda's attitude and asked her to explain. Linda looked at Joe hesitantly and then blurted her feelings: "I'm unhappy, that's what it is. Life is boring. I'm thirty-five and going nowhere."

Joe tried to reassure her. "I felt down in the dumps when I turned thirty-five, remember? I got over it—and you will too."

When she said that it wasn't a question of age, he became defensive. "Not happy? With me? With our wonderful kids?"

Linda took his hand and said, "That's not it. I love you. . . ." Joe interrupted. Pulling his hand away, he growled, "You sure pick a fine way of showing it, saying you're unhappy. If you didn't want kids, why didn't you say so before we married?"

That comment struck Linda where she was most vulnerable. She wept. Joe turned on the television.

That wasn't the end of it. Linda knew she would have to raise the issue again. The next time they were alone she asked him why he had gotten so angry. He got defensive again and said bitterly, "If you don't like being married to me, just leave." That closed this attempt. The third time, Linda started the conversation by telling Joe that he and the children were her number-one priority. She then detailed what she had been feeling and asked for his help.

Now, at last, Joe didn't feel rejected. On the contrary, by telling him of her pain and depression and her need for him, he felt very much wanted. She had turned to him seeking his assistance and approval and relying on his strength. He wanted to help her now. Her cause had become his. Her need would lead to a joint project that would add meaning and excitement to Linda's life and, in turn, to Joe's and the children's.

Joe and Linda engaged in a problem-solving procedure that helped her make a career choice and enroll for the necessary training. Getting Mom through school became a family enterprise. Joe and the children took over many of her household responsibilities. Further, they developed a routine. Within minutes after the family finished dinner, the table was cleared, the dishes were in the machine, and the kitchen was converted into a study hall. There, lined up in assigned places, sat Linda and the children, each surrounded by their own pile of books and assorted papers.

Joe felt great pride as he went from person to person, helping with math, spelling, or whatever was necessary. And when exam time came, Joe, Linda, and the children took turns quizzing each other.

The project fitted Linda and Joe's needs at this point in their marriage. Over the years of a family's development, the need for and nature of projects may vary.

TREATING THE TIRED MARRIAGE

If you look back on your personal history, you might observe that during childhood, adolescence, and early adulthood, you were automatically supplied with age-related challenges and opportunities for achievement. Between promotions to the next grade, sports activities, Sunday school and religious advancement, academic awards, certificates of recognition, and teen programs, you probably had ample activities offering you challenges. In contrast, as an adult you have fewer ready-made experiences with challenges, and those you do have happen less frequently.

Couples and families are no different from individuals in this regard because early in their history they are automatically presented with challenges and opportunities for progress. New lovers enjoy a stream of milestones, from the first long-stemmed rose to going steady, from becoming engaged to marriage and children, from renting a first apartment to buying a house. Each of these events and the projects typically associated with them challenge couples and bring them excitement. However, as the years pass, fewer changes and opportunities for projects come automatically to couples and families.

At a certain point, maybe from five to fifteen years after the wedding, many people, lacking excitment and challenge in life, come to feel stalled in their marriage or frustrated, bored, or displeased by the fact that certain goals apparently will never be realized. We call this the "tired marriage syndrome." Projects can have great value to couples encountering this difficulty, providing them with hope and opportunities to create their own challenges and excitement.

To help you better understand the tired marriage syndrome and its causes, we will trace the development of a love relationship. If you come to understand this syndrome, you can better cope with it or avoid it altogether. Moreover, you will be better able to help others who are trying to deal with it.

Dating days. In your early period together, you and your future spouse shared ever-increasing amounts of time, enjoyment, and affection. While you strived to convince your lover that you were a good catch, you busily scrutinized your mate to determine whether he or she was a good choice. Your spouse, of course, engaged in similar detective work.

As the family drama unfolded, you faced a challenge—

to discover beneficial, mutually satisfying ways of meshing your relationship scripts. As you interacted, every discussion, decision, and shared activity was important. They set precedents that shaped the set of rules you developed to govern your relationship. The rules, in turn, enabled you to function as a couple on a day-to-day basis with a comfortable predictability.

A flowering romance meant that you spent longer periods together, which brought new challenges. You had to create rules to guide interactions across a wider range of new settings. For example, if you shared meals, you needed a system for budgeting money and dividing the work of shopping, cooking, and washing dishes.

In time, you were ready for a major project, moving toward marriage. You remember the moment when you made the commitment and immediately improved your Happiness-Test outcomes. One increased benefit was that you could then introduce your sweetheart as your fiancé/fiancée. Once you set a wedding date, you had the opportunity to dive into other projects, such as making preparations for the ceremony, the celebration, and new living quarters.

The honeymoon bliss period. The words "I now pronounce you man and wife" almost always bring a Disneyland-like excitement to couples. Even cynics and those who have cohabited for years experience the personal satisfaction of committing to a lifelong mate, a feeling complimented by the pleasure of basking in the congratulations of people who care.

The honeymoon bliss period can last for months if couples master the challenges of a fully shared life. During this period, you establish patterns of interaction designed to bring personal and marital fulfillment, and you develop routines and rules to guide you in writing the new section of your family drama—the part in which you are married.

Besides working on your relationship, building your career, and establishing your household, you probably tackled other undertakings. Popular projects at this stage often involve vigorous exercise, activities that help families create a more useful living space, and those that can accommodate the needs of pregnant women, infants, and young children.

The early family phase.   As the wedding, honeymoon, and early days of marriage become photo-album history, the couple moves forward to accept new challenges, such as establishing a comfortable lifestyle and positioning itself to achieve desired goals. Projects are often used for these purposes.

While short-term projects are always popular at this stage, the spouses may also involve themselves in long-term undertakings like acquiring desired material goods, building a nest with suitable amenities, establishing kinship networks and friendship circles, and teaching children skills or shared hobbies.

If you have children, you know how their presence influences your family's projects. On the one hand, the children's ages, sleep schedules, and eating needs often restrict the time open for certain projects. On the other hand, children are a seemingly never-ending source of projects. They supply automatic projects centered around fostering their development, and generate opportunities for other projects through their involvement in school, church, music, and sports.

The mature family phase.   Most couples reach a point at which they feel settled. They have created a home that suits them, a set of rules that serves as their constitution, and a social network that provides support and friendship. They have established their lifestyle, acquired many wanted material goods, and positioned themselves as best they could for the years ahead.

If you have not yet reached this point, you can look forward to it. When you reach it, you will experience the satisfaction of achieving a milestone and, perhaps, relief that the quest is over. However, this point has special significance for another reason. After passing it, far fewer opportunities for projects are thrust upon or easily available to you. This means that, if you do not actively seek projects, you might find yourself in jeopardy from insidious threats. Boredom, feelings of emptiness, and dissatisfaction with your home life are just some of these. In other words, you are vulnerable to the tired marriage syndrome.

Pete and Tracy Miller had been using FDMs for years, and when their last children left home, they had no shared projects in operation. After more than twenty years of marriage, they came to us, complaining of a stale relationship and of lost intimacy. They felt stymied as individuals and powerless as a couple to remedy feelings of unhappiness and boredom in their marriage. Pete explained, "We started out as teenage sweethearts. My mother called us well-matched bookends. And, I must say, life has gone pretty well."

"We overcame an unplanned pregnancy that forced Pete to quit school," Tracy continued. "But for most of our years we were a typical, suburban couple—happy and busy. Then after the twins left home, life changed. Friends looked at us with envy. They figured we'd be pleased with our freedom and excited about the future. They didn't know we were in a rut."

"We weren't in any rut," Pete interrupted. "I spent my best years working hard to support the family. Now I want to relax at home with my wife. Is that wrong, doctor?"

Tracy jumped back in and continued her explanation. "We never go anywhere together. Pete bowls on Monday and Thursday nights and watches television every other night. We hardly talk and rarely have sex."

By learning the skills we have been describing, the Millers were able to attack their problem effectively. We taught them how to become aware of their feelings, express frustrations, and effectively plan their time. Over a period of weeks they used these skills to develop a new set of goals, some individual and some mutual.

The projects they selected brought zest back into their tired marriage. One courageous choice was buying a lot in the country and building a new home. They had never done anything like that before. The following Christmas, Tracy and Pete sent us a card. It read, "We're loving life as contractors. We study blueprints and instruction sheets together, talk about building techniques and our materials, and enjoy every minute of it. Thanks. You've done the trick. The spark is back!"

They deserve the credit. They had refused to let circumstances shape their future. They had refused to let emptiness and friction dominate their home. Instead, they took action and brought back the spark.

Couples who have been using projects over the years are less susceptible than the Millers to the tired marriage syndrome. Such couples can reduce their chances of later problems by renewing old interests or by finding new ones to share. Over the course of the mature family phase, the amount of time and money available for spouses to spend on projects often changes. Some couples, retired and with child-rearing obligations behind them, become more extravagant, taking cruises or purchasing a vacation condominium. In contrast, others, weary of retirement expenses looming ahead, limit their spending or focus their resources on money-making activities.

Finally, during this phase the spouses' children reach adulthood and this opens the door to an entirely new set of opportunities, ones with a new flavor and with benefits across generations. For instance, grown children can join with their parents in a project, and together, they can forge an intimacy based on healthy adult-to-adult interaction. Moreover, projects can serve as a bond between parents and their grown children's families. Well-selected activities can effectively link two or three generations of people who live in different households, providing them with opportunities to build intimacy and share excitement.

On a personal note, writing this book turned out to be a multi-generational project for our family. Even the two youngest members, Davy and Sara, helped with some of the details. Although we undertook the writing because of professional interest and commitment, the project provided us with a shared challenge and served us in many other ways as well. Like any good project, all of us had an equal stake in this one. Being able to work together productively, despite the geographical distance between us, heightened our positive feelings about our family and about the possibilities for all families.

NEW DIMENSION IN
TODAY'S FAMILIES

One more issue pertaining to projects and family development deserves mention. Today many families do not conform to the traditional mold established in the 1950s. Since then, significant social changes have taken place, and these have altered family life and created a variety of typical families.

One major social change is that large numbers of women work outside the home and postpone the arrival of children until after their careers are established. Because of this and other lifestyle changes, spouses' ages no longer predict their place in the family life cycle. If you married or remarried in your thirties or forties and have children, or if you married earlier and had children after establishing a career, your offspring may be younger than many of your agemates' and the projects you choose may differ greatly from theirs. Those differences can be enjoyable, however, and you may encounter situations like our next example.

Professor Roger Fisher, a former student, wrote to update us on what had happened to him over the past six years. In his lengthy letter, Roger explained what his life had been like, seemingly five to ten years behind most of his friends. He wrote:

> Getting my degree after eleven years work was my first cue. Being older than some profs was my second. It seems that Betty and I are destined to do everything a little later than

everybody else! I was thirty-nine when we married and balder than the minister. Betty was thirty-eight when Joshua was born, and both of us were older than the Doc. Betty was the oldest mother on her hospital floor and almost double the age of her roommate.

And so it continues. At every parents meeting we have attended since our first Lamaze class, we are the grayest. Luckily, we laugh at all this because we've done it our way. Most people we socialize with have kids ten to fifteen years older. Their families go to high-school activities together, we go to tot swims. They worry about paying for college, I worry about staying in shape so I can coach little league someday.

Betty and I are also involved with the parents of children the same age as ours. And we enjoy them too. I must share one funny incident, though. One day, right after work, I rushed to the first day-care center picnic of the year. I didn't have time to change, so I was still wearing a suit and a red tie. Before I was introduced to the others, one father there called me 'sir.' I don't know whether I looked old that day or whether he was especially polite and thought I was the teacher. Anyway, since then, that man and I have become friends.

Roger and Betty thrive on joint projects. In that respect they are not different from many couples. For them, however, as for others who become parents a dozen years after their contemporaries, the time schedule is different. But they're not unhappy about it. They laugh when they say that they'll be coaching little league together when their friends' children are playing varsity ball in college!

The principal purpose of projects is to add excitement and intimacy to family life. We also have seen that projects can be used as vehicles to revitalize tired marriages, foster personal fulfillment in family members, and manage conflict between people. Projects can help you rewrite your family drama, and they deserve a place in your arsenal of conflict-management techniques.

8

Learning Cooperative Negotiation

*I*n one sense, all families are created equal because every one of them has conflict. Sometimes conflict is sparked by routine matters such as a simple misunderstanding ("I thought you said you would call if you were going to be late"), or different desires ("I know you want to eat at home, but I feel like going out tonight"), or a set of circumstances ("Son, I'm terribly sorry that I can't attend your school play tonight, but my boss told me I have to go to a meeting").

Inevitably conflict occurs over the basic components of a family drama: goals and the family dream, work roles, the way in which affection and intimacy are expressed, and the establishment of rules that form the family constitution. This talk of conflict may sound ominous, but conflict actually adds spice to life. If every person had the same desires and thought and felt the same way about everything, we would live in a remarkably dull world.

The challenge you face as a family is not to avoid conflict, although it can be minimized, but to resolve it when possible and to learn to live together happily despite your differences. Family dramas can be written or rewritten to accommodate conflict—some families even thrive on it. In a well-constructed family drama, differences are clearly communicated and then resolved through cooperative negotiations. That is, each individual is satisfied with the way conflict is resolved.

Unfortunately, most relationship scripts do not prepare people with the attitudes and skills necessary for successful conflict resolution. Therefore, many families are torn apart by bitter fights, negative feelings, and severe antagonisms that make everyone unhappy.

If you have problems with conflict, you can learn how to rewrite your family rules to create the best possible results in your Happiness Test. We will introduce you to the Basic Cooperative Agreement (BCA), whereby family members make a conscious decision and a commitment to work together as a unit in which everyone has equal rights. The essence of the agreement is that every person in the family is committed to every other person's well-being. When conflict arises, no one will try to dominate and no one will disregard his or her own needs. Instead, the family cooperatively negotiates as a team to satisfy each individual.

A Basic Cooperative Agreement enables your family, as a unit, to generate more benefits than it could through individual effort. With a BCA, family members feel supported and are able to perform their work roles more effectively. For example, a mother who is largely responsible for the child-rearing role in her family will be supported by the rest of her family, enabling her to feel appreciated.

A very important assumption of a BCA is that the family can generate enough benefits to satisfy everyone. A family member may not always get what he or she wants at a particular moment (such is the nature of compromise), but in the long run, by pooling the family's energy and resources, the individual needs can be addressed and met satisfactorily.

Morale is high with a BCA because, even if you don't get exactly what you want, the negotiation process is fair. No one feels like a loser. Therefore, negotiation based on a BCA is called "win-win." This contrasts with most family dramas, which are win-lose.

THE COMPETITIVE WIN-LOSE
FAMILY DRAMA

In a win-lose negotiation, one person gets what he wants and feels like a winner, while the other does not and feels like a loser. Dominance is determined either by a competitive struggle to win or by both people agreeing, sometimes by default, about which one should get what he wants.

In the *competitive* win-lose family drama, each person is out for himself. So much energy is expended trying to beat the other person that neither one feels good in the end. Family members are constantly hurt, angry, and bitter. Yet each believes that to let down his guard would be to accept defeat. Because of the competitive struggle, the family attains poor results on the Happiness Test.

Martha and Mitchell, married eight years, the parents of a six-year-old daughter and an eight-month-old son, were caught in a competitive struggle. One evening Mitchell, an attorney, returned from work, grabbed a snack from the refrigerator, and went into the den. Martha approached him for a kiss at the door but was brushed aside. Then she followed him into the den.

Mitchell: I hate the way you follow me around the house as if you're a poor little kitten starved for affection. The kids are out of control. Go watch them. Just leave me alone and take care of your kids.

Martha: *My* kids! Don't forget who planted the seeds for these children, and quit being so damn nasty. You make it sound like my life is a piece of cake or something. By the time you come home, I'm sick of the children and the housework. Then you make your entrance, Mr. Grump, and I think. . . .

Mitchell: Yeah, yeah, tell me about it. You've been watching soap operas and playing with the baby all day while I work. You should give me a chance to relax.

Martha: You always imply that I'm loafing. It's hard taking care of a home and *our* children. You don't give me any credit.

Mitchell: Well, at least you could show some appreciation for the guy who earns the money to support our children.

Martha: Yeah, maybe when you get a promotion. And anyway, it wasn't my idea to quit my job. You insisted.

Martha and Mitchell are not interested in supporting or even understanding each other. They engage in an emotional free-for-all, devoid of intimacy, each struggling to outtalk and overpower the other. Because they are involved in a competitive, win-lose family drama, they make each other miserable. Mitchell doesn't get the relaxation he wants. Martha doesn't get the quality time she wants with him. Even if one of them gives in, the winner will feel guilty and the loser will resent it.

The origins of their family drama, as of any family drama, can be understood in terms of the relationship scripts of the individuals. People who want to win at someone else's expense are driven by a relationship script with an aggressive coping style. They are deficient in the ability to relate in a loving way. They don't recognize the value of cooperation. They use power plays to try to get their own way.

Typical messages in their relationship scripts include: "It's a dog-eat-dog world. You've to got to fight for what you want." "You have to look out for yourself, because if *you* don't, nobody will." "No one will listen to you unless you are aggressive."

If Martha and Mitchell had a Basic Cooperative Agreement and used the cooperative negotiation method, they could have found a satisfactory solution to their problem. Some couples spend a quick five minutes with each other when they first get together at the end of the workday. Others start with a momentary warm greeting, followed by a certain period of time apart, followed by time for closeness. There are many possibilities.

THE DOMINANT-SUBMISSIVE COMBINATION

Another win-lose family drama combines one person with a dominant relationship script and another with a submissive one. When they first meet, they fit together like pieces of a puzzle, each believing he or she has found an ideal partner. The dominant one enjoys getting his way. The submissive one expects that all of the love she gives (usually it is the woman) will be appreciated and reciprocated in the future.

But this family drama, in the long run, also produces poor results on the Happiness Test. The person in the submissive position eventually resents having her own needs ignored. Although results of the Happiness Test start well for the dominant person, his results decline drastically. He feels her resentment, so he may start to feel guilty about the way he is treating her.

In a classic example, a woman pampers her husband and never asks for what she wants. She becomes increasingly dissatisfied about her unmet needs. Her resentment is sometimes expressed through sarcastic humor in the presence of friends. Often, she doesn't say what she really feels, but picks on little things. She shows her resentment in subtle but passive ways, such as "accidentally" forgetting to pack his fishing equipment for the vacation at the lake. Sometimes she uses the credit card as a weapon of revenge. Her anger may eventually find expression in an affair or a divorce. Or she may internalize the anger and suffer a mental breakdown and, in the most extreme cases, attempt suicide.

The relationship scripts of submissive people are low in self-esteem. They misunderstand cooperation, thinking it means that they should always put the other person first and that sticking up for themselves is selfish. Their coping style is to please others and hope that eventually they will be rewarded for being so unselfish. They often confuse assertiveness with aggression and believe that, if they were to be strong, they would hurt others.

In thinking about cooperation gone awry, most people tend to think of the aggressive person using power plays to get his way. They overlook the equal participant in the problem—the person who gives away power. A person gives away power by not asking for what he wants and by giving in. This behavior is called a "rescue" because the rescuer saves others in the family from dealing with his or her needs. Rescuers may appear to be cooperative because their concessions temporarily avoid conflict. Contrary to appearances, such concessions undermine cooperation. Eventually a rescuer resents the lack of reciprocation.

WIN-WIN NEGOTIATION

The Basic Cooperative Agreement is a win-win approach to resolving conflict. In the words of the Three Musketeers, "One for all and all for one."

Making this agreement requires a vision of what is possible when people strive for win-win solutions. This can be seen in three major ways of resolving conflict through cooperative negotiation: compromise, trade-offs, and creative solutions. To illustrate, consider this situation: Miriam and David have been married for three years and finally have the time and money to take a vacation. He wants to go to the mountains. She wants to go to an ocean resort.

Compromise means meeting each other halfway. They might divide their time between the two different vacation sites. If that's not practical, they might find that they shared a common second choice, a trip to Mexico, which would make them both happy.

Trade-offs means doing it one way this time and another way next time. They go to the White Mountains this vacation and San Diego next time; or she gets her preference on choice of vacation, but he gets to choose how they spend their savings. Trading-off doesn't have to involve a rigid program of alternation. It is simply a statement of goodwill: "We can do it your way now, and I know in some future conflict situation, I'll get my way."

Creative solutions involve discovering a way to make each person satisfied without making substantial concessions. Miriam and David discovered that there are mountains along the coast in northern California that would fully satisfy both of them.

Most family drama tends to promote either/or solutions to conflict. That is, "We either do it your way or my way." Effective negotiation based on a BCA pushes people to look at their situation creatively. The first question to ask in searching for creative solution would be "Is there a way for everyone to get what he wants?" In a cooperative negotiation, no one loses. Winning doesn't mean that everyone necessarily gets exactly what he wants, it means that the process is fair, costs and benefits are balanced, and no one feels bullied or defeated.

A cooperative negotiation has five steps: identify the problem; ask for what you want; make offers and counter-offers; make win-win agreements; monitor, evaluate, and revise agreements.

Step 1: Identify the Problem

The first step in cooperative negotiation is for one person to say, "We have a problem. We need to talk." Because problems typically arise in connection with the following components of the family drama, we have chosen one example for each of them.

- *Work roles:* Someone might want to talk about how housework is divided.
- *Family goals:* Someone might want to talk about

allocation of limited resources such as money or vacation time.

- *Intimacy:* Someone might be dissatisfied with the level of emotional intimacy. A wife says, for example, "The only time you ever tell me you love me is while we're having sex."
- *Rules:* Someone may be concerned about decision-making about a particular issue. For example, a husband will say, "When it comes to whose parents we visit during the holiday, it seems that you always get the final say. I'm not happy with this arrangement."

Problems that require negotiation may concern day-to-day differences and misunderstandings, such as which video to rent or restaurant to choose. Seemingly routine problems can also signify deeper issues. With a couple that always goes to the restaurant one partner wants, there is probably a rules problem in the family drama. In identifying problems to negotiate, it is important not to lose sight of the forest for the trees. Sometimes what appears to be an isolated incident turns out to reflect deep-seated differences.

One night shortly after they were married, John complained to Blanche about dinner not being on the table when he came home from work. Blanche said his complaint was unreasonable because she holds a full-time job outside the home. Furthermore, she felt that John should help more with household chores. The issue wasn't isolated to that single night. They had very different relationship scripts about the division of work responsibilities, and they needed to negotiate an agreement.

In negotiation to divide work, such as in the assignment of household duties, part of identifying the problem is to list all the work that must be done and the amount of time required for each task. Then it can be determined who will do which tasks. The following are other examples of ongoing problems that require negotiation:

- What child-rearing practice should be used with a seven-year-old child who is having temper tantrums.
- One spouse likes to make love in the morning, while the other usually feels rushed to go to work.
- A teenage girl needs to talk about a new curfew because her friends laugh at her when she tells them that her parents expect her home at 11 P.M. on Saturday night.

Step 2: Ask for What You Want

After a problem is identified, the next step in cooperative negotiation is to ask for what you want. This involves each family member stating his own opinions and feelings. Many relationship scripts prevent people from doing this. Sometimes they don't ask because they think it would be selfish. They don't see the difference between asking for what they want and demanding it, grabbing it, or imposing their will on others.

Asking is essential: if a couple or a family is trying to take care of each other, then it is necessary to know what everyone wants. Family members who hide their desires are not giving other family members a fair opportunity to satisfy their needs. Furthermore, if compromises are to be made, the only way to know the middle point is to know where everyone starts.

In trying to decide where to eat, Tom suggested a Chinese restaurant but said he wasn't in a fussy mood. Roberta said she wanted a restaurant with salads because she was on a weight-loss diet. This was the starting point for a discussion. In a negotiation about dividing housework, Roberta, Tom, and their two children reviewed all the work that needed to be done and then each of them wrote down their preferred assignments.

Step 3: Making Offers and Counteroffers

Each person needs to listen attentively to the others, keeping the alternatives in mind—compromise, trade-offs, and creative solutions.

It wouldn't be negotiating to simply restate one's own position as a compromise or cooperative proposal. After preferences are stated, one person can take initiative by listing alternatives that he sees. Or someone will make a proposal, such as "Here's my idea. What do you think?" Notice that the second sentence indicates an openness to counterproposals. It starts a give-and-take process of proposing action plans.

Tom suggests a compromise to the restaurant quandary—Luigi's, an Italian restaurant that serves good salads. "I know you want a salad. They have good salads, and Italian food would be my second choice." Roberta says an Italian restaurant with good salads would be fine, but she doesn't like the atmosphere at Luigi's. She suggests the Roma Cafe. He agrees, and they go there, each satisfied with the outcome.

In dividing housework in Roberta and Tom's family, they went back and forth for an hour, making trades with each other based on the issues of time and desirability of tasks: "I'll empty the dishwasher every day," twelve-year-old Matthew said, "if I can avoid cleaning bathrooms."

Step 4: Making Agreements

Proposals and counterproposals are exchanged until you can find one that everyone accepts. It is important that everyone is satisfied that the process of negotiation is fair and reasonable. Such satisfaction increases compliance with the agreements and creates better results on the Happiness Test.

If there are problems in reaching an agreement, if one person is unclear about where he stands or is uncomfortable with the proposals, it makes sense to delay a decision or to make only temporary agreements. For example, "I'm not exactly sure if I'm happy with the idea of the family going out for dinner every Wednesday. But I'll be willing to try it for a month. Let's talk about it again after a month has passed. O.K.?"

If agreements concern important, long-term actions, we suggest you write them down. That makes it less likely that a family member will omit, distort, or forget parts of the agreement. After Roberta, Tom, and the children negotiated a division of household duties, they wrote down their agreement about who did what and how often and posted it on the refrigerator.

It is common, especially in families with teenagers, for parents to say, "We make agreements, but the children never keep them." The first issue to consider when agreements are broken is whether they were really valid in the first place. By "valid," we mean that all parties willingly committed to the agreement with the intention of working to fulfill their responsibilities. Often this is not the case.

Family members—children and adults alike—who are tired of arguing will sometimes agree to almost anything to end a dispute. Teenagers who feel that they don't have any real influence in their family and children who want to get parents off their backs will make agreements without intending to keep them.

"Yeah, yeah, sure I'll be home by the 11:30 P.M. curfew," said sixteen-year-old Mark to his parents, Joan and Steve, during a negotiation session. Eager to settle this matter, the parents were about to say, "Great, we have a deal." But Joan detected insincerity. She commented to Mark, "You don't sound very convincing to me. Do you really intend to come home by 11:30, or are you just trying to end this discussion?"

"I'm trying to get you guys off my back. You don't care what I think. You don't listen to me, so I'll come home at 11:30 if it's convenient. But if I'm having a good time, I won't."

At this point Joan suggested they "talk about talking."

She said, "Dad and I don't want you to give in. We want to talk until we all understand each other. We can't do that unless we *all* say what we really think and feel. We promise to listen to you."

Joan didn't mean that Mark had veto power. Her point was that the family needed an open discussion in which no one withheld information. With children, parents still have the ultimate power to set rules. But teenagers such as Mark are much more likely to comply if they feel they had an opportunity to express themselves and their parents listened.

To minimize the likelihood of making invalid agreements, we have four recommendations:

- After suggesting that the family agree upon a particular proposal, the person who makes the suggestion asks the others, "What do you think about this?"
- Before settling on an agreement, family members check with one another, "Did you say everything you need to say about how you feel?"
- If an agreement sounds like an insincere brush-off, as in, "Yeah, yeah, sure," express your doubt.
- After making an agreement, review your expectations by looking to the future—"This agreement means that when we check in with each other in a week, I will no longer be coming into your room to ask if you have done your homework. For your part, you will be doing homework without my asking. Is this correct?"

Step 5: Monitor, Evaluate, and Revise Agreements

After making agreements, the next step is to monitor what happens. For example, with household chores, family members can watch whether everyone is doing what they said they would do. You also need to evaluate the agreement in terms of costs and benefits. You need to ask if the agreement feels right once it is put into practice. A date should be set for your family to discuss how things are going and to make needed revisions. The basic questions for this discussion would be: "Is the agreement working?" "What changes, if any, do we need to make?"

KEEPING THE SPIRIT OF THE BASIC COOPERATIVE AGREEMENT

Once you and your family see the logic of a BCA, it still may be difficult to follow through. The difficulties you face in implementing the negotiation process will come from your relationship script and the already established patterns in your family drama. Some members will be resistant. Others will break agreements. Others will compete for the upper hand with power plays or to give away power by rescuing.

The ideal rules for BCA negotiation are (1) No rescuing. This means don't "save" the other person by putting aside your own desires. (2) No power plays. Don't try to dominate. (3) No lies. Be honest about what you consider a fair settlement. Don't agree to something that seems unfair.

The commitment with a BCA is *not* to keep agreements no matter what, or give up rescuing or power plays forever. That would be unrealistic. These behaviors don't go away just because you don't like them anymore. They are persistent old habits, and the goal is simply to engage in them less often. This means keeping an open mind—identifying impediments to cooperation and gradually overcoming them.

A Resistant Partner

The best way to convince a partner to establish a BCA is to explain that such an agreement provides the best possible results on the Happiness Test. Compared to win-lose family dramas, cooperative negotiation with a BCA creates the most benefits and incurs the least cost. In competitive win-lose situations each person suffers the hurt, guilt, anger, and frustration associated with competing for control. In the dominant-submissive combination, the high cost is incurred with hidden resentment, guilt, and loss of love. If these costs aren't immediately obvious to your partner, you can point them out as they have occurred in your life together in the past and as they may occur in the future.

A wife with a resistant husband was able to illustrate the benefits of a BCA when their income-tax refund arrived. She wanted to make household repairs, and he wanted to take a vacation. She gave her husband a choice. He could compete with her and see who prevailed; if he dominated as he usually did, she warned, she would feel angry, which would ruin their vacation. Or, she suggested, they could handle it calmly and respectfully with a BCA. He might still get his way. "If we cooperate," she said, "I'll support taking a vacation, either now or in the future. How about it?" The husband agreed. After negotiating cooperatively, they repaired the roof with the tax refund but immediately began saving money on a regular basis for a dream vacation in late summer.

Detecting Power Plays

People often use power plays without even realizing it. The rule against power plays in family life is best understood as a commitment to work toward the reduction and elimination of these abuses of power. That means having a willingness to look at your actions and to be self-critical. The easiest power plays to identify are those involving physical force or the threat of force.

Other types of threats are also fairly easy to catch; such as "If you walk out that door, don't bother to come back." But these behaviors are just the tip of the iceberg. Power plays come in many different forms. The most difficult power plays to identify are the subtle ones that may involve sulking,

the silent treatment, or passive withdrawal. Some power plays
rely on the arousal of guilt. Others are very rational and pick
apart a partner's point of view. To help you identify power
plays, we suggest looking for either of two indicators: (1) You
feel bullied, pushed, or coerced and don't know why. If this
occurs, think back over the previous interaction. (2) Take a
survey to see if either of you gets his/her way much more
than fifty percent of the time. If so, review recent decisions
with an eye for power plays.

To help you reduce the incidence of power plays in your
family, we will illustrate three subtle types of them below. We
will also show how a cooperative spirit based on a BCA can
lead to a reduction in the abuse of power.

Negative overkill.   In their discussion about where to spend
a vacation, Miriam picked apart David's suggestion: "Why
would anyone want to go to the mountains after the lousy trip
we had last time? It's expensive. It's too cold to do anything.
It's just a bad idea." Miriam and David had a BCA. David
said, "I'm willing to hear the negatives about my preference,
but I think you're going too far. It sounds like you're trying
to discredit my point of view. I think it's a power play."

Miriam hadn't realized what she was doing, but when
David pointed this out, she had to agree. In the spirit of the
BCA, she apologized. They continued their discussion in a
more respectful way. Miriam was able to see the merits of a
mountain trip, as well as the disadvantages.

Verbal maneuvering.   Another type of power play is outtalking a partner. Warren was a master at outtalking his wife,
Rochelle. He overwhelmed her with words. When she invited
her friend Sarah to the house on a Saturday morning, Warren
raised six objections to the visit: He likes to sleep in; Saturday
morning should be "family time"; she should have asked him
first; he would never invite friends over without checking with
her; she is selfish; and he doesn't like Sarah.

Accustomed to such power plays, Rochelle felt guilty

and was ready to cancel Sarah's visit. Then she realized that she felt bullied. "Warren," she said, "I think you are only looking at your own point of view about this. It's overwhelming. I'd like the two of us to consider this matter from my point of view and to consider my feelings. O.K.?"

Rochelle's remarks, supported by a BCA, were enough to make Warren back off. He realized he had been attempting to outtalk Linda to get his own way.

Manipulative actions.   Alice and Leo were discussing how to spend the money they budgeted for recreation. The last family expenditure had gone to skiing equipment, which Leo wanted. In fairness, they decided that this time the money would be spent on something Alice wanted, a family membership in an athletic club.

After they made this decision, Leo retired dejectedly to the bedroom and started to sulk. For the next three days he was quiet and withdrawn. Finally, Alice asked him if he was upset about the decision to join the athletic club.

"Yes," he whimpered.

"Well, I don't want you to feel so terrible," she said. She was about to suggest they take the winter ski trip he wanted when she realized she felt controlled. "I'm sorry you feel badly about our decision. But I think that you have been sulking about it, and that's a power play, isn't it? If you want to discuss our decision further, I'll talk. If not, I wish you would stop sulking."

With the BCA in mind, Leo was self-critical, realized that he had been sulking, and came to accept their decision.

Identifying Rescuing

Couples who want to negotiate cooperatively must look closely at their own behavior to see if they have a tendency to rescue. To find rescues, pay attention to these patterns: Do you usually *not* ask for what you want? Does your partner usually *not* ask for what he wants? Do you make more than

half the concessions? Does your partner make more than half
the concessions?

People who want to break the rescuing habit may be
helped by gaining awareness of certain thoughts in their
relationship script that promote rescuing.

- *Excessive fear of being selfish:* "It would be selfish
  to ask for what I want or to stick up for myself."
- *One-sided concern for the other's comfort or well-
  being:* When a husband told his wife to do something, as Archie Bunker used to tell Edith, "Go
  get me a beer from the refrigerator," the woman
  did as she was told because, "It's no big deal. I
  want him to have it. I can do it."
- *Resignation:* "No point in asking. I won't get
  what I want anyway."
- *Avoidance:* This means withdrawing from the
  fray to avoid trouble. "It's easier just to do what
  he wants and not to say what I want."

If your partner rescues, don't continue with a negotiation until he says what he wants. And don't settle negotiation
without double-checking that he isn't simply conceding in
order to avoid conflict or to be a nice guy. If you are the
rescuer, hold yourself to the same standard.

"No rescues" and "no power plays" are important rules
in cooperative negotiation. To rescue is to take a one-down
position. To use a power play is to fight for a one-up position.
It's not easy to share power when you start with a relationship
script for either dominance or submission, but that is precisely what cooperative negotiation is all about.

Broken Agreements

Although it is important that family members work hard to
meet their responsibilities, broken agreements are to be expected. Sometimes it is simply human error. Other times it

could indicate that the agreements weren't valid or that they were unreasonable or inadequate. Perhaps too much was expected too soon. Broken agreements often become grist for the fighting mill. This can be avoided by holding calm discussions or making gentle suggestions.

When Sandra, Tom, and their children negotiated household responsibilities, one of Matthew's jobs was to empty the dishwasher after school in the afternoon. But he was doing his dishwasher duty only fifty percent of the time. Sandra reminded Matthew once during the first week and twice during the second. When reminded, he did it, but he still forgot on other days. Sandra realized that this was the first regular work responsibility for Matthew. Some forgetting could be expected, but this seemed excessive.

Two weeks after the new work assignments began, the family members held a discussion to evaluate how the system was working. When asked why he wasn't doing well on the dishwasher duties, Matthew said he resented the assignment because it meant coming straight home after school every day. Sometimes, he said, he wanted to go out with his friends.

The family explained to him that if he wasn't happy with the agreement he should have said so, rather than simply ignoring his duties. He agreed. Then several options were listed. He could empty the dishwasher in the morning, he could trade jobs with someone else, or he could exchange favors and ask someone to cover for him on the days he was out with his friends. Matthew agreed to empty the dishwasher in the morning and did just fine with the revised agreement.

When Agreements Are Broken Repeatedly

When agreements are broken repeatedly, we recommend a systematic step-by-step effort to solve the problem, starting with a gentle reminder and escalating, if necessary, to a very strong position.

Step 1. Gentle reminders. "I noticed you didn't empty the dishwasher. Could you get to it please?"

Step 2. Express your feelings. "I'm frustrated that you haven't been emptying the dishwasher. I hope you will do it."

Step 3. A discussion. "You said you would empty the dishwasher but you haven't been doing it. What's the problem?"

Step 4. Second discussion. "We talked about the dishwasher last week. I thought we solved the problem, but apparently we didn't. We need to get to the bottom of it. What's wrong?"

Step 5. Express your frustration and serious resentment. "I'm concerned and annoyed that we have already talked about this twice. What's the problem? Please let's get to the bottom of this now. I'm not going to feel good about upholding my end of the agreement if you don't uphold yours."

Step 6. Either as a family or with the help of a professional, try to understand the underlying personal problems or relationship issues that prevent cooperation.

Step 7. If the problem persists and family members are unwilling to get professional help, the final measure is to make a threat. "This is the last time I will talk with you. Keep your agreement or work to change the agreement, but don't make promises you won't keep. If you don't do what you say you will do, I will begin to withdraw my cooperation. I'm not going to want to run errands for you if you're not doing what you've agreed to do for the rest of us. I want to cooperate. But I need you to cooperate with me too."

The process outlined above should be done with love and understanding. Usually there are good reasons for people not doing what they said they would, and a discussion can uncover them.

The final measure, the threat of withdrawing cooperation, is not retaliation. It is done only after a family member has demonstrated a clear unwillingness to cooperate. It may appear that such a threat opens the door to counterthreats and a power struggle. Actually, the person who is not cooperating and won't talk about resolving the problem has already begun a power struggle. Withdrawing cooperation is a positive response. It is a way to say, "I want to cooperate, but cooperation is two-way. I don't want to give without receiving. That's not right. I continue to desire cooperation, but it is your move now."

Families who want to rewrite their family dramas, who recognize the need for cooperative negotiation, and who are willing to overcome some of the limitations of their relationship scripts, will find that introducing these ideas into their routine will vastly improve the quality of family life. It will take practice, no doubt, but the Basic Cooperative Agreement provides an important structure for good communication.

9

Developing Intimate Communication

*A*lthough many volumes have been written about communication methods and skills, one of the most important issues is consistently overlooked—the *purpose* of communication. In families, the purpose should always be to understand, love, and support each other. Families that use communication methods without clarity of purpose are like mechanics who repair airplanes without realizing the machine is designed to fly. They can tinker around, but it won't get anything off the ground.

Families that communicate in order to understand, love, and support each other engage in what we call "intimate communication." In these families, everyone respectfully says what he thinks and feels, listens carefully to the others and negotiates fairly. We have just covered the third activity, negotiation. Now we will focus on the first two of these elements.

Unfortunately, most relationship scripts are deficient in the area of communication. We learn either to hide our thoughts and feelings or to blurt them out in sometimes harmful and offensive ways. The resulting family dramas are filled with unresolved conflict. Aggressive attacks create a family drama characterized by pitched battle. If one or more of the family members withholds negative thoughts and feelings, the battles will be quiet, passive, and subtle. But the conflict will linger, seething beneath the surface and bubbling up in indirect ways.

In presenting communications skills, we'll start on the

positive side with techniques that you can use to open up your family, get more involved in each other's lives and better support each other. Your ability to deal with difficulties in your family relationships is a function of the amount of love and support that you feel and express to each other on a day-to-day basis.

You will also find techniques for initiating discussions about emotionally charged family problems, a format for expressing resentments and other negative feelings, a method for giving and receiving constructive criticism, and suggestions about how to become a better listener. In learning these skills of intimate communication, you will be rewriting negative aspects of your relationship script and family drama. You may come to know each other more deeply and to communicate love and support. And, finally, your entire family will achieve better results on the Happiness Test.

GETTING PERSONAL

All too often we see couples and families who don't talk with each other. You probably see them face to face in restaurants contemplating their next forkful of food but not uttering a single word. In some families, silence is only broken by conducting business ("Who will go to the bank tomorrow?") or by a pastime such as a put-down session ("Did you notice that stupid outfit that Mildred was wearing?"). The relationship scripts of adults in these families are isolationist—"Keep to yourself. Don't be vulnerable."

Families with intimate communication are different. They openly share their thoughts and feelings because they feel safe and want to talk about the details of their daily lives. They are interested in what one another is thinking, feeling, and doing, and are supportive of what they hear. They will not make fun, put down, or attack a family member who has been open.

If you want to establish this sort of openness in your

home, we suggest you begin by using the practice of checking-in at dinnertime. "Checking-in" means you bring each other up to date about what happened during the day, talking about experiences and feelings and asking personal questions. The tone is supportive. If a discussion arouses negative thoughts or feelings, family members deal with them respectfully.

To involve children in checking-in, parents can ask questions such as, "What happened in school today?" "What happened after that?" "How did you feel about it?" "What did the other kids think?" "What else happened?" If the family has only been using "maintenance talk," the child might be on guard and give only brief, evasive answers:

Parent: How was your day?

Child: Fine.

Parent: What happened in school today?

Child: Nothing much.

Parents will have to be creative and persistent in responding to such uninformative answers, perhaps trying tactics such as these: "Was your day *that* unexciting? Can't you think of one interesting thing that happened?" Or, "Just a typical day, huh? Tell me what happens to you on a typical day." Or, "What have you been doing lately in phys-ed?" Or (with a smile), "You're holding your cards pretty close to your vest. How about telling me some of the details? I'm really curious."

Showing interest, being attentive, and offering encouragement help loosen up the atmosphere. But if children are criticized after opening up, they will pull back into their shell. To encourage discussions with children, it is important that parents talk about their own experiences, sharing what happened to them during the day. Children also appreciate it when parents talk about their own childhoods. In families that use a check-in routine, children benefit from the opportunity to discuss their day's experiences with an adult. They are more likely to discuss worries and troubles that otherwise might fester and remain unexpressed.

Intimate communication has a deeper dimension when people find special moments to share their innermost thoughts and feelings with each other. It is important that husbands and wives do this. One way to begin is for you to share some previously undisclosed thoughts or feelings. You might want to propose a discussion about a personal issue, such as your dreams for the future. Another way to begin is by asking personal questions. Here are examples:

"What do you think our life will be like together in five years?"

"How do you feel about my parents?"

"What are your fears?"

"What do you think about when you daydream?"

"What is important to you?"

These discussions continue with follow-up questions: "What makes you happy?" "When are you the happiest?" "What keeps you from being happy?"

A romantic candlelight dinner with flowers is a good way to start. It can be made into a game. Each person comes prepared to ask five personal questions and to reveal two details about themselves they have never discussed before. The revelations could be anything from a childhood memory of special significance to a previously unstated opinion about a current event. By doing this, you will develop trust and get to know each other better.

If a spouse resists, you can gently encourage him or her by setting a good example and sharing details about yourself. You can say that you want to get to know him or her better, that it's important to you. If the resistance continues, you can ask why he or she is unwilling to share more.

As you and your spouse become increasingly open with

each other, you might want to take an opportunity to put your family onstage, taking an objective look at your interactions. You can serve as supportive critics of your family drama as you get a clear picture of what happens when you are all together at meals, over the weekends, and on vacations. Talk about what happens during these important interactions.

Eventually you and your spouse can examine the effect of your respective parents on family life. You may discover current influences that had never been discussed, as in the case of the husband who routinely shared household responsibilities, but rebelled against them when his parents visited. He was afraid they would view him as weak. You may discover indirect parental influence, as in the case of the obsessively clean wife who learned that "your house must always be spic and span."

Giving and Receiving Strokes

One of the most important forms of intimate communication is "strokes," the expression of human warmth. Many relationship scripts prohibit the free expression of strokes. The rules against stroking have been called the "stroke economy" by psychologist Claude Steiner in his book, *Scripts People Live.* We focus on two of the rules that have a damaging effect on families: you can't ask for strokes, and you can't give the strokes you feel.

Why not? The reasons are varied. Perhaps you can't ask because that would mean you are needy or weak. If you have to ask, the strokes wouldn't count or wouldn't be real. You would be indebted. You have to earn strokes, not ask for them. You might not give strokes because you think people don't care how you feel. Or you would be embarrassed. Or people would think you are being manipulative. Or if you gave strokes freely, it would cheapen their value.

These terrible injunctions about the expression of human affection wreak havoc in family relationships. People need to know that they are loved. We need to be stroked. We need compliments. We need hugs. We need to be touched. Your family can't grow and flourish without the strokes of people who care. People who can't ask for strokes in direct and straightforward ways need them as much as anyone else. In the end, they will find themselves using manipulative and indirect ways to get attention and recognition.

The foundation of intimate communication is the ability to express love and affection. This means breaking the rules against freely giving and asking for strokes. In order to do this, you might ask yourselves what reasons you have for not exchanging strokes. Then, make a conscious effort to become aware of your positive feelings and to express them, as well as to gain awareness of your needs for affection and to ask for strokes.

We recommend that you and your family take time to make a list of all the qualities you like about each other and then make a point of expressing these strokes, most of all showing your love. Your ability to deal with the tough stuff in family relationships will be a function of the amount of love that you feel and express to each other on a daily basis. We also recommend that you make a commitment of asking for affection when you want it.

How to Start Difficult Communication

When it comes to communicating criticism, suspicion, and negative emotions, most relationship scripts encourage family members either to withhold their thoughts and feelings to keep the peace or to impose them on each other aggressively. The result is a family drama characterized either by wild emotional confrontations or by bitter feelings that are suppressed but felt by all.

The communication methods presented below, in the context of a BCA, will allow families to communicate their hurt, angry, and critical thoughts to each other in constructive and loving ways. Good timing is important in successful communication. Words are wasted if the person who is supposed to listen is not in a receptive mood, as in the following example.

Martha held her baby while she checked the boiling rice. The oven bell rang, signaling that the chicken was cooked. Her mother had phoned a minute ago and asked that she return her call. At that moment, Mitchell entered the kitchen and politely told Martha that he was annoyed to find the day's newspaper in the garbage.

"And I suppose you're mad that I didn't leave your slippers out for you, too?" she commented sarcastically.

Her response was provocative. But his timing was horrendous. People who want to communicate effectively have to use good judgment in selecting times. In general, we wouldn't recommend a heavy discussion right after a tough day of work, during dinner preparation, or while the children are getting ready for bed. Fatigue level, time of day, and experiences of the day need to be considered. Setting is also important: it isn't a good idea to have a serious discussion about a tense issue when the children are within earshot.

The only sure way to know of the appropriateness of time and setting for a discussion is to ask the question, "Can we talk?" This is an important formality before any serious discussion. It's a respectful way to find out if the other person is receptive. The message is: "I want to talk *with* you, not *at* you." Also, the question gives listeners a brief opportunity to prepare psychologically for a discussion. Without such warning, when listeners hear a resentment, criticism, or other negative feeling, they may experience a sense of intrusion and react defensively.

When asking permission, it is important to give an idea of what you want to talk about. For example: "I have a little resentment that I want to express. Can we talk?" "I've been suspicious about something. Can we discuss it?" "There has been something happening between us lately that has made me scared and angry. I need to talk with you about it." "I'm having trouble with. . . . I need to talk about it so we can work things out. Can we talk?"

If the other person is not receptive at the moment, either one can suggest an alternative time: "Not right now. I'm making dinner and need to return my mother's phone call. How about talking after dinner?"

KEEPING AN OPEN-MINDED ATTITUDE

Intimate communication of criticism and negative feelings requires an open-minded attitude. You can have a position, even a strong one, but you must allow for the possibility of other valid positions. This means you shouldn't assume that you are necessarily justified in your opinion. In the heat of conflict, there is a tendency to think in egocentric terms. These are the times to remind yourself that there can be different ways to look at your situation. Other family members may have different feelings about it.

Open-mindedness is communicated by statements such as these: "This is how I see things. How do you see them?" "These are my feelings. How do you feel?" "This makes me suspicious that . . . is happening. Is it?" "Let me tell you my opinion. I want to hear yours."

Handling Resentments

In many relationship scripts, people do not express their resentments because they are afraid of hurting other family members or of losing approval. Withheld resentments cause serious problems. It is like the stamps that are given in some supermarkets. Each one doesn't amount to much. But when many accumulate over time, the result is substantial. People save up resentments until they accumulate enough to cash them in for a big explosion, a temper tantrum, a spending binge, an affair, or a divorce. It's not calculated. They don't deliberately save up to get revenge. Rather, their feelings catch up with them.

Because unexpressed anger causes problems, you need

to learn to express resentments and deal with them construc-tively before the negative feelings accumulate. Furthermore, people in cooperative relationships want to know what other family members are feeling—they respect each other's feelings.

In rewriting your family drama to express resentments and other negative emotions, we recommend a very simple fill-in sentence: "When you did A, I felt B."

"A" is a description of a specific behavior, such as, "when you yelled at me last night," or "when you left dirty dishes in the sink after dinner."

"B" is a description of your feelings—anger, resent-ment, hurt, or fear.

Complete sentences go like this: "When you yelled at me last night, I was scared and very angry." Or, "When you left dirty dishes in the sink after dinner, I resented it."

In describing the event, it is important to be specific in order to be understood. For example, "when you leave dishes in the sink and crumbs on the counter" is a better description than the generalization, "when you leave the kitchen dirty." The beauty of this format is that the sentence constructed is indisputable. When A occurred, I felt B. This is a report of how one person felt when a particular event took place, not a judgment about an event that could be subject to debate.

The biggest mistake that people make with this commu-nication is to insert judgments. Sometimes a judgment is used instead of the description of behavior: "When you *acted like a slob,* I resented it."

Sometimes the judgment replaces the feeling: "When you left dirty dishes in the sink, it showed that you are a slob and that you have no respect for others."

Obviously both of these statements are provocative and more likely to start a fight than to clarify feelings.

Another common mistake in using this format is exag-geration, especially by using such terms as always and never. This may make the description of behavior inaccurate. For example: "You *never* clean up anything you say you will."

"When I suggest we visit my mother, you *always* have an excuse." "When we get our Christmas bonus, you *always* decide how to spend it. You *never* listen to me."

The extremes of "always" and "never" may be accurate, but usually are not.

One further caution about potential pitfalls: sometimes people start with a clear statement but attach an extra ending, an add-on, perhaps a justification for a feeling or some sort of comment that blames the other person. For example, Mitchell said to his wife Martha, "When you threw away the newspaper before I read it, it made me angry because it is inconsiderate. I never throw out anything of yours."

The first part of the statement stands alone. Mitchell should let Martha know how he feels. But the "because" clause is a judgment about her behavior. She may have been inconsiderate in this instance, but there are other possibilities: she may have thought that Mitchell had already read the newspaper; she may have thought that he wasn't interested; she may have thought it was yesterday's paper. Mitchell doesn't need to justify his feelings with an add-on. His justification only confuses matters.

Because people in cooperative relationships want to know what other family members feel, the most important part of a response to an expression of a feeling is acknowledgment. The speaker wants to be heard. Through words or gestures, the listener needs to communicate the following message: "I hear what you're saying. I will take it seriously."

The person who heard the feeling may take time to think it over. He may change his behavior. He may apologize. He may suggest a discussion.

Resentment and other feelings, even strongly felt ones, need not be a source of conflict. Couples and families can learn to express them in a disciplined way and to accept them without becoming defensive. Families who use this simple fill-in statement are surprised to discover that feelings that used to be a source of conflict can be easily communicated and understood most of the time.

Checking Out Suspicion

Even with the best communication, families cannot possibly know every detail of each other's lives. So we fill in the missing information with our own imaginations. Sometimes we have suspicions. We suspect something is happening, maybe that a child is experimenting with drugs or an elderly parent wants to visit but is too shy to say so or a spouse is having an affair. Suspicion is an entirely normal part of life. So in your most intimate relationships, you need a mechanism for checking out suspicions.

Unfortunately, most relationship scripts do not prepare people for dealing with suspicions. Many relationship scripts lead people to assume that their suspicions are true, act as if they are true, and stir up intense conflict: "If I think something is true, it must be so."

Martha accused Mitchell of giving up on their marriage and staying married because of the children. She didn't check out her suspicion. She simply assumed it was true and made an accusation. Although Mitchell was often upset about their relationship, he hadn't given up. Martha's accusation, based on her incorrect assumption, started a huge argument.

Some people do the opposite. They try to brush aside their suspicions, assuming they must be wrong. This doesn't work because suspicion is almost always based on at least a grain of truth. Without an adequate explanation, the suspicion will persist and become ever more intense and elaborate.

Good communication of suspicions means testing them out. So in rewriting your family drama, we recommend that couples and families share their suspicions with one another, put them forth tentatively, and seek validation. When Martha suspects that her husband has given up on the relationship, rather than acting on her assumption, she would put forth her feelings: "Mitchell, I have a suspicion. I don't know if it's true or not, but it's a feeling I have. I'm worried that you might have given up on our relationship. Have you? If you haven't, what do you think is happening that makes me feel this way?"

When someone checks out a suspicion and the family has a cooperative agreement, the listener will help find the validity of the suspicious feeling. If Mitchell has "given-up" on the relationship, he would have to say so. If he hasn't given up, using cooperative communication, Mitchell would need to say something besides a simple "It's not true."

This gets back to the basis for suspicion. There is almost always some grain of truth. Suspicions are based on something you detect but cannot necessarily explain fully. Mitchell would try to find the kernel of truth in Martha's suspicion in order to validate her feelings. He might say: "Martha, I have thought it through carefully, and I haven't given up on our relationship. I wonder if you think that I have because of my tendency to withdraw after big fights, and we've had some big ones lately. When I withdraw it's kind of like gasping for air. I have trouble with the intensity of emotions, so I need to cool off.

"When I do this, I feel distant. Sometimes I even fantasize about breaking up, but it's never a serious consideration. Maybe you sense this. Maybe this explains why you think I've given up. Clearly the kids are one good reason for our staying together. But I also stay with you because I believe we can work it out. I want to work things out."

This response validates Martha's suspicion. In a way Mitchell is saying, "I take your suspicion seriously. I want to help explain it and alleviate your uneasiness. I want to help you account for your feelings."

Sometimes people have trouble validating suspicions, not simply in admitting the truth to others, but in recognizing the truth within themselves. That makes this communication technique a particularly difficult one. But it is important to validate the truth of suspicions.

Family members who want cooperative communication will need to learn this technique, even if it is a struggle. It may require practice, but such effort will help stretch your perseverance in looking for your own hidden motivations and feelings. If you can't admit the truth to yourself, it will be impossible to have clear communication with other family members.

In the Schwebel family, we have had some first-hand experience with suspicions that other families living at a distance from one another may also have encountered. We talk on the telephone frequently and used to have a pattern of protecting each other from bad news, such as illness. Whenever we withheld information, we found that the person on the other end of the line could sense something was wrong and became suspicious. We also noticed that, because we knew information was withheld, we started to suspect trouble when everything was fine. In confronting this problem, we finally decided to tell it straight with each other. The pain of the truth can be less intense than the confusion and suspicion of keeping secrets.

OFFERING CONSTRUCTIVE CRITICISM

If your spouse or children haven't criticized you, you're missing something important—part of the truth of what your family thinks and an opportunity to work out your differences. Human beings cannot live with each other without criticism. No two people see everything exactly alike. Despite what some of us might feel at times, no one is all-knowing. Therefore, when we live together, our family members will make observations, some of them negative. If handled well, these observations constitute constructive criticism.

Unfortunately, the human ability to be critical is terribly abused. Many children experience insensitive and destructive criticism and consequently build walls against it. As adults, they send a signal: "Don't say anything negative about me." This defensiveness, incorporated in their relationship scripts, protects against harmful criticism but also shields them from accurate, helpful, and constructive suggestions.

In rewriting your family drama, it is important to learn to give and receive constructive criticism. To succeed, it is important to remind yourself that the purpose of communication in families is to foster love, support, and understanding. Constructive criticism always comes with love and positive intentions, not putting someone down but building him up.

Constructive criticism can be divided into two basic categories. One is criticism of something that affects other family members. Some examples:

"I've noticed that you leave dirty dishes in the sink when you have an evening snack, instead of putting them in the dishwasher as we have agreed."

"I think that you get grumpy at me when you've had a bad day at the office."

To a teenage son: "The last couple of times you borrowed my car keys, you didn't return them."

The other type of criticism is directed to the well-being of the person being criticized:

"I've noticed that you seem to feel kind of depressed after you speak with your parents. You get down on yourself."

To a nine-year-old daughter: "You seem to be shy about inviting your friends to visit. Is it hard for you?"

To a teenage daughter: "It seems that you put off doing your homework until you are tired and ready to go to bed. Maybe it would be better to do it when you first come home."

Often criticism combines the two categories:

"I've noticed that, when you feel bad, you usually cancel our social plans. I'm disappointed because we don't go out together and have fun. Then you feel lousy all night. I think we both would feel better if you'd push yourself to do things instead of staying home."

Giving and Receiving Criticism

When offering constructive criticism, be sure to raise issues in a calm and reasonable way without making threats. When family members listen to each other, simple and careful communication can resolve many problems and avert unnecessary escalation. Too often people start with an angry confrontation when a calm discussion would have produced better results.

People who start with a confrontation generally have a history of having been discounted in the past. Because they expect their concerns to be brushed aside, they get aggressive and sound accusatory. What they elicit is a defensive response, which then confirms their assumption that the other family member wouldn't listen. But if they had raised the issue in a calm and reasonable way, the other person might have responded more kindly and more cooperatively. Here is an example of the benefits of the calm approach.

A woman complained about her husband to her best friend. "He just doesn't help with the kids," she said. "I'm going to *confront* him about this. I'm going to give him an ultimatum." She sounded bitter and angry.

"Have you ever discussed the idea of sharing responsibility for the children with your husband?" the friend asked.

"No, but I'm ready now."

"I'd suggest," her friend said, "that you *discuss* the matter with your husband before you confront him about it. Confrontation sounds like overkill."

The disgruntled wife took her friend's advice and discussed the issue with her husband in a calm way. She said,

"I am concerned about our family life. I'm unhappy that you don't spend more time with the children and me. I want us to spend more time together as a family. I would like you to help more with some of the responsibilities. What do you think about that?"

She was surprised to discover that her husband never really thought about family time. He had been raised in a family with a father who was often absent. When his wife brought this issue to his attention in a calm, nonaccusatory way, he was appreciative of her needs. He too wanted to have more of a family life and share the responsibilities. The calm approach gave them an opportunity for thoughtful and unthreatened communication.

Below are ten additional guidelines for constructive criticism in the context of a Basic Cooperative Agreement:

- Ask permission to give criticism so that you offer it when the other person is receptive. The cooperative form begins, "I have a criticism (or an observation or an idea about something you are doing) that I would like to share with you. Do you want to hear it?" If the present moment is not a good time, ask when the other person would be ready to listen.
- Offer an opinion, not an absolute truth. "I," "me," and "my" statements are best: "I've noticed . . . ," "It is my opinion . . . ," "It seems to me . . . ," and "I think . . ."
- Keep a warm tone of voice. Avoid nastiness and accusations.
- Keep a positive perspective whenever possible. Point out positives too, so that your statements are balanced. Remember, criticism can be received only to the extent that there has been a positive exchange of good feelings now or in the past.

- No name-calling or put-downs.
- Avoid using extreme terms such as "always" and "never."
- Stay focused. Deal with issues one at a time, instead of letting one criticism lead to a whole onslaught of unrelated criticism and countercriticism.
- Give specifics for each issue. Generalizations about behavior are only helpful if they are explained with specific examples. If you make generalizations (such as, "You don't always do the work you promised to do"), give examples for clarity (such as, "You haven't been walking the dog in the mornings as you said you would" and "You didn't do the dishes last Tuesday").
- Distinguish fact from opinion. An opinion should be labeled as such. "I have noticed that you usually start your homework late at night (fact)." "It is my *opinion* that you would do better in school if you did your homework when you first got home."
- Show open-mindedness. In intimate communication it is important to find out what the other person is thinking. There is always room for differences of opinion. Ask for the other person's thoughts and feelings.

Some of these principles of constructive criticism are applied in the following example in which a husband lovingly discusses the issue of child-rearing with his wife.

"I have some constructive criticism. May I share it with you? I know that you love the children very much. I appreciate how hard you work with them, but I've noticed something that concerns me. You often pick up their messes. When Tammy leaves her clothing on the floor, you hang it up for her. When Tammy and Greg leave dishes around the house, you bring them to the kitchen and wash them. It's my opinion that the children need to learn to take responsibility for their own behavior. I think we should talk to them about it. What do you think?"

HELPFUL HINTS FOR GOOD LISTENING

Many relationship scripts leave people ill-prepared for good listening—that is, listening to understand, without defensiveness or distortions. Relationship script messages such as the following undermine good listening: "If I listen to criticism, I must accept it as true." "If I listen to what the other person wants, I'll have to do things his way." "If I listen to his feelings, my feelings will be ignored." "It's weak to listen." "I lose power if I listen." "I'll be hurt if I listen."

Under the influence of these messages, family members listen defensively, with an ear for cutting down what they hear. They fight and lose sight of the common good. The result is a family drama with lots of argument but little listening. In rewriting your family drama for better listening, the Basic Cooperative Agreement helps family members keep in mind the importance of knowing what their spouse, parents, or children are thinking and feeling.

To improve your listening skills, you can begin by taking inventory to see if you use any of the following indicators of poor listening. The clearest indication of poor listening is an interruption. People who interrupt are saying it is more important for them to speak than to listen.

Another indication of poor listening is an instant response. Before the speaker has taken a breath, the listener has already launched a reply. Often the response is a rebuttal: "I think you should cut back on your drinking," a husband says. "I only drink," his wife answers without a moment's thought, "because you don't pay any attention to me."

Still another indication of poor listening is changing the

topic, sometimes tit-for-tat. "I'm angry," Karen says, "that you came home late for dinner." Jay replies, changing the topic, "Well, I'm angry you didn't greet me with a kiss."

Even though Jay is angry, if he wants to communicate with Karen and work out their differences cooperatively, he needs to pay attention to her message. A good listener takes the other person's point of view seriously. Jay would say, "I can understand why you would be upset about my late arrival." He can deal with her feelings knowing that he will have an opportunity later to express his own. There is room enough for both to have feelings. Furthermore, when he shows his concern about her feelings, she will be more inclined to show concern about his.

Another example of tit-for-tat occurred later that evening with the same couple. Jay complained to Karen about the money she spent on clothing. Instead of listening to him, she retaliated with a saved-up resentment about the money he spent on his hiking equipment. Maybe she resented his spending habits, but she ignored his concerns by switching to her own.

A different and particularly troublesome indication of poor listening occurs when the spoken words are distorted in interpretations by the listener. Sometimes the interpretations are made privately, but not vocalized, as in the following situation. Jay says, "The lasagna is delicious." Karen starts thinking, "Well he likes the lasagna but doesn't like the vegetables." She's listening to her own mind, not his words. Although Karen doesn't say anything to Jay, she is grouchy after she receives the compliment, leaving her husband baffled by her reaction.

Sometimes the distorted interpretations are expressed. "I wish you wouldn't invite your parents for Thanksgiving," Karen says. "You mean," Jay replies, "you don't like my parents." She cuts back, "I didn't say that." And he responds, "You did too." He was listening to his own commentary, not Karen's words.

Good listeners don't distort. They can tell the difference

between what others say and how they interpret what was said. If they are confused, they will ask questions rather than make false assumptions.

Techniques for Better Listening

If you find that your listening skills need sharpening, we recommend a family commitment to listen carefully to each other and to resist the temptation to interrupt or answer immediately or discount or rebut what another family member has said. The most effective measure is to pause before responding. Take a moment to remind yourself of the purpose of communication, to calm your fears, and to think about what was said. By delaying your response, you will not be able to interrupt others or to jump into speedy answers. This is especially important when emotions are intense.

Sometimes it helps to take written notes. Write down what you hear, not your interpretations. The act of writing will slow down your response and help to avoid distortions. If you are confused, ask questions of the speaker to better understand the communication. This also slows you down and keeps you from starting a counterargument.

Another excellent technique to improve listening and prevent distortions is to paraphrase what was said: "Let me see if I understand you. It sounds like . . ." When paraphrasing, you don't want to agree, disagree, or interpret. You just do a "reality check" to see that you understand what was said.

To really appreciate what was said, sometimes it is important to take a hard look at yourself. Remember that you are probably biased in your own point of view. We all have a tendency to get egocentric, thinking that our own point of view is correct and rejecting what others say without giving it fair consideration. You can challenge yourself to listen better by asking yourself tough questions. Sometimes you need to force yourself to confront unpleasant thoughts in order to work out differences with family members.

A husband who angrily left home during a fight would

entertain these thoughts. "Maybe I shouldn't have stormed off. Even if I was rightfully angry, maybe that didn't justify my behavior. Did it?"

A wife tells her husband that she thinks he is trying to keep her from moving ahead in her career. She cites a few examples. The man who challenges himself considers these thoughts. "Maybe I am scared of her success. How would I really feel if my wife started earning more money than I did?"

A husband says that he thinks his wife has been angry all morning. She denies it right away. Then she reconsiders: "Even though I have been denying it, maybe I was angry at him. Maybe that was why I did what I did. Was I angry?"

In pushing yourself to listen better and to overcome negative relationship-script messages, it helps to keep reminding yourself of the benefits of listening when you have a BCA. You might tell yourself:

> When I listen, I don't give up power. Because no one is trying to dominate, I can listen even to strong feelings and serious criticism without feeling threatened and without losing anything. I will gain understanding. Whether I like what was said or not, what I hear has to be taken seriously. It's a statement of what my spouse or children think and feel. I'll have an opportunity to express myself after I listen. We all want to be happy in this family.

I've Been Wronged

One of the excuses people use for expressing themselves poorly or avoiding listening to each other is that of being wronged. A family member's alleged misbehavior is used to justify one's own. This is a serious breach of a BCA. Even if you feel wronged, you need to communicate cooperatively.

Martin and Janet's second anniversary fell on a Saturday. Martin played tennis in the morning and spent the early afternoon with a friend. When he came home, Janet gave him the cold shoulder at first and then lashed out at him for forgetting their anniversary. She said it showed that he really didn't care. He tried to explain, but she wouldn't listen. She insisted that he would have made plans for the occasion if he *really* cared.

Janet was so overbearing in her attack that she never found out that Martin had planned a surprise dinner for the evening. He finally canceled the reservations. With a little self-control, Janet could have calmly said what she felt. She would have been pleasantly surprised to discover the plans. But Janet was too caught up in her own feelings to pay any attention to Martin.

This sort of self-righteousness is a common problem. In another incident, one of us provided counseling to a family seeking help for a thirteen-year-old daughter who had run away from home. The parents began with the view of being wronged. In therapy the father asked his daughter, "How could you have done this to us?" But it was asked rhetorically, with no expectation of an answer. The parents weren't interested in listening to their daughter and understanding her motivation.

They didn't realize that to deal with the issue, they needed to open a dialogue. They needed to *really* ask their daughter why she ran away and *really* listen to her answer. Only when they could listen and make an effort to understand would they be able to address her feelings and help her learn more constructive ways to deal with them.

"I've been wronged" is too often used as an excuse to limit communications to one-way transmissions. When this happens, intimate communication ceases. As always, you need to remember that the purpose of communication in a family is to love, support, and understand each other.

10

Rewriting Your Relationship Scripts Together

*T*he relationship script of each individual in a family is tightly interwoven into the tapestry of the family drama. Change the family drama and you change the relationship scripts. When our clients, the Steins, rewrote their family drama using the cooperative negotiation method, John's relationship script for dominance and Blanche's for submission were changed dramatically. To negotiate cooperatively, they had to revise their scripts.

The process of change works the other way as well. Rewrite the relationship scripts of the individuals, and the family drama will be altered. For example, Janet, who learned to "please her man," realized that she had been discounting her own needs. She decided she wanted a more equal relationship, so she no longer ignored her own preferences, asserting herself more. As Janet revised her relationship script, the family drama changed.

So far in discussing rewriting, we have emphasized changing the family drama itself, thereby altering relationship scripts as a by-product. We have suggested activities and methods that, when put into practice, alter your relationship scripts. We will now discuss techniques for changing individual relationship scripts and altering your family drama as a result. This procedure requires more psychological sophistication; it involves assessing your own unique problem areas and learning to talk about them with your spouse and other family members.

We will focus on the need for family members to change together. Because change in one part of the family system will inevitably create changes in other parts, we emphasize how you and your family can support each other in rewriting relationship scripts. This process begins with the challenging task of recognizing self-defeating patterns.

DETECTING SELF-DEFEATING PATTERNS

Self-defeating patterns are those behaviors that are learned during childhood and are incorporated into a relationship script, causing problems for a person as an adult. As a child hungry for attention, Jill found that by crying she could get her father to rub her back and attend to her. As an adult, she had difficulty asking for the attention and recognition she wanted from her husband Ben. But by crying she was able to get Ben's affection and often get her own way about a particular decision. Superficially, it seemed that crying, an important part of Jill's relationship script, brought her significant benefits. However, a Happiness Test revealed serious costs associated with this behavior.

First, Jill felt badly about herself: she couldn't get her needs satisfied in a straightforward, mature manner. Second, her husband felt manipulated by her tears and started resenting her. Further, instead of respecting her, the children considered her weak. Jill's crying behavior was self-defeating. She could attain better results in the Happiness Test if she learned to assert her needs without crying.

Elliot was a single man. Whenever he felt threatened, he got aggressive. Although he never became violent, he would wave his fist and make threats. He learned this behavior as a child, and continued it in his adulthood. Many of the women he liked ultimately rejected him because he was so aggressive. It was a self-defeating behavior.

Identifying self-defeating patterns in a relationship script is difficult because, by definition, the script is what you take for granted. It's part of you. It defines what relationships are supposed to be. It tells you the way you are supposed to behave. When you follow the directives of a relationship script, you believe you are doing what is correct.

You have to gain an unusual measure of detachment to put yourself onstage, be a critic, and look objectively and self-critically at your own behavior. Several methods can be helpful in identifying self-defeating patterns.

The first and most obvious is simply to self-critically picture some of the interactions in your relationship with an eye for those that yield poor results in your Happiness Test. To help you identify self-defeating aspects of your own relationship script, we have listed common problems below. The list is not all-inclusive, but it identifies some of the most frequent problems. As you review it, consider whether any of the problem areas are part of your own relationship script and how they lead to poor results on your Happiness Test.

Self-Defeating Components of Relationship Scripts

Emotional Awareness

Not usually aware of your own feelings.

Not usually aware of family members' feelings.

Communication

Not a good listener.

Express feelings in undisciplined ways, such as temper tantrums.

Difficulty in expressing affection.

Indirect communication, such as expressing anger by sulking or sarcasm.

Give opinions as if they are indisputable facts.

Fear and Low Self-Esteem

Plagued with self-doubt. Doubt your own opinions. Doubt the validity of your own feelings.

Afraid to express feelings and/or opinions.

Afraid to ask for what you want.

Almost always the one who compromises and makes concessions.

Unable to recognize or respond to power plays of other family members.

Can't accept criticism or deal with conflict without going to pieces.

Self-Centered Thoughts and Actions

Closed-minded. Convinced that you are right and others are wrong.

Not showing interest in other family member's opinions or desires.

Difficulty seeing another person's perspective.

Always trying to get your own way, resorting to threats and other power plays.

Overly critical of family members.

Work and Play Issues

Inability to be spontaneous and have fun.

Inability to handle responsibilities at work or in household.

Overly focused on fun.

Overly focused on work.

Isolated. Can't make friends outside of family.

Unaware of importance of negotiating on issues such as division of labor, use of financial resources, use of recreational time.

Coping Styles

Cope by avoiding conflict.

Cope by withdrawing, physically or emotionally.

Cope by aggression.

Anger is the only emotion consistently expressed.

Dependent on spouse.

Unwilling to commit yourself. Fear of being hurt.

Excessive individualism. Cannot ask for help or offer it.

Another excellent method for identifying self-defeating patterns in your relationship script is to mentally review conflict situations in your family. Think about your major disputes, especially the recurring ones. Focus on how *you*— not your partner and not your children—contributed to the conflict.

This isn't easy. If you thought you were wrong, you probably wouldn't be arguing in the first place. People argue because they are convinced they are right. However, learning to recognize your own part in family conflict is one way to get a grasp on self-defeating aspects of your relationship script.

Yet another method is to examine occasions when you strived to attain a goal in your relationship, but failed. Also, if you tried and failed with some of the rewriting methods outlined earlier, take a look at what happened.

Ask yourself, "What is it about my relationship script that keeps me from succeeding?" For example, you might realize that you would achieve better results if you could express your resentments, but you are unable because your relationship script says that it is petty to express resentments.

Because your family of origin is the source of relationship scripts, think back to your childhood to see which behaviors and emotions were encouraged and which were discouraged. Then you can determine the self-defeating ones. Begin this process by taking the role of an objective critic, reviewing scenes from your childhood: How did you get attention? How did you get what you want? How did you handle feelings? How did you handle conflict? What types of fun were allowed? What were the messages about work? What were you allowed to say? What were you forbidden from saying? What was your idea of a good boy (or girl)?

Try to be open-minded in thinking about yourself. Which behaviors that worked as a child are self-defeating for you as an adult? For example, crying may have been a terrific way to get what you wanted when you were young. Now it may be fine for expressing sadness, but a weak and passive way of getting your needs met.

Another excellent method to gain self-awareness about your relationship script is to request the viewpoint of family members and to listen undefensively to what they say. Ask family members to serve as critics. Instead of finding what is wrong with their criticism, listen only for what is right. This might mean you have to push your limits in looking for possible justifications for what they say. Try to consider "Even if my initial reaction is defensive, I'm going to look for some truth in this criticism."

Sometimes criticism is easier to accept from an impartial third party—a professional or a friend. Ask for an objective appraisal of how you conduct yourself in relationships. If you ask friends, it's usually necessary to insist on honesty. Tell them that you don't want to be spared from constructive criticism. You want the truth.

NANCY AND MIKE REWRITE THEIR RELATIONSHIP SCRIPTS

Here is one woman's example of how she pinpointed her problems. Nancy had spent most of her seven years of married life walking on eggshells, quietly absorbing a great deal of criticism from her husband Mike. He always managed to find faults: Nancy didn't say the "right" things with his parents; she didn't clean the house properly; she didn't remember to pay the bills on time. All along, Nancy took the criticism to heart and felt that she wasn't careful enough with her husband's feelings. Yet in spite of her efforts to be a good wife, she could not please him.

Frustrated by her failures, Nancy asked a level-headed friend for honest, constructive criticism. To Nancy's surprise, her friend placed much of the responsibility for the marital unhappiness on Mike's shoulders. She pointed out that he consistently picked away at Nancy. He was impossible for her to please. Like a restaurant with a specialty of the day, Mike had a gripe of the day.

Through the discussion with her friend, Nancy realized that Mike did criticize her excessively. Nancy then blamed Mike for everything for a while. Her only self-criticism was that she had put up with this nonsense for so long. But she didn't want to go from one extreme of self-blame to the other of blaming him. She wanted to be objective, so she began to wonder about herself. She asked her friend to focus on her own contribution to the problem.

With her friend's help, Nancy realized that by accepting Mike's excessive criticism, she had half the responsibility for their downward spiral. She recognized several important shortcomings in her own relationship script:

- She lacked the ability to distinguish between constructive criticism and put-downs. She didn't recognize Mike's abusive criticism.

- Her tendency for most of her life had been to blame herself for everything. When Mike criticized her, she accommodated to his wishes. In doing this, she colluded with his blaming.
- She did not say what she wanted. She tried to please others and simply gave Mike whatever he wanted.
- She did not say how she saw things and could not disagree with Mike's assessment of a situation.

With these new insights, Nancy began to rewrite her relationship script by standing up for herself more. However, one nagging self-doubt persisted. She asked herself: "Why did I let this go on? How could I have let myself be such a doormat for so long?"

These are the self-doubts of a person lacking historical perspective, who is unaware of how she came to behave the way she did. She didn't understand the origin and impact of her relationship script.

Determined to feel better, Nancy started thinking about her childhood. She realized that she learned the traditional sex roles of her time, to try to please others, especially men, at any cost. "If you please your man," her mom had said "he'll take care of you." Her father said, "Never get angry. That would be unladylike."

Over and over again she heard these messages. She learned them from the people she trusted the most—her parents. The same messages were reinforced at church, in the classroom, and on the popular TV shows of her time. They became important directives in her relationship script. But this "good" behavior as a child became her self-defeating behavior as an adult.

It was only by thinking back on her childhood that Nancy was able to put her behavior in perspective. This allowed her to stop condemning herself for past mistakes and helped her feel better as she went forward with changing her relationship script.

TELLING YOUR SPOUSE

When you discover a change you want to make in your relationship script, it is important to tell your partner, because it will inevitably affect your family drama. In most cases, changes in one person's script will become pressure for changes in a partner's relationship script. You can see this with Nancy and Mike. As she becomes more assertive, he will feel pressured to become more respectful.

There is a certain art to discussing changes of these sorts with a spouse. We recommend a four-part process:

1. Can we talk?
2. Self-criticism. Take responsibility for your own problems.
3. Explain potential mutual benefits of your changes.
4. Ask for complementary changes.

Nancy's approach is to begin by asking permission to talk: "I've been unhappy for quite some time, and I need to talk with you. Is that all right?"

Once given the go-ahead, she talks about her own difficulty in assertiveness. She says that she has trouble asking for what she wants, that she tends to accept criticism without thinking about it, and that she quietly accepts put-downs when she should be standing up against them. She explains with examples. "The other day, when we went out for dinner, I didn't feel like going to a steak house. I wanted a restaurant with a salad bar. I never said so. And when you were angry on Tuesday that I didn't wait for you with dinner, I should have told you that the children were hungry. That's why we ate before you came home."

Then she says that she intends to change her own behavior and explains why it's not only in her best interest, but also in his, that she make these changes. "If I don't stand up for myself more, I'm going to be disappointed. We won't be doing the activities I want to do. I'll accept criticism that doesn't feel right, and I'll end up unhappy and angry at you. You may have noticed it already. I've kind of withdrawn. I haven't felt like having sex much lately. I want to reverse this trend and have a better relationship."

After this introduction, Nancy asks for complementary changes. "I'd like you to stop the harsh criticism you've been giving me. Sometimes I feel like I'm walking on eggshells. And I want you to listen to me when I say what I want to do."

Mike gives his opinion as they talk, but to be certain he has said everything he wants, Nancy asks, "What do you think?"

What to Do If Your Partner Stonewalls

In only the most unusual cases, one person will immediately see the light when a spouse raises a problem. It usually takes time, but eventually a couple can gain an understanding of the situation. However, sometimes this is difficult, especially when a spouse is defensive. Under these circumstances, the person who wants to make changes is working against both his own relationship script and his partner's. Although this is difficult, it can be done. Even if a partner won't admit to a share of the responsibility, the person who wants mutual change can at least change his own behavior.

This would mean that Nancy puts forth her needs with Mike. When Mike gets hypercritical, she would say, "I won't accept that sort of criticism." When he says, "You better," she says, "I won't. It's not good for me, and it's not good for this relationship."

If Nancy is strong and persistent, Mike will eventually see that his relationship script will no longer lead to the same family drama as in the past. He used to do what he wanted without opposition. In the new family drama, Nancy asserts her needs, feelings, and opinions. Mike can accept this revision and negotiate, or he can fight to get his own way. Either outcome is a new family drama.

Although there's no guarantee that Mike's new behavior will be better than the old, if Nancy continues to say that she's making changes for a better relationship for both of them, it's more likely that Mike will choose a positive alternative. If he becomes even more aggressive, Nancy will have to decide if she is willing to tolerate it. She may consider leaving the relationship.

Sometimes it takes the threat of leaving to wake up the other person and make him willing to budge. But such threats should be made only as a last resort, when you are ready for divorce, not as an idle power play.

GUIDELINES FOR CHANGING YOUR RELATIONSHIP SCRIPT

Once you have identified self-defeating aspects of your relationship script, the next task is to make a change. We provide the following guidelines that will prove helpful:

Set goals for yourself.   Nancy wanted to become more assertive. Her goals were to learn to recognize put-downs, to fight back when she was put down, and to ask for what she wants.

Make a plan with a reasonable pace.   The pace should be challenging but not overwhelming. An instant turnabout is an unreasonable expectation. Nancy's plan was to work gradually on all her problem areas at the same time. She decided to ask for what she wants at least once during the first week, to stay alert to put-downs, and to tell Mike assertively to stop criticizing her at least once. On several occasions during the initial week, she didn't ask for what she wanted, and a couple of times she quietly accepted harsh criticism. But Nancy considered herself successful because she accomplished her objectives. It was a first step in a positive direction. In the following weeks, she became increasingly assertive.

Expect negative reactions.   When you try new behaviors, people who are accustomed to your old ones will respond negatively. Also you will have an old part of you that will be critical of the new behavior. Prepare to stick up for yourself. Recruit the backing of friends and family who understand and support your new, positive changes.

You can also prepare a statement that you read to remind yourself of why you are making changes and what the benefits will be in terms of the Happiness Test. It will be an affirmation of your new relationship script. Nancy needed such a statement because the first few times she asserted herself, she started feeling guilty and selfish. But she was able to fight back. With the support of her best friend, she had prepared this statement. "I'm not being selfish. I remain loving and supportive of other family members. The only difference is that now I'm giving my own needs equal status. Because of what I'm doing, family life will improve for all of us. I'll feel better about myself. My family will feel my affection instead of the resentment that I have felt."

Practice constructive self-criticism.   This means recognizing and appreciating successes, even small ones. It also means tolerance for setbacks and learning from them. Just when Nancy thought she was doing well with Mike, her parents came to visit. She found herself slipping into old patterns. She was able to see how her parents' influence affected her and to adjust her strategy for their presence.

Changing Together

Once family members have enlisted the support of each other and agreed upon specific changes, they can work together to establish the new patterns. Mike and Nancy agreed that she would assert herself. He would listen to her and treat her more respectfully. She would let go of her accumulated anger and resentments.

They agreed to discuss problems as they occurred: When Mike would be unduly critical, Nancy would calmly point out what was happening. When Nancy would remain silent about her preferences, Mike would ask her what she wanted. The change would be gradual. When they fell short in some way, they would cooperatively help each other get back on track. They could do this because they both understood the importance of rewriting their family drama.

They recognized that the drama, as previously constituted, could lead to a terrible outcome. Either Nancy would become severely depressed, seek a divorce, or become so angry that she would do something spiteful. Meanwhile, Mike would be losing her affection and respect, and would lose all intimacy.

Adult Change Affects Children

When Nancy first started to make important changes in her life, the amount of overt confrontation between her and Mike increased. She was concerned about its impact upon her children. But the more she worked at changing, the more certain she became that it was all for the better for the children.

Conflict is inevitable. Nancy was showing her children that people who love each other can transcend their differences and solve their problems. She saw the mutual respect and closeness that evolved. She and Mike were good role models. She became an example of an assertive and loving woman. Mike became an example of a loving and cooperative man.

Changing Together with Children

Just as adults can make positive changes in their relationship scripts with regard to spouses, they can do the same with their children. The process begins similarly, by identifying self-defeating patterns. You may find that you are too strict or lose your temper too easily or don't spend enough time with your children. Anything that leads to poor results in the Happiness Test for you and your children is subject to scrutiny.

You may find that you behave with your children in some of the same self-defeating ways that your parents behaved with you. If that's the case, you can make changes. You have a unique opportunity, not only to rewrite your own relationship script, but also to consciously improve the relationship scripts of your children. For you, it's a rewrite. For them it's a "first edition." You can help your children form positive relationship scripts.

For example, if you tend to be overprotective of your children, when they reach the teen years they are likely to become either frightened and timid or rebellious, neither of which is desirable. If you are willing to rewrite your relationship script by giving up some control, you can talk with your teenagers about the sort of responsible behavior you expect from them. You can then give some freedom (for example, you stop supervising homework) and help them learn from their experiences by having mature discussions. In so doing, you will rewrite your relationship script for more trust and less control. You will help your children write their relationship scripts for self-assurance and trustworthiness. You agree *not* to check every night whether your teenagers have done their homework. They agree to do it without such supervision. Later, you evaluate the success of the agreement.

Adults and Their Parents

When adults make a commitment to changing an important aspect of their relationship scripts, they will probably find it extremely difficult to behave differently with their parents. This makes sense: parents were the major influences in the formation of the original relationship script; they expect and reinforce the very behavior that their grown children are trying to change.

Nancy found it difficult to be assertive in the presence of her parents. Even after she had begun to act assertively with Mike, when her parents visited, her newfound motivation seemed to fizzle. She didn't like how easily she slipped into old patterns. By watching closely, Nancy noticed how her parents discouraged her assertiveness. When she objected to her father leaving a mess in the living room, he grudgingly picked up after himself but flashed a disapproving look at his daughter. Nancy was angry about his critical gesture.

In another incident, after Nancy asked Mike to clean his mess in the living room, Nancy's mother privately suggested that Nancy could easily do it herself. These remarks began a long discussion. Nancy told her mom that she loved and respected her, but that she wanted a more adult relationship with her parents. Her mother said she would welcome that.

Nancy then explained why she wanted to become more assertive. Her mom patiently listened and claimed that she could see the point. But Nancy realized that her mother was troubled by what she considered to be her daughter's decision to be more "pushy." In her heart, Nancy recognized that her mother didn't agree with her. She realized that both her parents would probably maintain their existing attitudes. And that was O.K. with Nancy.

With Mike's encouragement, she became more self-assured. Eventually she was able to be her new self with Mike in the presence of her parents. Although she still was not highly assertive with them, she decided that it really didn't matter. Nancy's experience is typical. It's difficult to master new behaviors with parents. However, once you finally feel comfortable with your new behavior, you can be your new self with other people in their presence.

Occasionally parents understand the importance of personal changes and make parallel changes of their own. More often they don't, and as an adult child you have to find some middle ground, doing enough of your new behavior so you don't feel that you've compromised your integrity, while accepting your parents' long-standing attitudes and behaviors. Unless the parents are highly oppressive, grown children can make peace with them.

GETTING PROFESSIONAL HELP

Some strong and courageous couples can rewrite their relationship scripts and family drama unassisted. Others need the help of professionals. Our purpose with this book has been to encourage families to look at their problems and improve their family lives. We believe that for some families professional therapists can add further to these improvements. If you have trouble identifying the problems in your family drama or rewriting the scripts that produced the drama, we suggest that you seek help. It is a sign of strength to face personal problems directly. If you have family problems, we urge you to act now. Too often families wait for a serious crisis before they consider seeking assistance.

Helen and Joe Spencer's family experienced plenty of emotional outbursts. They were on the verge of divorce when they sought professional help.

The series of outbursts that led them to this point began at a party at their suburban home on Independence Day. The lawn, looking very much like a stage setting, was alive with relatives dressed in sundresses, shorts, and colorful shirts— some at the barbecue, others at the buffet table, and a few just strolling. Besides parents, uncles, aunts, and cousins, there were an uncounted number of nephews and nieces racing around the lawn, with Helen and Joe's thirteen-year-old, Billy, in the lead.

This peaceful scene, which an artist like Renoir might have painted, was suddenly disrupted when Helen's father got into a shouting match with his brother. All other conversation came to a stop, and even the children halted their play as the atmosphere, so warm and jovial before, chilled.

When someone tried to intervene, Helen's mother interrupted, saying the men had a right to their argument. Helen
urged the men to lower their voices, but was cut off by her
mother's stern look. Joe, who had been at the other end of
the lawn, came running over, pushed his mother-in-law aside,
and said to the men, "Quit it. Enough! Get yourselves a cold
drink and cool it."

Joe started leading them to the table. When his father-in-
law resisted, Joe added firmly, "Either cool it here or at
home." Gradually the children's games and the adult conversations resumed, and everything seemed to be peaceful again.
But not for Joe and Helen.

After Joe crossed the lawn to get more charcoal, Helen
approached him. Her lips pursed in anger, she said, "Where
do you get off telling my parents what to do?" And off she
went before he could answer her. He dropped the charcoal,
ripped off the dirty gloves, and headed after her, only to see
her pull the car out of the driveway as if she were in a race.
He remembered the last time this happened, when she ended
up spending the night at a girlfriend's apartment. "If that's
it again," he thought, "I've had it."

Helen returned early the next morning after going out
to a bar and staying overnight with her friend. She
flaunted her behavior, as if Joe had it coming to him. Joe
called her a slut and said he wanted her to leave the house
that day. She refused. Verbally, they lashed out at each
other. "I married a slut who has a crazy family," he said.
"I should have known better. Your father showed what
your family is really like. A grown man fighting like a ten-
year-old. And your brother. What was the longest he ever
lasted on a job?"

She shot back, "At least my brother isn't a moocher. He
didn't take his kids and move back with his parents like your
sister did."

Joe moved out the following day. Ten days later Helen
phoned to tell him that Billy was in trouble. He was caught

smoking pot and giving it to another boy. In the thirty-minute drive home, Joe had many thoughts. For the first time he realized that he and Helen were in over their heads. He wanted them to see a psychologist. Helen agreed.

Through family therapy, the Spencers recognized that they needed to tame their wild emotions. They had to solve some of the relationship problems that had led to bitterness and to find positive and nondestructive ways to communicate their negative feelings. They soon recognized a pattern of revenge in the family. Helen left the barbecue to punish Joe. Joe left home to punish Helen. Billy smoked pot to punish his father for moving out. They agreed to stop using revenge power plays.

Over several months' time, they learned to negotiate work roles and other sources of misunderstanding in their family. They learned communication methods, so that resentments and hurt feelings could be handled constructively. Helen and Joe realized they had different ideas about the family dream and were able to settle this difference and gain a common direction.

Finally, Helen and Joe saw that they were embroiled in problems with their parents. Joe had rebelled against his parents in quiet ways and then, after marriage, did it openly against Helen's parents. He showed contempt and no understanding for Helen's parents and brother. She, in turn, took it out on his family. Helen hated her parents' behavior and sometimes didn't like them as people. These feelings made her so guilty that she overprotected them against Joe and sometimes behaved with them as if she were still their little girl. Their immature behavior was denying Joe and Helen what they both wanted—warm but independent relationships with their parents. While in therapy, they came to accept their parents for what they were and began to lead their lives independently. By rewriting their relationship scripts, they greatly improved their family drama.

This was a success story, though it required professional help and many months of therapy. Sometimes people aren't as fortunate. They wait so long that all the good, loving feelings in the family have been permanently erased. Often, they end up in divorce court—another way of rewriting the family drama.

11

Parting in the Healthiest Way

*Y*ou are probably not surprised to find the topic of divorce covered in a book discussing today's family. Given the staggering number of divorces granted yearly and the millions of people affected, divorce is a significant issue in contemporary family life.

Psychologists and other investigators have conducted research examining the threat divorce poses to the mental health of children and adults. Based on those studies and on our concepts, we hope to provide you with a new understanding of divorce, explaining how people can manage divorce in ways that minimize the hurt and the negative psychological outcomes for all family members.

You will find some familiar terms and concepts—costs and benefits of family membership, happiness tests, relationship scripts, family drama, FDMs—and some new ones, such as goodbye-forever divorce and family-forever divorce.

DIVORCE: A LENGTHY PROCESS

What images or ideas come to mind when you hear someone say, "Betsy and Don recently divorced"? You may visualize a judge pounding his gavel. Or you may imagine a person walking out of the courtroom clutching a legal document that specifies who gets the children and how much one parent has to pay the other. Or you may think of the emotional costs to young children or to a spouse.

Most people conceive of divorce as a momentary event, not as a long-term process that affects family members for many years—perhaps a lifetime. Individuals develop this notion partly because of the way the word "divorce" is commonly used. People say, "I just got my divorce" or "The judge handed me a divorce."

From a psychological point of view, however, divorce is a lengthy process that stretches days into months and months into years. It begins when a relationship moves from being joyous, as evidenced by happiness-test results, to the point at which the costs of the marriage outweigh the benefits. After repeatedly failed efforts to correct matters with everyday problem-solving techniques, FDMs, and rewriting the family drama, a couple may consider divorce as a solution. The most time-consuming part of the divorce process is the personal psychological readjustment of each family member.

THE STAGES AND STEPS OF DIVORCE

The divorce process involves a set of steps people must inevitably take as they work toward terminating their marriage. These steps enable people to psychologically reshape their relationships and move forward in life. If you know about these steps, you can better help individuals—whether adults or children—who are trying to cope with a divorce.

We will illustrate these steps by tracing Neil and Penny's relationship from dating days through their post-divorce settlement. To provide a context for understanding why Neil and Penny divorced, we begin by outlining the early stages of their relationship.

Stage 1: Happy Times, Conflict, and Everyday Problem-Solving

Neil and Penny met at a surprise birthday party thrown by a mutual friend. There was an immediate attraction between them. They talked, danced, and finally exchanged telephone numbers, with the intention of taking a bike ride the following weekend. The very next morning, however, Neil called Penny and invited her to dinner and a movie.

The instant rapport between them suggested that their relationship scripts had meshed well. In fact, after a dozen dates they decided to see each other exclusively. During their eleven-month courtship, they had their ups and downs like every other dating couple, but mostly they were content. After a spring wedding and a mountain-resort honeymoon, they settled into a new suburban townhouse.

During the early months of marriage they took ample time to play, laugh, and enjoy each other's company. Almost every day they tackled the nearby bike trail that winds gracefully through the woods and along the riverbank.

Penny and Neil also encountered conflicts common to newlyweds. They fought about issues such as how much time to spend with relatives, how closely to adhere to the family budget, and how the home should be cared for. Each spouse's position was the same week after week: Neil wanted to share more time with his parents than Penny did. Penny consistently overspent, cutting into savings. And Neil griped about Penny's cooking and housekeeping.

During the first half-year or so, they handled differences with everyday problem-solving methods. One person would provoke a fight with a belittling comment; they would exchange criticisms; and finally one person would say, "It doesn't make sense to fight about this. Let's compromise." Or one would apologize. Either way, Penny and Neil would soon kiss and make up.

Even with the steady dose of conflict in their relationship, Penny's and Neil's happiness-test outcomes were relatively favorable. Beyond the direct benefits Penny and Neil supplied each other in day-to-day activities, they appreciated the pleasures typically associated with the honeymoon phase of a marriage. Neil doted on Penny. He showered her with affection and declared his love for her with words and weekly bouquets of freshly cut flowers. Although Neil was often critical of her, Penny accepted that cost because she was happy.

Penny provided Neil with an ongoing stream of care. Neil had never had this experience in a relationship before, and he valued it highly. Moreover, Penny attended to Neil's physical needs in ways he had not dreamed possible. Because of these benefits, Neil tolerated Penny's shopping sprees, which endangered their savings account, and her housekeeping habits, which he considered to be untidy.

As Neil told his mother, "Penny is such a caring wife— an absolute doll. A man could ask for little more. Of course, the one thing I'd like to change is her housekeeping. She rarely scrubs the kitchen floor with disinfectant. She never seems to polish the silver. And she uses store-bought mixes instead of baking from scratch."

Stage 2: Unfavorable Happiness Tests, FDMs, and Family Drama Rewriting

In five years, by the time they had two children, the excitement of the romance faded, and Penny and Neil's problems came to outweigh their pleasure. The marriage could be characterized as conflict-ridden, as arguments between them flared daily, marring the time they spent together. While everyday problem-solving techniques allowed Penny and Neil to reach accord on many issues, on other important issues they faced a stalemate.

As their unresolved problems multiplied and their everyday problem-solving techniques began to fail, neither one would give up. Few couples surrender easily. Like all living entities, marriages and families have survival instincts. When in danger, they mobilize to combat the threat with a full arsenal, including FDMs and family drama rewriting, which Penny and Neil discovered.

As Neil explained to his mother, "Last week I got very upset watching Penny cook. She opened a few cans, threw together a bunch of packages, and microwaved what she jokingly called a 'chef's surprise.' Some surprise, especially since that very night I had brought home a fine bottle of French wine. Can you imagine?

"Saturday I worked at home and watched Penny clean house. I was so bothered by her superficial job of dusting and vacuuming I told her that from now on I'd take over the housecleaning [family drama rewrite].

"Penny didn't object, but when she saw me dust behind the books and polish the basement floor, she complained. She argued that by taking over I was criticizing her in the harshest way possible. So she left the house to go shopping. Now, every Saturday I clean, and she and the children spend the day at the mall [FDM of physical escape]."

Before Neil assumed the Saturday housecleaning chores, he had tried many approaches to change Penny's housekeeping habits. He had pleaded, begged, cajoled, intimidated, and used logic and charm to try to convince Penny to keep the home spotless. He wondered, "Will she ever change? If she won't, will it be worthwhile for me to stay in the relationship?" He puzzled over these questions and searched for ways to reduce this cost in the marriage until he found a solution in family drama rewriting.

Penny, although not aware of it, had reacted to Neil just as she had responded to her mother during her teenage years. Specifically, following the dictates of her relationship script, Penny said yes to every request but actually completed only those that paralleled her wishes. However, her unfulfilled promises soon brought criticism, which in turn led Penny to decide that her husband treated her unfairly, an attitude she used to justify her continued pattern of agreeing to requests but carrying through only when they coincided with her wishes.

The pain of being criticized was a major cost to Penny in the marriage. One way she handled it was to go to her mother's house (the escape FDM). After spending a few hours with her mother, Penny would return home, believing she had again swallowed her pride and forgiven her husband—sacrifices she felt she had to make for her children.

Penny recognized that the children, even at their ages, were aware of the marital friction. In fact, Jimmy, for the first time in his young life, had gotten into trouble at the day-care center. Penny wondered whether his problems were related to what was happening in the marriage. She had read about children who manage to fail schoolwork in order to create a crisis to unite parents and distract them from marital woes.

Stage 3: Deterioration of the Intact Family

Let's pause for a moment in our discussion of Penny and Neil to consider the thought processes that lead to a decision to divorce.

Family problems are inevitable and pose no threat as long as they can be managed. Sometimes, however, even with the full utilization of everyday problem-solving techniques, FDMs, and family drama rewriting, a couple may determine that it's impossible to cope with the continuing marital conflicts. Feeling discouraged and restricted by their inability to improve family life, a husband and wife begin to consider what single life would be like and how divorce would affect their individual happiness-test outcomes.

The single alternative.   Initially, the pros and cons of remaining married are weighed against the anticipation of what single life would offer. Often the comparison is done blindly, leading to an idealized picture of single life. You may envision a busy social calendar, freedom from the boredom and constraints of marriage, and your children easily adjusting to this change (and to a new stepparent someday). You are less likely to imagine yourself facing a string of lonely nights, dealing with unhappy children, and overloaded by household chores.

When the comparison is made more realistically, however, it becomes clear that, besides the opportunity for a fresh start, divorce brings stress, fear, anger, and a host of other negatives, including economic hardships. The children may suffer for several years, faced with the task of having to grow up more quickly. Would they do better in a healthy single-parent home or in a troubled two-parent home? Many such difficult questions must be asked.

The climate of the times also affects the decision to divorce. With each decade since the 1950s, the costs of divorce have dropped because it has become more prevalent and less stigmatized. The increased numbers of single adults, both divorced and never married, provide social support through a large pool of available unmarried people who form what is termed "the singles community."

During the mid-1980s, popular ideas about the quality of single life in the United States began to shift. The divorce rate appeared to level off, and more attention was paid to the family. While it is unclear what direction social attitudes will take during the 1990s, one factor will be the prevalence of sexually transmitted diseases, especially AIDS. This threat challenges our society ethically, medically, and socially and will undoubtedly affect how people weigh the costs and benefits of marriage and divorce.

Choosing divorce. At the point you decide that the single alternative is more appealing than marriage, you choose divorce as a means to regain a favorable outcome on your Happiness Test. No remedy can fix the marriage once you reach this point. You've quit. The search for solutions within the home is over: you are unwilling to extend yourself further because the pain in the relationship has defeated the family survival instinct.

People give up on preserving their marriages for as many different reasons as they have for marrying in the first place. There may be an identifiable threshold point. A wife may conclude it's not worth bouncing back from an unforgivable incident of verbal or physical abuse or of unfaithfulness. Perhaps they suffer from a husband's chronic unemployment or alcoholism or a wife's unacceptable treatment of the children. Maybe another potential mate appears far more attractive. Or the spouses are growing at different rates or in different directions, causing an emotional obstacle. For some, there is no signpost to precisely mark when a person reaches the threshold point.

Many people reach the threshold after careful thought and analysis, but others make this decision in a seemingly irrational way. For instance, one man retreated from his marriage three weeks after being fired from his executive position. He mistakenly assumed that, if his wife was as bright as he thought she was, she would no longer respect and love him. A woman left her husband of six years because she incorrectly convinced herself that he deeply resented her inability to conceive. With surprising frequency, spouses decide to end relationships because friends stir feelings and push, pull, or coerce them into this action.

Penny could easily identify why and when she reached the threshold point. If asked, Penny would be quick to label the towel incident as "the capper." On that afternoon, Neil exploded when he discovered Penny had forgotten to remove towels from the washing machine after the cycle had finished. "Penny, Penny, Penny," he wailed, "how could you? We'll have to run them through the machine again."

Over the years Penny had wished that Neil was less finicky, but nonetheless, she adjusted and came to accept this quality in him. Although Neil's reaction to the towels was not significantly different from a string of others, this criticism broke Penny's morale. It convinced her that divorce was the only way to correct her unhappiness.

At the threshold point, Penny decided a trial separation was a logical next step and the right one for her. Everything else had failed, and she had no evidence to convince her that the situation could be rectified in a less wrenching way. Although separation would have the cost of undermining family cohesion, it would provide immediate relief to Penny and Neil from ongoing interpersonal conflict by physically and psychologically separating them. Separation offered a clear-cut, ready-made vehicle to improve her happiness-test outcome. She also thought that in the long run separation would do no harm to the children's happiness-test results.

Penny had to deal with a resistant husband who wanted to remain married. She knew the transition would be difficult but realized that, if she and Neil proceeded in a constructive way, they would cause each other and the children the least possible distress. For this reason she proceeded patiently, allowing Neil to slowly adjust to the fact that she intended to have a separation and then a divorce.

Separation. The deterioration phase ends when spouses physically separate, extricating themselves from an unacceptable and unchangeable home environment. When this moment arrives, both husband and wife usually encounter intense feelings: stark pain, profound emptiness, and seething anger, sometimes tempered by deep and fond memories of what was once shared. As they look ahead, each partner may also feel hope, along with fear and an uncertainty about the future.

Significant changes take place in family relationships once the members dwell in separate residences. As your relationship scripts rub together in changed ways, you will develop new rules to govern your family drama. As a set, these rules eventually become the family's amended constitution. To write the best version, each partner alone, and the two of you together, must search for the elusive pattern of rules to guide interactions in ways that will produce the best happiness-test outcomes. This difficult task is made somewhat easier by the fact that you are separated and therefore interact less frequently, less intimately, and in ways that require fewer joint decisions.

Uncertainty prevails, and the family drama reaches its most chaotic state during this early stage of separation. Children look to parents and expect guidance and support. However, what you can offer is often limited by your own distress and confusion. For instance, children want to know what rules will govern life in each household and what consequences will be associated with violating them. But typically, you have limited ideas about new household rules and are inconsistent in enforcement, partly because you want to win the children's favor and partly because frustration may lead you to react harshly at times. An important task is to clarify the rules that will guide parent-parent and parent-child interactions.

It takes time to establish rules to regulate family interactions under the new circumstances. Some rules in your modified family are selected through discussion and some through arguments, but most develop as you act according to the dictates of your relationship scripts and unintentionally establish patterns that persist over the years.

In the first few months of Neil and Penny's separation, Neil set a precedent by calling every night to speak to the children. He asked each whether they had cleaned their plates at lunch and dinner, who they had played with after school, and whether their homework was done. Penny did not interfere with the calls. A pattern was established, and Neil continued to make these calls even after Penny remarried.

During the rule-rewriting process, you and your spouse must take care to avoid making big mistakes that could shatter the remaining trust each of you has in the other. One client's case illustrates how, in a moment of weakness, an unwise act intensified bitterness and caused long-term harm. After Harold packed his belongings and left home, he went to a downtown bar for a drink. There he met an intoxicated man who had left his wife a few years earlier. After hearing the details of the case, the man instructed Harold to empty the family's joint savings and checking accounts and convert the funds into traveler's checks. "This way," the man explained, "you control your money. Nobody can take it away."

Harold followed this advice and, although he ultimately returned the funds to the joint accounts, his poor judgment made cooperation with his wife Selma much more difficult. It took countless dollars wasted on court battles and a half-dozen years before Selma came to trust Harold again.

In most cases, it is far better for the spouses to develop the new rules themselves than to leave the task to judges, who lack a full knowledge of individual needs and sometimes make mistakes that cause substantial problems.

Stage 4: Writing the Post-Divorce Family Drama

Separated spouses are handicapped in the most crucial task of bringing a degree of predictability into redefined family relationships. Specifically, the pain, anger, and sense of failure you feel makes high-quality, rational work on this job difficult. Moreover, your thinking may be clouded by feelings of panic as you contemplate the changed family drama and the uncertainty ahead.

Selecting the style of divorce.   Even though you are under less than ideal circumstances as separated spouses, you must face the challenge of determining how you will relate to each other immediately and in the future. These choices are often made thoughtlessly, and may even be shaped by one act that causes irreparable harm. For example, permanent damage to prospects for a reasonable relationship can be inflicted by a spouse who, perhaps acting in a fit of anger, sells a piece of jewelry, flaunts a new lover, or threatens the partner.

In essence, you must determine how you are going to reach a legal settlement and how you are going to relate to each other afterward. Regarding the legal settlement, you have these options: you can elect to work cooperatively; you can fight like a gladiator down to possession of the last videotape; or you can use an approach somewhere in between these two extremes.

The second decision, how you will relate to each other for the rest of your lives, is heavily influenced by the first choice. Two types of post-divorce arrangements represent reasonable alternatives among the options possible: *goodbye forever* and *family forever.* If there are children involved, goodbye forever usually is not a viable option.

A goodbye-forever divorce, as the name suggests, specifies no future interaction between the ex-spouses. It is well illustrated in a description provided by a friend of ours, Allan Merck: "Mary was driving me nuts, and I didn't even know it. I'd come home from a twelve-hour workday, and she'd nag and nag. I got so used to the aggravation, headaches, and hassles that I thought that was part of marriage. It was like my army days. You ate in the mess tent, and you had heartburn. You got so used to upset stomachs that, when you ate in town and didn't have heartburn, you thought something was wrong.

"Well, it was like that with Mary, until one day, with a catlike grin on her face, she lowered the boom. She told me she had a boyfriend. Then she threw clothes into a suitcase and announced she had issued herself walking papers.

"For months I had a terrible time. I couldn't eat or sleep. I'd imagine that she would change her mind and come back to me. And I was haunted with thoughts about how terrific Mary's life was and how awful mine was.

"But she didn't come back, and I finally realized that, though I still loved Mary, her affair did everlasting damage. I could never trust her again. It took a year for me to be pain-free, but eventually I discovered leaving was the best thing Mary ever did for me. When I fell in love with Barb and found genuine happiness, my anger toward Mary evaporated. I honestly hope Mary is doing as well as I am. But I'll never know, because I doubt if we'll ever talk again."

Because Allan and Mary were childless, the good-bye-forever revision of their family drama was entirely acceptable. This approach makes much sense for people who have little or no ability to interact without causing each other grief and who have no continuing business that demands their joint effort.

A goodbye-forever divorce is not beneficial if children

are involved, except in extremely unusual conditions. Instead, we recommend a family-forever approach.

The family-forever divorce is illustrated in a description provided by Pam Thompson, a former client, who after her fortieth birthday was promoted to principal of a school. A trim brunette, Pam, a mother of five, was married to the manager of a local baseball team for nearly twenty years until, as she put it, "things soured." Before the divorce Pam explained:

"Mom and Dad are super-religious. I never missed one Sunday service during all my years growing up. They have one very clear idea about divorce—it's for the weak and irreverent. So here I am. Charley hates living with me. He wants a divorce. But, if we divorce, my folks will kill me.

"I guess I'd disappoint myself, too. My first year teaching I discovered that the school secretary marked a big red ink 'D' on a child's permanent folder if the parents were divorced. It sent shudders up my spine. It reminded me of Hester in *The Scarlet Letter,* who had that letter 'A' for 'adultery' emblazoned on her dress.

"So now I hold back, picturing that horrible 'D' on my children's records. I imagine the awful things Mom and Dad and the children's teachers will think. Poor Charley and me. The pain would be incredible, and I can't imagine the hurt ever fading."

Months later, Pam related the following: "Charley ended up dragging me into court and comparing our divorce to an extra-inning World Series game. Using baseball mentality, he said he intended to do everything to win. That infuriated me. After the settlement, Charley refused to speak to me and communicated through the children. As a result, on the night of his sixth or seventh scheduled visitation, I was stranded with a pair of expensive theater tickets, the children, and no baby-sitter. The children had forgotten to convey information about Charley's changed plans.

"I blew up. But I made two mistakes in expressing my fury. I told the children that their father was an irresponsible

so and so, and I mailed a note to Charley that read, 'Don't
bother coming for the kids if you can't follow our initial
agreement.'

"Charley decided to show me who was boss. He skipped
several visits with the children. Evidently, he decided it was
worth relinquishing them to teach me a lesson. The children,
however, missed their dad and hammered reality home to him
and to me in a letter drafted by the oldest, age fifteen."

Dear Mom and Dad:

Mom sees "the family" as us and her. Dad sees it as
us and him. That's fine for the two of you. Each one of us
see our family as Mom, Dad, and all us brothers and
sisters. Your divorce ended your marriage but it did not
end our family. That's all.
We Love You.

Sincerely,
Adam, Ben, Lynne, Cora, Chris

"In essence, the children told us to develop a family-
forever relationship. I knew they were right. Although I
wanted to be rid of Charley, I knew that such an arrangement
would be detrimental to our kids. Persuaded by the letter, I
called Charley to have coffee with me. We met several times
and eventually learned to cooperate on children-related issues. That's the only thing we ever talk about. Fortunately,
I'm able to talk with my parents. By the time Charley and I
separated they were convinced that I was well rid of him."

The Thompsons managed to build a family-forever divorce. While most couples encounter some difficulties in
building this style of divorce, the experience is often easier
than it was for the Thompsons. With this arrangement, their
family continues to exist, but in a new physical form. Instead
of living under one roof, the redefined Thompson family
consists of the same people split into two groups housed in
two dwellings, one headed by Mom and one by Dad. This

arrangement supports continued involvement of both parents in the lives of the children, a significant factor in reducing the negative effects children experience when their parents divorce.

Family-forever divorces generally work best if the spouses limit their contact to necessary, children-related business. With interactions accordingly reduced, most ex-spouses can tolerate the pain or discomfort involved in relating to each other. We advise couples to formally agree upon what we call the "limited contact rule." An example of what can happen when the rule is *not* used is presented below.

Beginning at the time of their separation, Penny and Neil argued every time one of them picked up the children at the other's home. Neil always had advice for Penny on how she should live her life, and she came to dread the exchange, a feeling certainly detected by the children.

One evening Penny decided to dodge Neil by feigning illness and escaping to bed just before he came to fetch the children. That failed. Neil charged into Penny's bedroom with medicine and hot chicken soup. Another time Penny plotted to leave the children with Neil for an extra day, so her sister could pick them up from him.

During a women's support-group meeting, Penny heard about the limited-contact rule and decided to explain it to Neil. Although he balked at the concept, claiming that even if the marriage was over he still cared about her, the two tried to practice the idea.

After several months of following the new rule, Penny no longer detested their meeting, largely because Neil had learned to control himself. The two of them simply smile at each other, and if discussion about child-related business is necessary, they talk briefly while the children march by them in or out of the house.

Directing a healthy post-divorce drama. Former spouses can help themselves and their children by being vigilant during the readjustment period—from the time of separation until two years or so after the divorce is finalized. By being on guard, you can capitalize on opportunities to actively promote a healthy post-divorce drama and protect yourselves and your children from unhealthy situations.

You'll benefit by having a support group of family members and friends to aid you in navigating a safe course through the choppy waters of this period. Support includes love and caring, which are commodities that divorcing people usually feel are in short supply. Support-group members also help by insuring that you are being an effective problem-solver, applying a measure of reason rather than pure emotion in making key decisions.

Former spouses can also help themselves by remembering to apply reason in the post-divorce family drama. You can avoid unhealthy episodes by reminding yourself of these catchphrases: "I can think myself into feeling miserable; I can think myself into feeling good." "Every behavior of mine has the potential to improve matters or make them worse." Some examples will illustrate these.

Feel-miserable thought: How can I be happy? Madeline doesn't love me anymore, so I'm a nobody.

Feel-good thought: Only I can make myself happy, not Madeline. My happiness and self-worth are not dependent on her evaluation of me.

Feel-miserable thought: If I don't get to have the children an extra hour on my birthday, it will ruin the whole visit.

Feel-good thought: The children and I will have a wonderful time on my birthday.

Behavior that worsens matters: Bringing the children home late or having the children available late because the promised child-support check arrived late.

Behavior that improves matters: Helping the children to buy, write, and mail a birthday card to an ex-spouse.

Thought and behavior that worsen matters: Suspecting that the young woman with Hank is his new lover and therefore ordering Hank to leave that "blankety-blank" home when he comes for the children.

Thought and behavior that improves matters: Recognizing that feeling jealous of Hank is the same old trap and forbidding yourself to feel jealous, while investing energy in building your own happiness. Smile at Hank when he comes for the children and think a thought like, "Maybe having a woman friend will make him a better dad."

The divorced person's question.   Negative and positive thoughts and behaviors shape the course of the post-divorce family drama. So do former spouses' reactions to a question that is commonly asked, which we call "the divorced person's question." Over and over again, people ponder, "Are things fair, or am I getting the shaft compared to my ex-spouse?"

Returning to Neil and Penny's case, you can see how much power is packed into their answers to the divorced person's question. Although Penny wanted the divorce, soon after Neil moved out, she began to worry that he would end up with a better outcome. It seemed to her that he had fewer costs and more benefits. She imagined him running around free and easy after work, while she struggled from dawn to midnight trying to keep up with her responsibilities. Initially, Penny's response to this question was simple: she worked toward stopping Neil from making gains, rather than toward her own welfare and a fair distribution of the benefits and costs.

Neil also fell victim to the divorced person's question at

first. Although he moved into a roomy apartment, he felt
deprived living there compared to their comfortable home.
Feeling less well-off than Penny, he seized every opportunity
to complain to her about his housing accommodations. Furthermore, he felt entitled to provoke energy-draining ex-
changes to make Penny pay for her harshness in deciding to
divorce. This conflict misdirected Penny and Neil into spending resources to get even instead of to get on with readjustment and the pursuit of life's tasks.

The healing quickened for Penny and Neil when they
came to realize, with unsolicited help from Neil's mother,
what harm they were doing to each other. After that, although
there were moments when one or the other nearly succumbed
to anger and struck out vengefully, mostly they resisted temp-
tations to hurt each other.

Neil and Penny's strength came partly from recognizing
that it would not be in their children's best interest if they
simply stumbled through the years ahead. Instead, they
agreed to have limited but ongoing discussions to monitor the
children's adjustment and plan for their future. Toward this
end, they tried to stay reasonable and self-disciplined so they
could make arrangements that empowered, rather than ham-
pered, each family member's development. Though they were
able to cooperate and act in everybody's best interests most
of the time, there were occasional slip-ups followed by a few
days of intense anger. Like the initial pain of the divorce,
these eventually came to pass.

Stage 5: Maintaining a
Two-Household Family

People who have successfully built the healthiest post-divorce
family dramas are easily identified. Children from such families, for instance, often have a sparkle in their eyes, indicating
that they have regained their sense of security and have been
able to resume the job of childhood—learning and experiencing the magic of life. Most likely these youngsters have en-

joyed the continued involvement of both parents, a factor that convinced them that the divorce was a marital affair, not a parental one in which they lost love or esteem.

Their parents helped them adjust by allowing them to remain children. This means that, whatever feelings Mother and Father had, they avoided serious argument and putting each other down within their youngsters' earshot. By hiding open conflict, screaming, and criticism from children, they spared them unneeded nightmares.

These parents undoubtedly made other sacrifices in the interest of their children's mental health. First of all, they avoided rushing them into adulthood by treating them like children, not like friends or confidants. Second, they effectively resisted the temptation to force the youngsters to choose one parent over the other. Third, they did not try to win their children's approval by easing up on rule enforcement. Instead of letting their children run wild, these parents continued to deliver effective discipline, meaning that they told their children in a straightforward way what the rules and consequences were and dealt with violations in a consistent manner.

Adults who have created effective post-divorce dramas are also easily identified. They have allowed themselves an ample period of readjustment, which might have stretched as long as two years, and sought support from others when needed. They have mostly come to terms with the end of their marriage, which enables them to enjoy the present rather than feeling trapped in reliving the past. They are in control of their lives, and this makes them optimistic about the kind of future they can build.

To maintain a healthy two-household family, you need to take the critic's role from time to time. Think about your revised family drama and how it serves your happiness-test results.

Also, consider what you can do to maintain equity with the other parent. If parts of the family drama are perceived as unfair—if one person feels the other is receiving a better shake as a result of the divorce process—then the divorced person's question may come into play, leading the person feeling deprived to agitate the other. Taking the critic's role might enable you to help everybody avoid the unnecessary heartaches such a provocation can cause.

ADDITIONAL ADVICE

If you are now in the process of rewriting your family drama by divorce, you are probably wondering what steps you might take to build the healthiest possible drama replacement. The first step is to recognize that you and your spouse initiated the divorce for a purpose: to deal with an otherwise unsolvable problem. In other words, the goal of the divorce is to rearrange your family's lifestyle and interaction to make it more comfortable or at least more tolerable. By cooperating, you can reduce the harshness of the rearrangement process.

You may wonder, if you couldn't cooperate when you were married, how you can cooperate when you are getting divorced. It's not easy, but people can do it. We've seen it over and over again. The cooperation needed takes much less skill and energy than what was needed during the marriage.

With that as background, the following advice depends on the circumstances—whether you are willing to cooperate or not.

Advice for Those Willing to Cooperate

First, confirm that you both are interested in developing a nonadversarial settlement. You will need to agree on key goals such as the following.

- Creating a healthy revised post-divorce family drama that fosters equity and enables you to cooperate on child-related business.
- Creating a settlement on child custody, property

division, and child support that is fair and in the children's best interests.

- Proceeding in a logical manner by settling what you can and then seeking the advice of attorneys who favor negotiated, out-of-court agreements. Such people will help you keep legal costs down and contain the hurt and psychological damage as much as possible.
- Recognizing that the process will be stressful and obtaining psychological support and encouragement from others to make the uncertainty and pain more bearable.

Second, determine the best way to reach shared goals. You maximize chances for ideal settlements by devising them together, with or without assistance from a neutral third party. As long as you both negotiate in good faith and retain control and decision-making power, the future is in your hands. This option is lost once you turn the conflicts over to a court.

Seek advice from others, but weigh the information you receive in terms of your needs. Family members, friends, pastors, attorneys, and other third parties can provide useful ideas.

Plan for the present and prepare for the future. The future will bring changes: the children reaching adolescence, your ex-spouse moving out of state, a remarriage, or a new job situation. Spell out what will happen when these events occur or, better yet, agree on how you will make such decisions when the need arises.

Finally, if an adversarial battle develops, consider hiring a mediator to help you iron out agreements. Mediators are neutral third parties trained in conflict management and problem-solving.

Many types of mediation are available. We practice Psychological/Mediation Intervention (PMI) to help divorcing spouses shape equitable settlements and formulate a healthy post-divorce family script. PMI permits ex-spouses to vent old hurts. With these removed, they are encouraged to cooperatively hammer out acceptable compromises with regard to child-rearing responsibilities and property. Usually after several sessions, the divorcing couple has reduced crippling animosities, produced a significantly revised family drama, and freed themselves from old conflict sufficiently to use common sense in future problem-solving.

Gail and Jason illustrate the potential power of mediation. Gail's attorney, who referred them for mediation, told us, "The couple's hopelessly mired in conflict for conflict's sake. They trap themselves. Every decision is monumental."

Consistent with the attorney's observations, the couple began mediation by raising such questions as who would get each tape, album, and CD and how would the photo collection be split.

PMI revealed that the real issue was not photos or music, but rather who had been unfaithful. Each believed the other had ruined the marriage and so deserved nothing at its dissolution. But by the end of the first PMI session, each person had discussed old incidents and vented anger that they had been storing for years. Each also divulged suspicions they had entertained about the partner's fidelity. With many disruptive feelings released, during a second session the spouses began making compromises on the photos and records and then moved on to developing equitable agreements about property division, child support, and visitation rights. A final session aided them in firming up a revised family drama.

Advice for Those Who Cannot Cooperate

If you can't agree on a set of goals like those spelled out above or if one of you is unwilling to try a nonadversarial settlement, each person should immediately hire an attorney.

Avoid taking actions that will provide momentary satisfaction but that might foster long-term harm. The temptation to vent anger is great. But you will have difficulty reestablishing trust and cooperation if one of you commits a vindictive act, like embarrassing the other in public or hiding the children for a few days. It's also difficult to regain trust if one of you seeks legal assistance before discussing it or seeks an advantageous judicial decision, such as prohibiting the other spouse from living in the family home.

If direct cooperation will not work for you, consider an indirect approach, such as using attorneys to negotiate or using a mediator who will work with attorneys. After every other method of resolution has been exhausted, your last resort is an adversarial courtroom confrontation. This means that you will give the final decision-making power to the judge. If you reach this point, you should consider whether your children's interests are best served if matters are settled by the court as soon as possible or if matters are delayed a few months. In some cases, settlement brings relief and is preferable. In other cases, the wait reduces the intensity of the feelings and produces better outcomes.

Whichever method you use to develop settlements and to forge your new family drama, you will have difficult moments. At these points you will benefit by remembering that life will improve if you keep stepping forward. That means knowing your deepest hurts will heal and the most awful parts of your family drama will be revised, at least to be tolerable if not ideal. And sometime in the future, you may decide to remarry and to strive together with a new partner toward your joint vision of the family dream.

Epilogue

*I*magine that you are in a theater. The curtain rises, and you recognize the stage setting because it is a cross section of your home. All the rooms are visible, and at the moment, they are deserted. Now bring onstage the members of your family, including yourself, one at a time. They are the characters in your family drama as you would like to see it written. You are the writer of the script, and you are the director of the performance.

How will your spouse interact with you? How intimate will your relationship be? If there is a scene at the dinner table, what will you, your spouse, and your children be doing besides eating? Will there be interesting conversation and happy laughter? And will some of it focus on your family dream?

The images you put onstage represent your vision of your family drama, and that vision is to be treasured. For after sharing it with your mate and perhaps modifying it as you both think best, it should be one of the goals toward which your family strives. Using the skills we have taught you about rewriting your family drama, the job ahead is to continue narrowing the gap between your vision of your family— the one you have put onstage—and your current family drama. Your family's objectives are to make life better by working toward a clearly defined target.

Some who see a wide gap between their dream and their reality may wonder whether it is worth the effort, but most people think marriage itself is indeed worthwhile. According to the National Center for Health Statistics, for both men and women, the percentage of adults up to age fifty-four who have been married has been higher in the 1980s than at any other time in the century. Three decades after the beginning of the sexual revolution and unprecedented freedom to create new lifestyles, marriage is still a social ideal.

Family life has received special notice recently. Leonard A. Sagan, an epidemiologist at the Electric Power Research Institute, in Palo Alto, California, who wrote the book *The Health of Nations: True Causes of Sickness and Well-Being,* gives high honors to families. He argues that increased life expectancies can be traced to quality of family life—not improvements in medicine, diet, or sanitation. He says, "Good health is as much a social and psychological achievement as a physical one. And the preservation of the family is not so much a moral issue as a medical one."

Our families give us the feeling that we are masters of our own destinies. Those feelings, in turn, give us self-esteem. There is no better way to develop that sense of mastery than by raising the quality of your family life.

You may wonder how much you can hope for. Or as one couple asked, "What is *good* family life really like?" In writing this book we had in mind a vision of the fulfilled family. Our years of experience, as well as several studies, helped to shape a picture of such families. Dr. W. Robert Beavers, a psychiatrist on the faculty of the University of Texas Health Center, outlined the characteristics of families that range from optimally functional to severely dysfunctional. His description of the healthy family is similar to our vision of the fulfilled family whose members enjoy life while they are striving for their dream.

Such family members take joy and comfort in relating to each other. They are sensitive to each other's feelings and show interest in what others are doing and saying. They feel close to each other, loyal to the family, but free to be involved in the outside world. Their individual accomplishments give pride to everyone in the family.

Leadership is unquestionably in the hands of the parents who provide solid, unified guidance while encouraging their children to contribute to decision-making and to become autonomous individuals. Power is shared, so there are rarely self-defeating power struggles. Family members are skilled at negotiating differences, with parents helping children to voice their ideas and to learn to compromise on differences. The family knows it is strong, yet dependent on a network of relationships, including those with grandparents, siblings, other relatives, and friends. Healthy family members know that everything changes, that illness and death are part of life, and they learn to cope with them. They see life as exciting and satisfying.

Don't get the wrong impression. Satisfied family members don't go around with halos over their heads! They have arguments, get angry, and sometimes say hurtful things. But they deal with their problems promptly and don't allow bad feelings to linger and grow worse. They bring their feelings out into the open and settle their differences then and there. They manage to handle the delicate balance between the needs for individual freedom and family togetherness. Such families are good models.

But they are only models. It is your vision alone—not any other family's vision—that will guide you as you take greater control of your family's future. If you haven't already done so, the time to begin taking control and raising the quality of your family life is now. The first step is communication with your spouse about your drama. As we have shown, this first step, the most important one, may be the most difficult. Yet once you and your spouse agree to rewrite your family drama, you are over the highest hurdle. You are ready to plan your steps and take them one at a time.

The little progress you make with each step can be a big morale booster, giving you greater incentive to move on to the next one. Patience and perseverance pay off. Your family may have a history of one, eight, or fifteen years. Don't expect to change long-established behavioral patterns—your relationship scripts and family drama—with the snap of a finger. Instead, look at the process of working on family relationships as a lifelong one in which family life continues to improve. One goal is reached and a new one set, and then another.

Every close relationship requires attention. The more we nourish it, the deeper the love and the greater our experience of joy. With that kind of tender care, as we age and children come and go, family relationships get stronger with time. Like an aging violin that has carefully been attended to, the music gets more beautiful. This is our hope for you in your quest for a happier family life.